Contemporary Authors of the German-Speaking Countries of Europe

A Selective Bibliography

Margrit B. Krewson

Library of Congress   Washington   1988

Library of Congress Cataloging-in-Publication Data

Krewson, Margrit B. (Margrit Beran).
  Contemporary authors of the German-speaking countries of
Europe.

  Supt. of Docs. no.: LC 1.12/2:G31/4
  1. German literature—20th century—Bibliography—
Catalogs. 2. German literature—Europe, German-speaking—
Bibliography—Catalogs. 3. German literature—20th
century—History and criticism—Bibliography—Catalogs.
4. German literature—Europe, German-speaking—History
and criticism—Bibliography—Catalogs. 5. Library of
Congress—Catalogs. I. Title.
Z2233.K79   1988   016.83′08′00914   88-600010
[PT401]
ISBN 0-8444-0613-9

For sale by the Superintendent of Documents,
U.S. Government Printing Office,
Washington, DC 20402

CONTENTS

INTRODUCTION

Although contemporary German literature draws on a long and distinguished intellectual tradition, it is largely the product of Post-World-War II experience. Germany's contemporary authors are predominantly the children of the postwar reconstruction and the *Wirtschaftswunderjahre* (economic miracle years) of the Federal Republic of Germany (FRG). This literary demarcation date—roughly 1945—can also be applied to the work of the Austrian and Swiss authors.

The Library of Congress has received a large volume of requests for information on contemporary German authors, such as criticism, bibliography, and biography, revealing both the high level of interest and the scarcity of currently available source material. This bibliography represents one small effort to remedy the situation. It is a compilation of the holdings of the Library of Congress for some of the more prominent writers of the German-speaking countries of Europe. The authors selected were chosen on the basis of their critical recognition rather than their commercial success. While some of the more widely known have seen their works translated into English and other languages, most of the contemporary works are available only in the original German.

In this bibliography, authors are listed under the country of their birth or the country in which they produced the main body of their work. The majority of these writers are natives or residents of the Federal Republic of Germany. This is attributable to that country's larger population and readership, its dynamic publishing industry, and its position as the primary recipient of authors expelled from the German Democratic Republic for political nonconformity. Several Austrian and Swiss writers have also taken up residence in the FRG, though for different reasons. Despite this prevalence of West Germans, it is important to note that most of those who write in German do so for a transnational audience. This is particularly true of the Austrians and the Swiss, whose smaller domestic literary markets make publication abroad a necessity rather than a luxury. By the same token, each writer is shaped by his or her unique and divergent national reality.

German-speaking authors, like those of many other countries, have a tendency to be defined by generations or groups. In the case of the FRG, the most influential postwar group was Gruppe 47, formed by Hans Werner Richter, Alfred Andersch, and Walter Kolbenhoff. All had suffered during the years of Nazi rule and reacted to that traumatic experience by rejecting strictly structured literary forms as a reflection of the fascist mindset. They also questioned the social role of literature, owing to their experience with officially approved propagandistic works during the Nazi period.

The Gruppe 47 was for some two decades the leading West German literary group and came to include such prominent novelists as Heinrich Böll and Günter Grass. However, it eventually fell victim to the shifting tides of political opinion. The Gruppe 61, a smaller and less prestigious association, criticized the more established authors for their lack of commitment to the depiction and advancement of the working class. This radical approach, influenced by Marxist theory, found a resonance among West German university students. The students so vehemently urged the Gruppe 47 to adopt a more pronounced political consciousness and to achieve a *Fernwirkung,* or social impact, that the group eventually divided into two camps. This dichotomy led to the dissolution of the group in 1967. Grass would achieve worldwide recognition with the publication of *The Tin Drum* in 1958 and Böll would go on to win the Nobel Prize for literature in 1972.

The initial postwar literary prospects in the German Democratic Republic were promising, as many writers exiled under the Nazi regime returned home to Berlin. Bertolt Brecht was among their number, as were Arnold Zweig and Anna Seghers. The majority of these writers held political convictions of a socialist or antifascist nature, and most accepted the premise that art should contribute to the establishment and strengthening of the socialist state. In the earnest atmosphere of the immediate postwar period, the prevailing school of writing was that of social realism. However, as the East German state consolidated and began to find its separate identity, the strict artistic parameters of socialist realism were realigned in what came to be known as the *Tauwetter,* or thaw, of GDR literature beginning about 1956. Among the new crop of artists encouraged by the thaw were the poets Volker Braun and Stefan Heym, and poet/novelist/children's author Franz Fühmann.

East German literature has gone on to reflect the evolving nature of society in the German Democratic Republic (GDR). By the late 1980's, there were indications that the *Tauwetter* might give way to further artistic liberalization in the spirit of *glasnost* encouraged by Soviet leader Mikhail Gorbachev. In general, East German writers have tended to be forward-looking in their approach to their subject matter, rarely looking back to the pre-socialist past for their raw material. In this respect, they resemble their colleagues in the FRG, who for years appeared unwilling or unable to come to grips with the past, particularly the World War II period.

Austrian writers on the other hand, have shown a greater tendency to delve into their national history for inspiration. Since the Allies absolved Austria of responsibility for World War II, Austrian writers, unlike their German counterparts, felt little or no compulsion to prod the national conscience. Rather, Austrian authors sought refuge in the pre-Anschluss period and, veering away from political activism, looked to the pre-Anschluss period for inspiration.

The postwar Austrian authors, many of whom associated to varying degrees with what became known as the Wiener Gruppe, revived such experimental approaches as surrealism in an effort to understand some of the seeming contradictions in Austrian life: the peaceful postwar country which had voted for the *Anschluss* with Nazi Germany, the prosperous commercial center with a lingering air of provincialism. Another literary group, the Grazer Gruppe, included such notables as Alfred Kolleritsch, Barbara Frischmuth, and Peter Handke.

These efforts to revitalize Austrian tradition produced a backlash among the younger generation of writers. Yet as these authors themselves later found recognition and approval, their need to challenge authority and tradition gradually disappeared. Today, Austrian literature is rich in both tradition and diversity, and one may say that no one particular trend or genre prevails.

The multiplicity of languages in Switzerland has had a strong effect on its literature. Equally influential has been the split between generations and political perspectives. The language question involves not only the major European tongues of German, French, and Italian but also some regional dialects which claim their own limited but growing bodies of literature. The clash between generations can be more or less equated to the conflict between classicists and modernists. There has also been a political dimension to this split, with the modernists representing more leftist/progressive tendencies and the classicists following a more conservative line. These artistic schools have even disagreed over the very existence of a "Swiss literature," with younger writers arguing that such a small body of work represents nothing more than a sub-classification of German literature.

It is hoped that the present bibliography, although by no means complete, will serve the reader as an introduction to a major body of literature. The bibliography is divided into four major sections, arranged alphabetically by country. At the head of each section are general reference works followed by works of the individual authors and by works about them. They include belles lettres, selected music, radio plays, social criticism, travelogues, and even children's literature in a few instances, when the author is known for a significant contribution to adult literature. All items can be found in the collections of the Library of Congress.

I wish to acknowledge the advice and help of Dr. Elke Frederiksen, University of Maryland; Rose Ullmer and Ingrid Kohlmeyer, Heidelberg City Library; Dr. Axel Frohn and Jacqueline Taylor, German Historical Institute, Washington; and the embassies of Austria, the Federal Republic of Germany, the German Democratic Republic, and Switzerland.

Margrit B. Krewson
May 1988

AUSTRIA

General Reference Works

1

Anthology of modern Austrian literature/ compiled and edited with
an introduction by Adolf Opel. London: Oswald Wolff, 1981.
viii. 257 p.   PT3823.A58 1981
   Bibliography: p. 248-251.

2

Durzak, Manfred. Peter Handke und die deutsche Gegenwartsliteratur: Narziss auf Abwegen. Stuttgart: Kohlhammer, 1982.
186 p. (Sprache und Literatur; 108)   PT2668.A5 Z62 1982
Includes bibliographical references and index.

3

Für und wider eine österreichische Literatur/ herausgegeben von
Kurt Bartsch, Dietmar Goltschnigg, Gerhard Melzer.
Königstein/Ts.: Athenäum, 1982. 192 p.   PT3813.F87 1982
One contribution translated from the English.
Includes bibliographical references and index.

4

Literatur aus Österreich, österreichische Literatur; ein Bonner Sym-
posion/ herausgegeben von Karl Konrad Polheim. Bonn:
Bouvier, 1981. 241 p.   PT3813.L55 1981
Includes bibliographical references.

5

Literatur der Nachkriegszeit und der fünfziger Jahre in Österreich/
herausgegeben von Friedbert Aspetsberger, Norbert Frei und
Hubert Lengauer. Wien: Österreichischer Bundesverlag, 1984.
380 p. (Schriften des Instituts für Österreichkunde: 44/45)
                             PT3818.L53 1984
Includes bibliographical references and index.

6

Literatur in Österreich: Rot ich weiss Rot/ herausgegeben von Gustav Ernst und Klaus Wagenbach. Berlin: Wagenbach, 1979. 126 p. (Tintenfisch; 16)   PT3823.L58

7

Literatur und Literaturgeschichte in Österreich/ herausgegeben von Ilona T. Erdelyi. Budapest: Akadémiai Kiadó, 1979. 343 p.
     PT3813.L57
    Includes bibliographical references.

8

Major figures of contemporary Austrian literature/ edited by Donald G. Daviau. New York: Lang, 1987. 413 p.
     PT3818.M35 1987
    Includes bibliographies and index.

9

Prokop, Hans F. Österreichisches Literaturhandbuch. Wien, München: Jugend & Volk, 1974. 253 p.   PT3822.P7
    Lists Austrian authors, Austrian literary prizes, Austrian literary societies.
    Includes index.
    Bibliography: p. 22.

10

Ruiss, Gerhard. Literarisches Leben in Österreich: ein Handbuch. Herausgeber, Interessengemeinschaft Österreichischer Autoren. Wien: Die Interessengemeinschaft, 1985. 466 p.
     PT3818.R85 1985

11

Suchy, Viktor. Literatur in Österreich von 1945 bis 1970. 2. überarb. Aufl. Wien: Dokumentationsstelle für Neuere Österreichische Literatur, 1973. 160 p.   PT3818.S8 1973

12

Ungar, Frederick. Handbook of Austrian literature. New York: Ungar, 1973. xvi, 296 p.   PT155.U5
    Includes bibliographies.

13
Wagner, Karl. Niederösterreichische Gegenwartsliteratur. St. Polten, Wien: Verlag Niederösterreichisches Pressehaus, 1980. 29, 1 p. (Wissenschaftliche Schriftenreihe Niederösterreich; 48)
PT3827.A8 W33
Bibliography: p. 28–30.

14
Die Zeitgenössische Literatur Österreichs/ herausgegeben von Hilde Spiel. Zürich, München: Kindler, 1976. 758 p.: ill.
PT3811.Z4
Includes bibliographical references and index.

Individual Authors

15
Aichinger, Ilse. Auckland. 4 Hörspiele. Frankfurt am Main: Fischer, 1969. 151 p.   PT2601.I26 A6 1969

16
————. The bound man, and other stories. Freeport, N.Y.: Books for Libraries Press, 1971, c1956. 100 p.   PZ3.A2878 B06
Translation of: Der Gefesselte, Erzählungen.

17
————. Dialoge. Stuttgart: Reclam, 1971, c1965. 110 p.
PT2601.I26 D5 1971

18
————. Eliza, Eliza. Frankfurt am Main: Fischer, 1965. 166 p.
PT2601.I26 E4

19
————. Der Gefesselte: Erzählungen. Frankfurt am Main: Fischer, 1953. 102 p.   PT2601.I26 G4

20
————. Die grössere Hoffnung. Frankfurt am Main: Fischer, 1966. 236 p.   PT2601.I26 G7

21

——. Herod's children. New York: Atheneum, 1963. 238 p.
PZ3.A2878 He

22

——. Hörspiele. Frankfurt am Main: Fischer, 1965. 203 p.
PN6120.R2 H57

23

——. Der junge Roth: Erzählungen. München: Deutscher
Taschenbuch-Verlag. 1974. 185 p.   PT2662.I38 A6 1974

24

——. Knöpfe: Hörspiel. Düsseldorf: Eremiten-Presse, 1980,
c1955. 72 p.: ill.   MLCS 87/2004 (P)

25

——. Meine Sprache und ich: Erzählungen. Frankfurt am Main:
Fischer, 1978. 221 p.   PT2601.I26 M4

26

——. Nachricht vom Tag. Frankfurt am Main, Hamburg:
Fischer, 1970. 190 p.   PT2601.I26 N3

27

——. Schlechte Wörter. Frankfurt am Main: Fischer, 1976.
133 p.   PT2601.I26 S3

28

——. Selected poetry and prose. Durango, Colo: Logbridge-
Rhodes, 1983. 141 p.   PT2601.I26 A23 1983

29

——. Selected short stories and dialogs. Oxford, New York: Per-
gamon Press, 1966. viii, 130 p.: port.   PT2601.I26 A6 1966

30

——. Spiegelgeschichte: Erzählungen und Dialoge. Leipzig:
Kiepenheuer, 1979. 284 p.   MLCS 84/11074 (P)

31

————. Verschenkter Rat: Gedichte. Frankfurt am Main: Fischer, 1978. 99 p.   PT2601.I26 V47

32

————. Zu keiner Stunde: Szenen und Dialoge. Frankfurt am Main: Fischer, 1980. 143 p.   MLCS 87/2670 (P)

33

Alldridge, James C. Ilse Aichinger. Chester Springs, Pa.: Dufour Editions, 1969. 128 p. (Modern German authors, texts and contexts; v. 2)   PT2601.I26 Z58
    Translations: p. 48–125.
    Bibliography: p. 126–128.

34

Ilse Aichinger: Ansprachen und Dokumente zur Verleihung des Kulturpreises der Stadt Dortmund, Nelly-Sachs-Preis, 1971. Dortmund: Literaturarchiv Kulturpreis der Stadt Dortmund, Nelly-Sachs-Preis, 1971. 56 p.: ill.   PT110.N4 I4

35

Kleiber, Carine. Ilse Aichinger: Leben und Werk. Frankfurt am Main, New York: Lang, 1984. 180 p. (Europäische Hochschulschriften. Reihe I, Deutsche Sprache und Literatur; Bd. 743)   PT2601.I26 Z75 1984
    Bibliography of works by and about I. Aichinger: p. 167–180.

36

Lorenz, Dagmar C. G. Ilse Aichinger. Königstein/Ts.: Athenäum, 1981. 259 p.   PT2601.I26 Z77
    Bibliography of works by and about I. Aichinger: p. 254–259.

****

37

Artmann, Hans Carl. Der aeronautische Sindtbart: oder, Seltsame Luftreise von Niedercalifornien nach Crain. München: Deutscher Taschenbuch-Verlag, 1975. 126 p.: ill.
PT2661.R75 A68 1975

38

————. Allerleirausch: neue schöne Kinderreime. Erlangen:
Renner, 1978. 56 p.   PT2661.R75 A8 1978

39

————. Aus meiner Botanisiertrommel: Balladen und
Naturgedichte. Salzburg: Residenz, 1975. 95 p.
                                            PT2661.R75 A95

40

————. Christopher und Peregrin und was weiter geschah: ein
Bären-Roman in drei Kapiteln. Frankfurt am Main: Insel
Verlag, 1975. 45 p.: ill.   PZ36.3.A73

41

————. Drakula, Drakula. Berlin: Rainer; Meilen bei Zürich:
Magica-Verlag, 1966. 33 1.: ill.   PT2661.R75 D7

42

————. Die Fahrt zur Insel Nantucket. Neuwied: Luchterhand,
1969. 500 p.   PT2661.R75 A19 1969

43

————. Fleiss und Industrie. Frankfurt am Main: Suhrkamp,
1967. 67 p.   PT2661.R75 F55

44

————. Frankenstein in Sussex. München: Lentz, 1974. 50 p.:
numerous ill.   PT2661.R75 F7 1974

45

————. Gedichte über die Liebe und über die Lasterhaftigkeit.
Frankfurt am Main: Suhrkamp, 1975. 190 p.
                                          PT2661.R75 A6 1975
     Includes index.

46

————. Grammatik der Rosen: gesammelte Prosa. Salzburg,
Wien: Residenz, 1979. 3 v.   PT2661.R75 A15 1979
     Issued in a case.
     Includes index.

47

―――. Grünverschlossene Botschaft. Frankfurt am Main: Suhrkamp, 1972. 90 p.: ill.

PT2661.R75 G7 1972

48

―――. Der handkolorierte Menschenfresser. Stuttgart: Collispress, 1968. 31 p. (on double leaves): col. ill.

PT2661.R75 H3

49

―――. How much, Schatzi? Frankfurt am Main: Suhrkamp, 1971. 170 p.   PT2661.R75 H6

50

―――. Im Schatten der Burenwurst: Skizzen aus Wien. Salzburg: Residenz, 1983. 134 p.: ill.   PT2661.R75 I37 1983

51

―――. Die Jagd nach Dr. U.: oder, Ein einsamer Spiegel, in dem sich der Tag reflektiert. Salzburg: Residenz, 1977. 157 p.

PT2661.R75 J3

52

―――. Kleinere Taschenkunststücke. Fast eine Chinoiserie. Wollerau, Wien, München: Georg Lentz, 1973. 47 p.

PT2661.R75 K5 1973

53

―――. Ein lilienweisser Brief aus Lincolnshire: Gedichte aus 21 Jahren. Frankfurt am Main: Suhrkamp, 1969. 529 p.

PT2661.R75 L5

54

―――. Nachrichten aus Nord und Süd. Salzburg, Wien: Residenz, 1978. 178 p.   PT2661.R75 N3

55

―――. Ompul. Zürich, München: Artemis, 1973. 24 p.: ill.

PZ36.3.A74

56

————. Die Sonne war ein grünes Ei: von der Erschaffung der Welt und ihren Dingen. Salzburg: Residenz, 1982. 98 p.

MLCS 84/5443

57

————. Das Suchen nach dem gestrigen Tag; oder, Schnee auf einem heissen Brotwecken. München: Goldmann, 1978. 159 p.

PT2661.R75 S9 1978

58

————. Überall wo Hamlet hinkam. Stuttgart: Collispress Eckhardt, 1969. 30 p.   PT2661.R75 U3

59

————. Unter der Bedeckung eines Hutes. Montagen und Sequenzen. Salzburg: Residenz, 1974. 107 p.

PT2661.R75 U5

60

————. Die Wanderer. München: Renner, 1979. 54 p.: ill.

PT2661.R75 W3

61

————. Yeti; oder, John, ich reise . . . München: Willing, 1970. 48 p.: ill.   PT2661.R75 Y4

———————————

62

Bisinger, Gerald. Über H. C. Artmann. Frankfurt am Main: Suhrkamp, 1972. 195, 1 p.   PT2661.R75 Z6

63

Pabisch, Peter. H. C. Artmann: ein Versuch über die literarische Alogik. Wien: Schendl, 1978. 145 p. PT2661.R75 Z84 1978

A revision of the author's thesis, University of Illinois, 1974, under the title: Das Alogische im literarischen Werk von Hans Carl Artmann.

Includes index.

Bibliography: p. 126–140.

64

Pose, Possen und Poesie: zum Werk Hans Carl Artmanns/ herausgegeben von Josef Donnenberg. Stuttgart: Akademischer Verlag Heinz, 1981. iv, 185 p. (Stuttgarter Arbeiten zur Germanistik: Nr. 100)　　　　PT2661.R75 Z86 1981
　　"Literatur von und über Hans Carl Artmann:"—p. 181–184.

＊＊＊＊＊＊＊＊＊＊＊＊＊＊＊＊＊＊＊

65

Bachmann, Ingeborg. Das dreissigste Jahr. München: Piper, 1961.
　243 p.　　　　　　　　　　　PT2603.A147 D7

66

———. Der Fall Franza: Requiem für Fanny Goldmann. München: Piper, 1979. 192 p.　　　PT2603.A147 F3 1979

67

———. Frankfurter Vorlesungen: Probleme zeitgenössischer Dichtung. München: Piper, 1980. 104 p.　　PT552.B27 1980
　Lectures given at the University of Frankfurt am Main, 1959–1960.
　Includes bibliographical references.

68

———. Gedichte, Erzählungen, Hörspiel, Essays. München: Piper, 1964. 346, 1 p.　　　　　PT2603.A147 A6 1964

69

———. Die gestundete Zeit, Gedichte. Frankfurt am Main: Frankfurter Verlagsanstalt, 1953. 60 p.　　PT2603.A147 G4

70

———. Der gute Gott von Manhattan. Stuttgart: Reclam, 1970.
　85 p.　　　　　　　　　　　PT2603.A174 G8 1970

71

———. Das Honditschkreuz. München: Piper, 1983. 114 p.
　　　　　　　　　　　　　PT2603.A147 H6 1983

72

————. Die Hörspiele. München: Piper, 1976. 171 p.

PT2603.A147 A6 1976

73

————. In the storm of roses: selected poems. Princeton, N.J.:
Princeton University Press, 1986. x, 210 p.: port.

PT2603.A147 A23 1986

74

————. Malina: Roman. Frankfurt am Main: Suhrkamp, 1977,
c1971. 355 p.   PT2603.A147 M3 1977

75

————. Ein Ort für Zufälle. Berlin: Wagenbach, 1965. 70 p.: ill.

PT2603.A147 O7 1965b

76

————. Simultan: neue Erzählungen. München: Piper, 1972.
233 p.   PT2603.A14 S5

77

————. The thirtieth year: stories. New York: Holmes & Meier,
1987. xvii, 181 p.   PT2603.A147 D713 1987
Translation of: Das dreissigste Jahr.

78

————. Undine geht: Erzählungen. Leipzig: Reclam, 1976, c1961.
237 p.   PT2603.A147 U5 1976

79

————. Die Wahrheit ist dem Menschen zumutbar: Essays,
Reden, Kleinere Schriften. München: Piper, 1981. 189 p.

PT2603.A147 W3 1981

80

————. Werke/ herausgegeben von Christine Koschel, Inge von
Weidenbaum, Clemens Münster. München, Zürich: Piper,
1978. 4 v.   PT2603.A147 1978
Includes indexes.

81

————. Wir müssen wahre Sätze finden: Gespräche und Interviews. München: Piper, 1983. 164 p.

PT2603.A147 Z477 1983

82

Angst-Hürlimann, Beatrice. Im Widerspiel des Unmöglichen mit dem Möglichen. Zürich: Juris-Verlag, 1971. 129 p.

PT2603.A147 Z57

83

Bareiss, Otto. Ingeborg Bachmann: eine Bibliographie. München, Zürich: Piper, 1978. xxxv, 343 p.: ill.   Z8056.B37
Includes indexes.

84

Bothner, Susanne. Ingeborg Bachmann, der janusköpfige Tod: Versuch der literaturpsychologischen Deutung eines Grenzgebietes der Lyrik unter Einbeziehung des Nachlasses. Frankfurt am Main, New York: Lang, 1986. 394 p. (Europäische Hochschulschriften. Reihe I, Deutsche Sprache und Literatur; Bd. 906)   PT2603.A147 Z59 1986
Originally presented as the author's thesis (doctoral)—Universität Würzburg, 1985.
Bibliography: p. 364–394.

85

Gürtler, Christa. Schreiben Frauen anders?: Untersuchungen zu Ingeborg Bachmann und Barbara Frischmuth. Stuttgart: Heinz, 1983. 417 p. (Stuttgarter Arbeiten zur Germanistik; Nr. 134. Salzburger Beiträge; Nr. 8)   PT3818.G8 1983
Originally presented as the author's thesis (doctoral), 1982.
Bibliography: p. 392–417.

86

Hapkemeyer, Andreas. Die Sprachthematik in der Prosa Ingeborg Bachmanns: Todesarten und Sprachformen. Frankfurt am Main:

Lang, 1982. ii, 123 p. (Europäische Hochschulschriften. Reihe
I, Deutsche Sprache und Literatur; Bd. 496)
                                          PT2603.A147 Z647 1982
Originally presented as the author's thesis (doctoral)—
Universität Innsbruck, 1981.
Bibliography: p. 118–123.

87

Henze, Hans Werner. Der junge Lord: komische Oper in zwei
Akten von Ingeborg Bachmann nach einer Parabel aus Der
Scheik von Alexandria und seine Sklaven. Mainz: Schott's
Söhne; New York: Schott Music Corp., 1965. 43 p.
                                          ML50.H519 J44 1965 (Case)

88

Henze, Hans Werner. Nachtstücke und Arien, nach Gedichten
von Ingeborg Bachmann, für Sopran und grosses Orchester.
Mainz: Schott's Söhne, 1958. 92 p.   M1613.H54 N3

89

Jakubowicz-Pisarek, Marta. Stand der Forschung zum Werk von
Ingeborg Bachmann. Frankfurt am Main, New York: Lang,
1984. 115 p. (Europäische Hochschulschriften. Reihe I, Deutsche
Sprache und Literatur; Bd. 753)   PT2603.A147 Z69 1984
Bibliography: p. 98–114.

90

Jürgensen, Manfred. Ingeborg Bachmann: die neue Sprache. Bern,
Las Vegas: Lang, 1981. 109 p.   PT2603.A147 Z7 1981
Bibliography: p. 107–109.

91

Mechtenberg, Theo. Utopie als ästhetische Kategorie: eine
Untersuchung der Lyrik Ingeborg Bachmanns. Stuttgart:
Akademischer Verlag Heinz, 1978. 138 p. (Stuttgarter Arbeiten
zur Germanistik; Nr. 47)   PT2603.A147 Z77
Summary in English.
Bibliography: p. 129–138.

92

Reinert, Claus. Unzumutbare Wahrheiten?: Einführung in
Ingeborg Bachmanns Hörspiel „Der gute Gott von Manhattan.''

Bonn: Bouvier, 1983. 267 p. (Abhandlungen zur Kunst-, Musik-
und Literaturwissenschaft; Bd. 346)

PT2603.A147 G837 1983

Includes index.
Bibliography: p. 251–263.

93

Thau, Bärbel. Gesellschaftsbild und Utopie im Spätwerk Ingeborg
Bachmanns: Untersuchungen zum ,,Todesarten-Zyklus'' und
zu ,,Simultan.'' Frankfurt am Main, New York: Lang, 1986.
166 p. (Europäische Hochschulschriften. Reihe I, Deutsche
Sprache und Literatur; Bd. 893)   PT2603.A147 Z89 1986
Bibliography: p. 151–166.

****

94

Bauer, Wolfgang. All change and other plays. London: Calder and
Boyars, 1973. 179 p.   PT2662.H85 M313
Translations of 3 plays originally published in German with
English titles: Magic afternoon. Change. Party for six.

95

————. Der Fieberkopf. Frankfurt a. M.: Barmeier & Nikel, 1967.
157 p.   PT2662.A85 F5

96

————. Gespenster: Silvester oder, Das Massaker im Hotel Sacher:
Film und Frau: drei Stücke. Köln: Kiepenheuer & Witsch, 1974.
151 p.: port.   PT2662.A85 G4

97

————. In Zeiten wie diesen: ein Drehbuch. Salzburg: Residenz,
1984. 91 p.: ill.   MLCS 84/8678 (P)

98

————. Katharina Doppelkopf, und andere Eisenbahnstücke.
Dornbirn: Vorarlberger Verlagsanstalt, 1973. 80 p.: ill.

PT2662.A85 K3

99

————. Magic afternoon. Change. Party for six. Drei Stücke.
Köln: Kiepenheuer & Witsch, 1969. 185 p.: port.

PT2662.A85 M3

100

————. Romeo und Julia. Drama in 5 Bildern. München: Hanser,
1969. 34 l. of ill. with text. PT2662.A85 R6 (Rare Bk Coll)

101

————. Die Sumpftänzer: Dramen, Prosa, Lyrik aus 2
Jahrzehnten. Köln: Kiepenheuer und Witsch, 1978. 403 p.

PT2662.A85 S8

102

————. Woher kommen wir? wohin gehen wir?: Dramen und
Prosa mit bisher unveröffentlichten und neuen Stücken.
München: Heyne, 1982. 591 p.: 1 port. (Neue Literatur; Bd. 14)

PT2662.A85 W6 1982

103

Melzer, Gerhard. Wolfgang Bauer: eine Einführung in das
Gesamtwerk. Königstein/Ts.: Athenäum, 1981. 170 p.

PT2662.A85 Z77 1981

    Includes index.
    Bibliography: p. 162–167.

****

104

Bernhard, Thomas. Alte Meister: Komödie. Frankfurt am Main:
Suhrkamp, 1985. 310 p.   PT2662.E7 A75 1985

105

————. Am Ziel. Frankfurt am Main: Suhrkamp, 1981. 151 p.

MLCS 81/473

106

————. Amras. Frankfurt am Main: Insel-Verlag, 1964. 79 p.

PT2662.E7 A78

107

————. An der Baumgrenze. Salzburg: Residenz, 1969. 94 p.

PT2662.E7 A8

108

————. Der Atem: eine Entscheidung. Salzburg, Wien: Residenz, 1978. 157 p. PT2662.E7 Z513

Continuation of the author's Die Ursache and Der Keller.

109

————. Auf der Erde und in der Hölle: Gedichte. Salzburg: Müller, 1957. 125 p. PT2662.E7 A9 1957

110

————. Auslöschung: ein Zerfall. Frankfurt am Main: Suhrkamp, 1986. 650 p. PT2662.E7 A95 1986

111

————. Die Berühmten. Frankfurt am Main: Suhrkamp, 1976. 130 p. PT2662.E7 B4

112

————. Die Billigesser. Frankfurt am Main: Suhrkamp, 1980. 150 p.: port. PT2662.E7 B5

113

————. Concrete. New York: Knopf, 1984. 155 p.

PT2662.E7 B4413 1984

Translation of: Beton.

114

————. Correction. New York: Vintage Books, 1983, c1979. 271 p. PT2662.E7 K613 1983

Translation of: Korrektur.

115

————. Einfach kompliziert. Frankfurt am Main: Suhrkamp, 1986. 70 p. MLCS 86/7006 (P)

116

————. Ereignisse. Berlin: Literarisches Colloquium, 1969. 43 p.

PT2662.E7 E7

117
————. Die Erzählungen. Frankfurt am Main: Suhrkamp, 1979.
607 p.   PT2662.E7 E79

118
————. Ein Fest für Boris. Frankfurt am Main: Suhrkamp, 1970.
106 p.   PT2662.E7 F4

119
————. The force of habit: a comedy. London: Heinemann, 1976.
x, 94 p.   PT2662.E7 M313
Translation of: Die Macht der Gewohnheit.

120
————. Frost. Frankfurt am Main: Suhrkamp, 1972. 315 p.
PT2662.E7 F7 1972

121
————. Gargoyles. Chicago: University of Chicago Press, 1986,
c1970. 208 p.   PT2662.E7 V413 1986
Translation of: Verstörung.
Includes index.

122
————. Gathering evidence: a memoir. New York: Knopf, 1985.
viii, 340 p.   PT2662.E7 Z46413 1985
Contains translations of the 5 works which comprise the
author's memoirs.

123
————. Gehen. Frankfurt am Main: Suhrkamp, 1971. 100 p.
PT2662.E7 G4

124
————. Holzfällen: eine Erregung. Frankfurt am Main:
Suhrkamp, 1984. 320 p.   PT2662.E7 H65 1984

125
————. Der Ignorant und der Wahnsinnige. Frankfurt am Main:
Suhrkamp, 1972. 98 p.   PT2662.E7 I45

126.

————. Immanuel Kant: Komödie. Frankfurt am Main: Suhrkamp, 1978. 132 p.   PT2662.E7 I5

127

————. Der Italiener. Salzburg: Residenz, 1971. 94 p., 16 1. of ill.   PN1997.B397

128

————. Ja. Frankfurt am Main: Suhrkamp, 1978. 147 p.   PT2662.E7 J2

129

————. Die Jagdgesellschaft. Frankfurt am Main: Suhrkamp, 1974. 112 p.   PT2662.E7 J3

130

————. Das Kalkwerk. Frankfurt am Main: Suhrkamp, 1970. 269 p.   PT2662.E7 K3

131

————. Die Kälte: eine Isolation. Salzburg: Residenz, 1981. 150 p.   MLCS 87/3459 (P)

132

————. Der Keller: eine Entziehung. Salzburg: Residenz, 1976. 167 p.   PT2662.E7 Z52

Continuation of the author's Die Ursache and continued by Der Atem.

133

————. Ein Kind. Salzburg: Residenz, 1982. 166 p.   MLCS 84/5558

134

————. Korrektur. Frankfurt am Main: Suhrkamp, 1975. 362 p.   PT2662.E7 K6

135

————. Der Kulterer: eine Filmgeschichte. Salzburg: Residenz, 1974. 118 p.   PT2662.E7 K8

136

————. The lime works. Chicago: University of Chicago Press,
1986, c1973. 241 p.   PT2662.E7 K313 1986
Translation of: Das Kalkwerk.

137

————. Die Macht der Gewohnheit: Komödie. Frankfurt am
Main: Suhrkamp, 1974. 144 p.   PT2662.E7 M3

138

————. Midland in Stilfs: drei Erzählungen. Frankfurt am Main:
Suhrkamp, 1971. 116 p.   PT2662.E7 M5

139

————. Minetti: ein Portrait des Künstlers als alter Mann.
Frankfurt am Main: Suhrkamp, 1977. 57 p.: ill.
                                             PT2662.E7 M55

140

————. Der Präsident. Zürich: Suhrkamp, 1975. 163 p.
                                             PT2662.E7 P67

141

————. Ritter, Dene, Voss. Frankfurt am Main: Suhrkamp, 1984.
163 p.   PT2662.E7 R58 1984

142

————. Die Rosen der Einöde; fünf Sätze für Ballett, Stimmen
und Orchester. Frankfurt am Main: Fischer, 1959. 58 p.
                                             ML52.B465 R7

143

————. Die Salzburger Stücke. Frankfurt am Main: Suhrkamp,
1975. 196 p.   PT2662.E7 A19 1975
Bibliography of works by B. Thomas; p. 202.

144

————. Der Schein trügt. Frankfurt am Main: Suhrkamp, 1983.
112 p.   PT2662.E7 S3 1983

145
———. Der Stimmenimitator. Frankfurt am Main: Suhrkamp,
1978. 179 p.   PT2662.E7 S7

146
———. Die Stücke. Frankfurt am Main: Suhrkamp, 1983. 1064 p.
                                               PT2662.E7 A19 1983

147
———. Der Theatermacher. Frankfurt am Main: Suhrkamp,
1984. 161 p.   PT2662.E7 T5 1984

148
———. Über allen Gipfeln ist Ruh: ein deutscher Dichtertag um
1980: Komödie. Frankfurt am Main: Suhrkamp, 1981. 143 p.
                                                  MLCS 83/1947 (P)

149
———. Ungenachl: Erzählung. Frankfurt am Main: Suhrkamp,
1968. 92 p.   PT2662.E7 U5

150
———. Der Untergeher. Frankfurt am Main: Suhrkamp, 1983.
242 p.   MLCS 84/5200 (P)

151
———. Die Ursache: eine Andeutung. Salzburg: Residenz, 1975.
159 p.   PT2662.E7 Z524
Continued by the author's Der Keller and Der Atem.

152
———. Verstörung. Frankfurt am Main: Suhrkamp, 1969. 193 p.
                                                PT2662.E7 V4 1969

153
———. Vor dem Ruhestand: eine Komödie von deutscher Seele.
Frankfurt am Main: Suhrkamp, 1979. 120 p. PT2662.E7 V6

154
———. Watten: ein Nachlass. Frankfurt am Main: Suhrkamp,
1969. 88 p.   PT2662.E7 W3

155

————. Der Weltverbesserer. Bochum: Schauspielhaus Bochum,
   1980. 268 p.: ill.   PT2662.E7 W35 1980

156

————. Der Wetterfleck: Erzählungen. Stuttgart: Reclam, 1976.
   76 p.   PT2662.E7 W4

157

————. Wittgensteins Neffe: eine Freundschaft. Frankfurt am
   Main: Suhrkamp, 1983, c1982. 163 p.
                                                   PT2662.E7 Z475 1983

158

————. Woodcutters. New York: Knopf, 1987. 181 p.
                                                   PT2662.E7 H6513 1988
   Translation of: Holzfällen.

————————————

159

Bernhard: Annäherungen/ herausgegeben von Manfred Jürgensen.
   Bern: Francke, 1981. 245 p.: ill. (Queensland studies in German
   language and literature; v. 8)   PT2662.E7 Z53 1981
   Includes bibliographical references.

160

Bohnert, Karin. Ein Modell der Entfremdung: eine Interpretation
   des Romans ,,Das Kalkwerk'' von Thomas Bernhard. Wien:
   VWGO, Verbindung der Wissenschaftlichen Gesellschaften
   Österreichs, 1976. v, 160 p. (Dissertation der Universität Wien;
   130)   PT2662.E7 K332 1976
   Originally presented as the author's thesis, Vienna, 1973.
   Bibliography: p. 254–260.

161

Bugmann, Urs. Bewältigungsversuch: Thomas Bernhards
   autobiographische Schriften. Bern, Las Vegas: Lang, 1981.
   369 p.: ill. (Europäische Hochschulschriften. Reihe I, Deutsche
   Sprache und Literatur; Bd. 435)   PT2662.E7 Z62 1981

Originally presented as the author's thesis (doctoral)—
Universität Zürich.
Bibliography: p. 356-369.

162

Dittmar, Jens. Thomas Bernhard: Werkgeschichte. Frankfurt am
Main: Suhrkamp, 1981. 318 p.   PT2662.E7 Z64
Includes excerpts from T. Bernhard's works.
Includes index.
Bibliography: p. 232-312.

163

Fischer, Bernhard. ,,Gehen'' von Thomas Bernhard: eine Studie
zum Problem der Moderne. Bonn: Bouvier, 1985. 185 p.
(Bonner Arbeiten zur deutschen Literatur; Bd. 43)
          PT2662.E7 G434 1985
Bibliography: p. 182-185.

164

Kohlenbach, Margarete. Das Ende der Vollkommenheit: zum
Verständnis von Thomas Bernhards ,,Korrektur.'' Tübingen:
Narr, 1986. ix, 245 p. (Mannheimer Beiträge zur Sprach- und
Literaturwissenschaft; Bd. 10)   PT2662.E7 K635 1986
Revision of the author's thesis (doctoral)—Freie Universität
Berlin, 1984.
Bibliography: p. 241-245.

165

Lindenmayr, Heinrich. Totalität und Beschränkung: eine
Untersuchung zu Thomas Bernhards Roman ,,Das Kalkwerk.''
Königstein/Ts.: Forum Academicum, 1982. 128 p. (Hochschul-
schriften Literaturwissenschaft; Bd. 50)
          PT2662.E7 K334 1982
Includes index.
Bibliography: p. 121-126.

166

Meyerhöfer, Nicholas J. Thomas Bernhard. Berlin: Colloquium
Verlag, 1985. 91 p. (Köpfe des 20. Jahrhunderts; Bd. 104)
          PT2662.E7 Z78 1985
Bibliography: p. 89.

* * * * * * * * * * * * * * * * * *

167
Busta, Christine. Inmitten aller Vergänglichkeit: Gedichte.
Salzburg: Müller, 1985. 96 p.   MLCS 87/547 (P)

168
———. Lampe und Delphin. Gedichte. Salzburg: Müller, 1966.
94 p.   PT2603.U89 L3 1966

169
———. Der Regenbaum: Gedichte. Salzburg: Müller, 1977. 134 p.
                                             PT2603.U89 R4 1977

170
———. Salzgarten: Gedichte. Salzburg: Müller, 1975. 92 p.
                                                PT2603.U89 S2

171
———. Die Scheune der Vögel. Salzburg: Müller, 1968. 121 p.
                                             PT2603.U89 S3 1968

172
———. Die Sternenmühle. Salzburg, Wien, Freilassing: Müller,
1970. 16 l. col. ill.   PZ34.3.B87 1970

173
———. Unterwegs zu älteren Feuern; Gedichte. Salzburg: Müller,
1965. 92 p.   PT2603.U89 U5

174
———. Unveröffentlichte Gedichte. Wien: Höhere Graphische
Bundes- Lehr- und Versuchsanstalt, 1965. 17 p.
                                               PT2603.U89 U53

175
———. Wenn du das Wappen der Liebe malst: Gedichte.
Salzburg: Müller, 1981. 121 p.   PT2603.U89 W4 1981

****

176
Eisenreich, Herbert. Die abgelegte Zeit: ein Fragment. Wien:
Wiener Journal, Herold, 1985. 612 p. PT2609.I73 A63 1985
  „Biographische und bibliographische Hinweise": p. 611–612.

177

————. Der alte Adam: aus dem Zettelkram eines Sophisten. Mühlacker: Stieglitz, 1985. 119 p.   MLCS 86/3307 (B)

178

————. Die blaue Distel der Romantik: Erzählungen. Graz, Wien, Köln: Styria, 1976. 160 p.   PT2665.I8 B55

179

————. Carnuntum: Geist und Fleisch. Graz, Wien, Köln: Styria, 1978. 61 p.: ill.   DB879.C3 E38 1978

180

————. Die Freunde meiner Frau und 19 andere Kurzgeschichten. Zürich: Diogenes Verlag, 1966. 396 p.: ill.   PT2665.I8 F7

181

————. Grosse Welt auf kleinen Schienen: das Entstehen einer Modellanlage. Salzburg: Residenz, 1963. 219 p.: ill., plans (in pocket).   TF197.E35

182

————. Ich im Auto. Salzburg: Residenz, 1966. 179 p.
GV1023.E37

183

————. Das kleine Stifterbuch. Salzburg: Residenz, 1967. 122 p.
PT2525.Z4 E35

184

————. Das Leben als Freizeit. Düsseldorf: Edition Freizeit, 1976. 40 p.   HD5106.E35

185

————. Reaktionen: Essays zur Literatur. Gütersloh: Mohn, 1964. 357 p.   PN710.E4

186

————. Ein schöner Sieg, und 21 andere Missverständnisse. Graz: Styria, 1973. 163 p.   PT2665.I8 S3

187

————. Sebastian. Gütersloh: Mohn, 1966. 67 p.   PT2665.I8 S4

188

————. Sozusagen Liebesgeschichten. Gütersloh: Mohn, 1965.
199 p.   PT2665.I8 S6

189

————. Verlorene Funde: Gedichte 1946–1952. Graz, Wien,
Köln: Styria, 1976. 84 p.   PT2665.I8 V4

———————————

190

Basil, Otto. Das grosse Erbe: Aufsatz zur österreichischen Literatur.
Graz: Stiasny, 1962. 127 p.   PT3813.B3
Includes Herbert Eisenreich.

****

191

Fried, Erich. Angst und Trost: Erzählungen und Gedichte über
Juden und Nazis. Frankfurt am Main: Alibaba, 1983. 100 p.: ill.
                                                   PT2611.R596 A6 1983
Bibliography of the author's works: p. 2.

192

————. Aufforderung zur Unruhe. München: Deutscher
Taschenbuch-Verlag, 1972. 161 p.   PT2611.R596 A9

193

————. Befreiung von der Flucht: Gedichte und Gegengedichte.
Erw. Neuaufl. Düsseldorf: Claassen, 1983. 150 p.
                                                   MLCS 84/7232 (P)

194

————. Die Beine der grösseren Lügen. Berlin: Wagenbach, 1969.
66 p.   PT2611.R596 B45

195

————. Beunruhigungen. Berlin: Wagenbach, 1984. 90 p.
                                                   MLCS 86/5364 (P)

196

————. Die bunten Getüme. Berlin: Wagenbach, 1977. 76 p.: ill.

PT2666.R4846 B8

Bibliography of E. Fried's works: p. 76.

197

————. Es ist was es ist: Liebesgedichte, Angstgedichte, Zorngedichte. Berlin: Wagenbach, 1983. 105 p.

PT2611.R596 E8 1983

198

————. Fast alles Mögliche: wahre Geschichten und gültige Lügen. Berlin: Wagenbach, 1975. 143 p.   PT2611.R596 F3

Bibliography of the author's works: p. 143.

199

————. Die Freiheit den Mund aufzumachen: achtundvierzig Gedichte. Berlin: Wagenbach, 1972. 67 p.   PT2611.R596 F7

200

————. Frühe Gedichte. Düsseldorf: Claassen, 1986. 119 p.

MLCS 87/1031 (P)

201

————. Gegengift. Berlin: Wagenbach, 1974. 78 p.: ill.

PT2611.R596 G4

202

————. Höre Israel. Hamburg: Verlag Association, 1974. 154 p.: ill.   PT2611.R596 H6

203

————. Hundert Gedichte ohne Vaterland. Berlin: Wagenbach, 1978. 126 p.   PT2611.R596 H8

204

————. Kampf ohne Engel. Berlin: Verlag Volk und Welt, 1976. 214 p: ill.   PT2611.R596 K35

205

————. Kinder und Narren. München: Hanser, 1965. 192 p.

PT2611.R596 K5

206
————. Last honours. London: Turret, 1968. 31 p.

                                    PT2611.R596 L3

Poems.

Parallel German text, English translation.

Limited ed. of 150 copies, 50 signed and numbered.

207
————. Lebensschatten. Berlin: Wagenbach, 1981. 104 p.

                                   MLCS 87/3549 (P)

208
————. Liebesgedichte. Berlin: Wagenbach, 1979. 102 p.

                                   PT2666.R4846 L5

209
————. Das Nähe suchen. Berlin: Wagenbach, 1982. 91 p.

                                   MLCS 84/11166 (P)

210
————. On pain of seeing. London: Rapp & Whiting, 1969. 72 p.
  (Poetry Europe series; 11)   PT2611.R596 O5
    Bibliography: p. 71–72.

211
————. One hundred poems without a country. London: Calder,
  1978. 147 p.   PT2611.R596 H813
    Translation of: Hundert Gedichte ohne Vaterland.
    Includes bibliographical references.

212
————. So kam ich unter die Deutschen. Hamburg: Verlag
  Association, 1977. 122 p.: ill.   PT2611.R596 S6

213
————. Überlegungen. München: Hanser, 1964. 22 p.

                                     PT2611.R596 U3

214
————. Um Klarheit: Gedichte gegen das Vergessen. Berlin:
  Wagenbach, 1985. 75 p.   MLCS 86/1440 (P)

215

————. Und alle seine Mörder. Wien: Promedia, 1984. 87 p.

MLCS 86/3708 (P)

216

————. Und Vietnam und. Berlin: Wagenbach, 1966. 70 p.

PT2611.R596 U5

217

————. Unter Nebenfeinden: fünfzig Gedichte. Berlin: Wagenbach, 1970. 66 p.

PT2611.R596 U54

218

————. Wächst das Rettende auch?: Gedichte für den Frieden. Köln: Bund-Verlag, 1986. 110 p.: ill.

MLCS 87/414 (P)

219

————. Warngedichte. Erich Fried. München: Hanser, 1964. 128 p.

MLCS 85/576 (P)

220

————. Zeitfragen und Überlegungen: 80 Gedichte, sowie ein Zyklus. Berlin: Wagenbach, 1984. 118 p.

MLCS 86/7937 (P)

221

————. Zur Zeit und zur Unzeit. Köln: Bund-Verlag, 1981. 148 p.

MLCS 82/2425

* * * * * * * * * * * * * * * * * *

222

Frischmuth, Barbara. Amoralische Kinderklapper. Frankfurt am Main: Suhrkamp, 1975. 117 p.

PT2666.R558 A8 1975

223

————. Amy: oder, Die Metamorphose: Roman. Salzburg, Wien: Residenz, Verlag, 1978. 296 p.

PT2666.R558 A84

Continuation of the author's Die Mystifikationen der Sophie Silber and continued by Kai und die Liebe zu den Modellen.

224
————. Bindungen: Erzählung. Salzburg: Residenz, 1980. 125 p.
MLCS 87/2162 (P)

225
————. Entzug, ein Menetekel der zärtlichsten Art. Pfaffenweiler:
Pfaffenweiler Presse, 1979. 41 p.: ill.   MLCS 84/12585 (P)

226
————. Die Ferienfamilie: Roman. Wien: Residenz, 1981. 131 p.
MLCS 81/1043

227
————. Die Frau im Mond: Roman. Salzburg: Residenz, 1982.
154 p.   MLCS 84/5478

228
————. Haschen nach Wind: Erzählungen. Salzburg: Residenz,
1974. 143 p.   PT2666.R558 H3

229
————. Herrin der Tiere: Erzählung. Salzburg: Residenz, 1986.
140 p.   MLCS 86/7099 (P)

230
————. Ida und Ob. Wien: Jugend und Volk, 1972. 143 p.
PZ33.F718

231
————. Kai und die Liebe zu den Modellen: Roman. Salzburg,
Wien: Residenz, 1979. 207 p.   PT2666.R558 K3
    Continuation of the author's Die Mystifikationen der Sophie
Silber and Amy.

232
————. Die Klosterschule; Das Verschwinden des Schattens in der
Sonne. Berlin: Verlag Volk und Welt, 1976. 289 p.
PT2666.R558 A15 1976

233
————. Kopftänzer. Salzburg: Residenz, 1984. 268 p.
MLCS 87/339 (P)

234

———. Die Mystifikationen der Sophie Silber. Salzburg: Residenz, 1976. 319 p.   PT2666.R558 M9

Continued by Amy and Kai und die Liebe zu den Modellen.

235

———. Der Pluderich. Frankfurt am Main: Insel-Verlag, 1969. 8 1. of ill.: text.   PZ33.F72

236

———. Rückkehr zum vorläufigen Ausgangspunkt: Erzählungen. Salzburg: Residenz, 1973. 129 p.   PT2666.R558 R8

237

———. Tage und Jahre. Salzburg: Residenz, 1971. 111 p.   PT2666.R558 T3

238

———. Traumgrenze: Erzählungen. Salzburg: Residenz, 1983. 138 p.   MLCS 84/7217 (P)

239

———. Das Verschwinden des Schattens in der Sonne. Frankfurt am Main: Suhrkamp, 1973. 232 p.   PT2666.R558 V4

240

Gürtler, Christa. Schreiben Frauen anders?: Untersuchungen zu Ingeborg Bachmann und Barbara Frischmuth. Stuttgart: Heinz, 1983. 417 p. (Stuttgarter Arbeiten zur Germanistik; Nr. 134. Salzburger Beiträge; Nr. 8)   PT3818.G8 1983

Originally presented as the author's thesis (doctoral), 1982. Bibliography: p. 392–417.

241

Khaled, Muhammad Abu-Hatab. Oesterreichische Literatur in Aegypten: kritische Gedanken zu Barbara Frischmuths Roman „Das Verschwinden des Schattens in der Sonne." Kairo: Deutschabteilung der Al-Azhar Universität, 1978. 46 p.   PT2666.R558 V434 1978

Includes bibliographical references.

****

242
Handke, Peter. Across. New York: Collier Books, Macmillan,
1987, c1986. 137 p.   PT2668.A5 C4513 1987
Translation of: Der Chinese des Schmerzes.

243
———. Als das Wünschen noch geholfen hat. Frankfurt a. M.:
Suhrkamp, 1974. 121 p., 2 leaves of plates, ill. (2 col.).
                                           PT2668.A5 A78

244
———. Die Angst des Tormanns beim Elfmeter. Frankfurt am
Main: Suhrkamp, 1970. 125 p.   PT2668.A5 A8

245
———. Begrüssung des Aufsichtsrats. Salzburg: Residenz, 1967.
126 p.   PT2668.A5 B4

246
———. Der Chinese des Schmerzes. Frankfurt am Main:
Suhrkamp, 1983. 254 p.   PT2668.A5 C45 1983

247
———. Chronik der laufenden Ereignisse. Frankfurt am Main:
Suhrkamp, 1971. 139 p.: ill.   PT2668.A5 C5

248
———. Deutsche Gedichte. Frankfurt am Main: Euphorion-
Verlag, 1969. 1 v. (unpaged).   PT2688.A5 D4

249
———. Das Ende des Flanierens. Wien: Davidpresse, 1976. 28
double leaves: ill.   PT2668.A5 E5
Limited ed. of 150 copies; this is no. 52.

250
———. Das Ende des Flanierens. Frankfurt am Main: Suhrkamp,
1980. 169 p.   MLCS 87/3502 (P)

251
———. Falsche Bewegung. Frankfurt am Main: Suhrkamp, 1975.
80 p.   PT2668.A5 F3

252

————. Gedicht an die Dauer. Frankfurt am Main: Suhrkamp, 1986. 54 p.   MLCS 87/776 (P)

253

————. Die Geschichte des Bleistifts. Salzburg: Residenz, 1982. 249 p.   PT2668.A5 G37 1982

254

————. Das Gewicht der Welt: ein Journal (November 1975—März 1977). Salzburg: Residenz, 1977. 324 p.
         PT2668.A5 G4 1977

255

————. Der gewöhnliche Schrecken. Salzburg: Residenz, 1969. 184 p.   PT1340.H6 H3

256

————. The goalie's anxiety at the penalty kick. New York: Farrar, Straus and Giroux, 1972. 133 p.   PZ4.H2363 Go
Translation of: Die Angst des Tormanns beim Elfmeter.

257

————. Der Hausierer. Frankfurt am Main: Suhrkamp, 1967. 200 p.   PT2668.A5 H3

258

————. Die Hornissen. Reinbek bei Hamburg: Rowohlt-Taschenbuch-Verlag, 1968. 150 p.   PT2668.A65 H6 1968

259

————. Ich bin ein Bewohner des Elfenbeinturms. Frankfurt am Main: Suhrkamp, 1972. 232 p.   PT2668.A5 I3

260

————. Die Innenwelt der Aussenwelt der Innenwelt. Frankfurt am Main: Suhrkamp, 1969. 149 p.: ill.   PT2668.A5 I5

261

————. The innerworld of the outerworld of the innerworld. New York: Seabury Press, 1974. 172 p.   PT2668.A5 I5213 1974

Poems.
English and German.
Selected from Die Innenwelt der Aussenwelt der Innenwelt.
Bibliography: p. 171–172.

262
————. Kaspar and other plays. New York: Farrar, Straus, and
Giroux, 1969. 139 p.   PT2668.A5 A27

263
————. Kindergeschichte. Frankfurt am Main: Suhrkamp, 1981.
137 p.   HQ756.H36

264
————. Der kurze Brief zum langen Abschied. Frankfurt am
Main: Suhrkamp, 1972. 194 p.   PT2668.A5 K8

265
————. Langsame Heimkehr. Frankfurt am Main: Suhrkamp,
1979. 199 p.   PT2668.A5 L3 1979

266
————. The left-handed woman. New York: Farrar, Straus, and
Giroux, 1978. 87 p.   PZ4.H2363 Le
Translation of: Die linkshändige Frau.

267
————. Die linkshändige Frau. Frankfurt am Main: Suhrkamp,
1979, c1976. 130 p.   PT2668.A5 L5 1979

268
————. A moment of true feeling. New York, Farrar, Straus and
Giroux, 1977. 133 p.   PZ4.H2363 Mo 1977
Translation of: Die Stunde der wahren Empfindung.

269
————. Nachmittag eines Schriftstellers. Salzburg: Residenz, 1987.
90 p.   MLCS 87/3652 (P)

270

————. Nonsense and happiness. New York: Urizen Books, 1976.
93 p.   PT2668.A5 A7813
Translation of: Als das Wünschen noch geholfen hat, with
original German text.

271

————. Offending the audience; and, Self-accusation. London:
Methuen, 1971. 57 p.   PT2668.A5 P813
Translations of: Publikumsbeschimpfung and Selbstbe-
zichtigung.

272

————. Phantasien der Wiederholung. Frankfurt am Main:
Suhrkamp, 1983. 99 p.   PT2668.A5 P48 1983

273

————. Prosa, Gedichte, Theaterstücke, Hörspiel, Aufsätze.
Frankfurt am Main: Suhrkamp, 1969. 350 p.
                                         PT2668.A5 A6 1969

274

————. Publikumsbeschimpfung und andere Sprechstücke.
Frankfurt am Main: Suhrkamp, 1971. 95 p.
                                         PT2668.A5 P8 1971

275

————. The ride across Lake Constance and other plays. New
York: Farrar, Straus and Giroux, 1976. 258 p.
                                         PT2668.A5 A274

276

————. Der Ritt über den Bodensee. Frankfurt am Main:
Suhrkamp, 1971. 101 p.   PT2668.A5 R5

277

————. Short letter, long farewell. New York: Farrar, Straus and
Giroux, 1974. 167 p.   PZ4.H2363 Sh 1974
Translation of: Der kurze Brief zum langen Abschied.

278

———. A sorrow beyond dreams: a life story. New York: Farrar, Straus and Giroux, 1975, c1974. 69 p.   PT2668.A5 W813 1975
Translation of: Wunschloses Unglück.

279

———. Stücke. Frankfurt am Main: Suhrkamp, 1972. 2 v.
PT2668.A5 S8 v. 1–2

280

———. Die Stunde der wahren Empfindung. Frankfurt am Main: Suhrkamp, 1975. 166 p.   PT2668.A5 S85

281

———. They are dying out. London: Eyre Methuen, 1975, c1974. 63 p.   PT2668.A5 U513 1975
Translation of: Die Unvernünftigen sterben aus.

282

———. Über die Dörfer: dramatisches Gedicht. Frankfurt am Main: Suhrkamp, 1981. 105 p.   MLCS 81/177

283

———. Die Unvernünftigen sterben aus. Frankfurt am Main: Suhrkamp, 1973. 99 p.   PT2668.A5 U5

284

———. The weight of the world. New York: Farrar, Straus, and Giroux, 1984. 243 p.   PT2668.A5 G413 1984
Translation of: Das Gewicht der Welt.

285

———. Wind und Meer. Frankfurt am Main: Suhrkamp, 1970. 127 p.   PT2668.A5 W5 1970

286

———. Wunschloses Unglück. Boston: Suhrkamp/Insel Publishers, 1985. xiv, 123 p.   PT2668.A5 W8 1985
Annotated ed. in the original German, with English notes and vocabulary.
Bibliography: p. 105–106.

287

Bartmann, Christoph. Suche nach Zusammenhang: Handkes Werk
als Prozess. Wien: Braumüller, 1984. 250 p. (Wiener Arbeiten
zur deutschen Literatur; 11)   PT2668.A5 Z57 1984
   Bibliography: p. 243–250.

288

DeMeritt, Linda C. New subjectivity and prose forms of alienation:
Peter Handke and Botho Strauss. New York: Lang, 1987. n.p.
   PT735.D 1987
   Includes index and bibliography.

289

Dinter, Ellen. Gefundene und erfundene Heimat: zu Peter Handkes
zyklischer Dichtung „Langsame Heimkehr," 1979–1981. Köln:
Böhlau, 1986. vii, 297 p. (Kölner germanistische Studien; Bd.
22)   PT2668.A5 L334 1986
   Bibliography: p. 279–297.

290

Durzak, Manfred. Peter Handke und die deutsche Gegenwartsliteratur: Narziss auf Abwegen. Stuttgart: Kohlhammer, 1982.
186 p. (Sprache und Literatur; 108)   PT2668.A5 Z62 1982
   Includes bibliographical references and index.

291

Falkenstein, Henning. Peter Handke. Berlin: Colloquium-Verlag,
1979. 98 p. (Köpfe des zwanzigsten Jahrhunderts; Bd. 75)
   PT2668.A5 Z63 1979
   Bibliography: p. 95–96.

292

Gabriel, Norbert. Peter Handke und Österreich. Bonn: Bouvier,
1983. 265 p. (Abhandlungen zur Kunst-, Musik- und Literaturwissenschaft; Bd. 334)   PT2668.A5 Z64 1983
   Bibliography: p. 257–265.

293

Klatzkin, Amy. Peter Handke, the first five plays. Stanford:
Humanities Honors Program, Stanford University, 1979. 71 p.

(Stanford honors essay in humanities; no. 23)   PT2668.A5 Z74
    Bibliography: p. 67–70.

294

Klinkowitz, Jerome. Peter Handke and the postmodern trans-
formation: the goalie's journey home. Columbia: University of
Missouri Press, 1983. vii, 133 p.   PT2668.A5 Z75 1983
    "Books by Peter Handke"—p. 131–133.
    Includes bibliographical references.

295

Putz, Peter. Peter Handke. Frankfurt am Main: Suhrkamp, 1982.
    124 p.   PT2668.A5 Z82 1982

296

Renner, Rolf Gunter. Peter Handke. Stuttgart: Metzler, 1985. ix,
    204 p.   PT2668.A5 Z83 1985
        Includes index.
        Bibliography: p. 183–202.

297

Schlueter, June. The plays and novels of Peter Handke. Pittsburgh:
    University of Pittsburgh Press, 1981. xiii, 213 p.
                                    PT2668.A5 Z877 1981
        Includes index.
        Bibliography: p. 195–208.

298

Sergooris, Günther. Peter Handke und die Sprache. Bonn: Bouvier,
    1979. 138 p. (Abhandlungen zur Kunst-, Musik- und Literatur-
    wissenschaft; Bd. 270)   PT2668.A5 Z883 1979
        Bibliography: p. 135–138.

****

299

Hergouth, Alois. Flucht zu Odysseus: Gedichte. Graz, Wien, Köln:
    Styria, 1975. 111 p.   PT2668.E726 F4

300

————. Der Mond im Apfelgarten: aus meinem Leben. Graz: Styria, 1980. 198 p.: ill.   PT2668.E726 M6 1980

301

————. Stationen im Wind. Gedichte, 1953–1973. Graz, Wien, Köln: Styria, 1973. 82 p.   PT2668.E726 S8

****

302

Innerhofer, Franz. Beautiful days. New York: Urizen Books, 1976. 170 p.   PZ4.I5446 Be 1976
  Translation of: Schöne Tage.

303

————. Der Emporkömmling. Salzburg: Residenz, 1982. 133 p.   MLCS 84/5202 (P)

304

————. Die grossen Wörter. Salzburg: Residenz, 1977. 175 p.   PT2669.N6 G7

305

————. Innenansichten eines beginnenden Arbeitstages. Pfaffenweiler: Pfaffenweiler Presse, 1976. 35 p.: ill.   PT2669.N6 I5

306

————. Schattseite. Salzburg: Residenz, 1975. 257 p.   PT2669.N6 S28

307

————. Schöne Tage. Salzburg: Residenz, 1974. 239 p.   PT2669.N6 S3

****

308

Jandl, Ernst. Andere Augen. Wien: Bergland Verlag, 1956. 61 p.   PT2670.A483 A7

309

————. Aus der Fremde: Sprechoper in 7 Szenen. Darmstadt:
Luchterhand, 1980. 107 p.   PT2670.A483 A9

310

————. Die Bearbeitung der Mütze. Darmstadt, Neuwied:
Luchterhand, 1978. 162 p.   PT2670.A483 B4

311

————. Dingfest. Darmstadt: Luchterhand, 1973. 190 p.
                                                   PT2670.A483 D5

312

————. Flöda und der Schwan. Stierstadt i. Ts.: Eremiten-Presse,
1971. 20 double 1.: ill.   PT2670.A483 F6

313

————. Für Alle. Darmstadt, Neuwied: Luchterhand, 1974. 263 p.
                                                   PT2670.A483 F84
Bibliography of E. Jandl's works: p. 260.

314

————. Der gelbe Hund. Darmstadt: Luchterhand, 1980. 231 p.
                                                   MLCS 87/2207 (P)

315

————. Der künstliche Baum. Neuwied, Berlin: Luchterhand,
1970. 155 p.   PT2670.A483 K8 1970

316

————. Laut und Luise. Stuttgart: Reclam, 1976. 159 p.
                                                   PT2670.A483 L3 1976

317

————. Die Männer: ein Film. Düsseldorf: Eremiten-Presse, 1973.
40 p.   PT2670.A483 M3

318

————. Das Öffnen und Schliessen des Mundes: Frankfurter
Poetik-Vorlesung. Darmstadt: Luchterhand, 1985. 132 p.: ill.
                                                   PT2670.A483 Z74 1985

319
———. Die schöne Kunst des Schreibens. Darmstadt:
Luchterhand, 1983. 150 p.: ill.   PN1044.J3 1983
  Bibliography: p. 148–150.

320
———. Selbstporträt des Schachspielers als trinkende Uhr.
Darmstadt: Luchterhand, 1983. 91 p.   PT2670.A483 S35 1983

321
———. Serienfuss. Darmstadt: Luchterhand, 1974. 81 p.
                                        PT2670.A483 S4

322
———. Übung mit Buben. Berlin: Berliner Handpresse, 1973.
73 p. (On double leaves).   PT2670.A483 U35

323
———. Der versteckte Hirte. Düsseldorf: Eremiten-Presse, 1975.
43 p.: ill.   PT2670.A483 V4

324
———. Wischen möchten. Berlin: Literarisches Colloquium
Berlin, 1974. 48 p.   PT2670.A483 W5
  ,,Dieser Band enthält Gedichte aus zwanzig Jahren
(1952–1972).''

———

325
Für Ernst Jandl: Texte zum 60. Geburtstag. Werkgeschichte/
  herausgegeben von Kristina Pfoser-Schewig. Wien:
Dokumentationsstelle für Neuere Österreichische Literatur, 1985.
180 p.: ill.   PT2670.A483 Z64 1985
  Bibliography of works by and about E. Jandl: p. 167–180.

* * * * * * * * * * * * * * * * * * *

326
Jandl, Hermann. Kernwissen. Baden bei Wien: Grasl, 1985. 63 p.
  (Reihe Lyrik aus Österreich; Bd. 33)   MLCS 86/3184 (P)

327
————. Leute, Leute. Frankfurt am Main: Fischer, 1970. 87 p.
                                            PT2670.A484 L4

328
————. Ein Mensch: oder, Das Leben ist eines der schwersten.
St. Pölten: Niederösterreichisches Pressehaus, 1979. 53 p.: port.
                                            PT2670.A484 M4
Niederösterreich-Gesellschaft für Kunst und Kultur.

329
————. Storno. Wien: Jugend und Volk, 1983. 102 p.
                                            MLCS 84/5215 (P)

330
————. Die Übersiedlung. Wien: Niederösterreichisches Pressehaus, 1985. 83 p.   MLCS 86/1484 (P)

****

331
Jelinek, Elfriede. Die Ausgesperrten. Reinbek bei Hamburg:
Rowohlt, 1980. 265 p.   PT2670.E46 A97

332
————. Ende: Gedichte von 1966–1968. Schwifting: Schwiftinger
Galerie-Verlag, 1980. 76 p.: ill.   PT2670.E46 E5

333
————. Die endlose Unschuldigkeit. Schwifting: Schwiftinger
Galerie-Verlag, 1980. 82 p.   MLCS 87/1521 (P)

334
————. Die Klavierspielerin. Reinbek bei Hamburg: Rowohlt,
1983. 351 p.   MLCS 84/2169 (P)

335
————. Die Liebhaberinnen. Reinbek bei Hamburg: Rowohlt,
1975. 121 p.   PT2670.E46 L5

336

————. Materialien zur Musiksoziologie. Wien, München: Jugend & Volk, 1972. 60 p.   ML55.J44

337

————. Michael. Ein Jugendbuch für die Infantilgesellschaft. Reinbek bei Hamburg: Rowohlt, 1972. 116 p.

PT2670.E46 M5

338

————. Oh Wildnis, oh Schutz vor ihr. Reinbek bei Hamburg: Rowohlt, 1985. 281 p.   MLCS 86/1155 (P)

339

————. Wir sind Lockvögel Baby. Reinbek bei Hamburg: Rowohlt, 1970. 257 p.   PT2670.E46 W5

* * * * * * * * * * * * * * * * * *

340

Jonke, Gert. Die erste Reise zum unerforschten Grund des stillen Horizonts: von Glashäusern, Leuchttürmen, Windmaschinen und anderen Wahrzeichen der Gegend. Salzburg: Residenz, 1980. 387 p.: ill.   MLCS 87/2347 (P)

341

————. Erwachen zum grossen Schlafkrieg. Salzburg: Residenz, 1982. 213 p.   MLCS 82/6612

342

————. Der ferne Klang. Salzburg, Wien: Residenz, 1979. 263 p.
PT2670.O5 F4

343

————. Geometrischer Heimatroman. Frankfurt am Main: Suhrkamp, 1969. 143 p.: ill., music.   PT2670.O5 G4

344

————. Schule der Geläufigkeit. Frankfurt am Main: Suhrkamp, 1977. 176 p.   PT2670.O5 S3

* * * * * * * * * * * * * * * * * *

345
Kolleritsch, Alfred. Absturz ins Glück. Salzburg: Residenz, 1983.
  96 p.   PT2671.O418 A63 1983

346
————. Augenlust. Salzburg: Residenz, 1986. 111 p.
                                          MLCS 86/7536 (P)

347
————. Einübung in das Vermeidbare. Salzburg, Wien: Residenz,
  1978. 105 p.: port.   PT2671.O418 E3

348
————. Gespräche im Heilbad: Verstreutes, Gesammeltes.
  Salzburg: Residenz, 1985. 162 p.   PT2671.O418 G4 1985
  Collection of papers written and published in the last 10 years.

349
————. Die grüne Seite. Salzburg: Residenz, 1974. 219 p.
                                          PT2671.O418 G7

350
————. Im Vorfeld der Augen. Salzburg: Residenz, 1982. 83 p.
                                          MLCS 84/5922

351
————. Die Pfirsichtöter. Seismographischer Roman. Salzburg:
  Residenz, 1972. 163 p.   PT2671.O418 P4

****

352
Mayröcker, Friederike. Die Abschiede. Frankfurt am Main:
  Suhrkamp, 1980. 258 p.   MLCS 87/2002 (P)

353
————. Arie auf tönernen Füszen: metaphysisches Theater.
  Neuwied: Luchterhand, 1972. 79 p.   PT2625.A95 A85

354

————. Augen wie Schaljapin bevor er starb. Dornbirn: Vorarlberger Verlagsanstalt, 1974. 64 p.: ill.   PT2625.A95 A94

355

————. Ausgewählte Gedichte: 1944–1978. Frankfurt am Main: Suhrkamp, 1979. 238 p.   PT2625.A95 A6 1979

356

————. Fantom Fan. Reinbek bei Hamburg: Rowohlt, 1971. 107 p.: ill.   PT2625.A95 F3

357

————. Fast ein Frühling des Markus M. Frankfurt am Main: Suhrkamp, 1976. 104 p.   PT2625.A95 F37 1976

358

————. Gute Nacht, guten Morgen: Gedichte 1978–1981. Frankfurt am Main: Suhrkamp, 1982. 139 p.   MLCS 82/6432

359

————. Heiligenanstalt. Frankfurt am Main: Suhrkamp, 1978. 109 p.   PT2625.A95 H4 1978
Includes bibliographical references.

360

————. Heisse Hunde. Pfaffenweiler: Pfaffenweiler Presse, 1977. 22 p.: ill.   MLCS 85/10916 (P)

361

————. In langsamen Blitzen. Berlin: Literarisches Colloquium Berlin, 1974. 38 p.   PT2625.A95 I5

362

————. Je ein umwölkter Gipfel. Darmstadt: Luchterhand, 1973. 130 p.   PT2625.A95 J4

363

————. Larifari, ein konfuses Buch. Wien: Bergland Verlag, 1956. 49 p.   PT2625.A95 L3

364
————. Das Licht in der Landschaft. Frankfurt am Main:
Suhrkamp, 1975. 137 p.   PT2625.A95 L5

365
————. Magische Blätter. Frankfurt am Main: Suhrkamp, 1983.
129 p.: ill.   PT2625.A95 M3 1983

366
————. Meine Träume, ein Flügelkleid. Düsseldorf: Eremiten-
Presse, 1974. 72 p. (on double leaves): ill.   PT2625.A95 M36

367
————. Metaphorisch. Stuttgart: Walther, 1964. 8 1.
                                                   PT2625.A95 M4

368
————. Minimonsters Traumlexikon. Reinbek bei Hamburg:
Rowohlt, 1968. 90 p.: ill.   PT2625.A95 M5

369
————. Reise durch die Nacht. Frankfurt am Main: Suhrkamp,
1984. 135 p.   MLCS 86/7932 (P)

370
————. Rot ist unten. Wien, München: Jugend und Volk, 1977.
93 p.   PT2625.A95 R6 1977
Bibliography of the author's works: p. 93.

371
————. Schriftungen oder Gerüchte aus dem Jenseits.
Pfaffenweiler: Pfaffenweiler Presse, 1975. 48 p.: ill.
                                                   PT2625.A95 S3
Limited ed. of 200 numbered and signed copies. This is no. 61.

372
————. Schwarmgesang: Szenen für die poetische Bühne. Berlin:
Rainer-Verlag, 1978. 219 p.: 1 ill.   PT2625.A95 S34 1978

373
————. Sinclair Sofokles, der Baby-Saurier. Wien: Jugend und
Volk, 1971. 37 p.: ill. (some col.).   PZ36.3.M35

374

————. Sinclair Sophocles, the baby dinosaur. New York: Random House, 1974. 39 p.: ill. (part col.).   PZ7.M47376 Si
Translation of: Sinclair Sofokles, der Baby-Saurier.

375

————. Tod durch Musen: poetischer Text mit einem Nachwort. Darmstadt: Luchterhand, 1973. 198 p.   PT2625.A95 T6 1973

376

————. Winterglück: Gedichte, 1981–1985. Frankfurt am Main: Suhrkamp, 1986. 136 p.   MLCS 86/5861 (P)

————————

377

Friederike Mayröcker/ herausgegeben von Siegfried J. Schmidt. Frankfurt am Main: Suhrkamp, 1984. 387 p.: ill.
                    PT2625.A95 Z64 1984
    Bibliography of works by and about F. Mayröcker: p. 354–386.

* * * * * * * * * * * * * * * *

378

Merkel, Inge. Das andere Gesicht. Salzburg: Residenz, 1982. 313 p.   MLCS 84/2020 (P)

379

————. Eine ganz gewöhnliche Ehe: Odysseus und Penelope. Salzburg: Residenz, 1987. 429 p.   MLCS 87/3651 (P)

380

————. Die letzte Posaune. Salzburg: Residenz, 1985. 403 p.
                    MLCS 86/1109 (P)

381

————. Zypressen: drei Erzählungen. Salzburg: Residenz, 1983. 147 p.   MLCS 84/7226 (P)

* * * * * * * * * * * * * * * *

382
Scharang, Michael. Bericht an das Stadtteilkomitee: politische
  Lesebuchtexte. Darmstadt, Neuwied: Luchterhand, 1974. 98 p.
                                         PT2680.A68 B4

383
———. Charly Traktor. Darmstadt, Neuwied: Luchterhand,
  1973. 140 p.   PT2680.A68 C48

384
———. Das doppelte Leben: ein Drehbuch. Salzburg: Residenz,
  1981. 92 p.: ill.   MLCS 82/4205

385
———. Einer muss immer parieren: Dokumentationen von
  Arbeitern über Arbeiter. Darmstadt: Luchterhand, 1973. 132 p.
                                         PT2680.A68 E5

386
———. Harry: eine Abrechnung. Darmstadt: Luchterhand, 1984.
  113 p.   MLCS 86/5222 (P)

387
———. Der Lebemann. München: List, 1979. 255 p.
                                         PT2680.A68 L4

388
———. Schluss mit dem Erzählen und andere Erzählungen.
  Neuwied, Berlin: Luchterhand, 1970. 111 p.   PT2680.A68 S3

389
———. Der Sohn eines Landarbeiters. Darmstadt: Luchterhand,
  1976. 196 p.   PT2680.A68 S6

390
———. Verfahren eines Verfahrens. Neuwied: Luchterhand,
  1969. 95 p.   PT2680.A68 V4

****

391

Schwaiger, Brigitte. Die Galizianerin. Wien: Zsolnay, 1982. 221 p.
PT2680.W26 G3 1982

392

———. Der Himmel ist süss: eine Beichte. Hamburg: Knaus,
1984. 222 p. MLCS 84/13227 (P)

393

———. Lange Abwesenheit. Wien, Hamburg: Zsolnay, 1980.
123 p. PT 2680.W26 L36

394

———. Malstunde. Wien: Zsolnay, 1980. 118 p.
ND511.5.R3 S38 1980

395

———. Mein spanisches Dorf. Wien, Hamburg: Zsolnay, 1978.
198 p. PT2680.W26 M4

396

———. Wie kommt das Salz ins Meer? Wien, Hamburg: Zsolnay,
1977. 167 p. PT2680.W26 W5

397

———. Why is there salt in the sea? Lincoln: University of
Nebraska Press, 1988. 126 p. PT2680.W26 W513 1988
Translation of: Wie kommt das Salz ins Meer?

****

398

Turrini, Peter. Erlebnisse in der Mundhöhle. Reinbek bei Hamburg:
Rowohlt, 1972. 87 p. PT2682.U7 E7

399

———. Ein paar Schritte zurück. Wien: Europaverlag, 1986. 51 p.
MLCS 87/75 (P)

400

————. Sauschlachten: ein Volksstück. Wien: Lentz, 1974. 59 p.

PT2682.U7 S3 1974

401

————. Der tollste Tag: Theaterstück frei nach Beaumarchais. Wollerau, Wien, München: Lentz, 1973. 76 p.   PT2682.U7 T6

402

————. Turrini Lesebuch: Stücke, Pamphlete, Filme, Reaktionen etc. Wien, München, Zürich: Europaverlag, 1978. 414 p.: ill.

PT2682.U7 T8

Bibliography of the author's works: p. 399–400.

403

————. Turrini Lesebuch: zwei Stücke, Film, Gedichte, Reaktionen, etc. Wien: Europaverlag, 1983. 408 p.: ill.

PT2682.U7 T82 1983

„Werkverzeichnis'': p. 403.

404

————. Zero, Zero. Wien: Universal Edition, 1971. 81 p.

PT2682.U7 Z3

****

405

Wolfgruber, Gernot. Ankunftsversuch. Pfaffenweiler: Pfaffenweiler Presse, 1979. 50 p.: ill.   MLCS 84/12577 (P)

406

————. Auf freiem Fuss. Salzburg: Residenz, 1975. 164 p.

PT2685.O395 A93

407

————. Herrenjahre. Berlin: Verlag Neues Leben, 1979. 327 p.

PT2685.O395 H4 1979

408

————. Der Jagdgast: ein Drehbuch. Salzburg, Wien: Residenz, 1978. 130 p.: ill.   PT2685.O395 J3

409

————. Die Nähe der Sonne. Salzburg: Residenz, 1985. 345 p.
MLCS 86/997 (P)

410

————. Niemandsland. Salzburg: Residenz, 1978. 391 p.
PT2685.O395 N5

411

————. Verlauf eines Sommers. Salzburg: Residenz, 1981. 339 p.
MLCS 81/1762

412

————. Wiener Schnitzel, oder, High noon. Baden: Grasl, 1981.
68 p.: ill.
MLCS 84/9372 (P)

FEDERAL REPUBLIC OF GERMANY

General Reference Works

413

Deutsche Literatur in der Bundesrepublik seit 1965/ herausgegeben von Paul Michael Lützeler und Egon Schwarz. Königstein/Ts.: Athenäum, 1980. 318 p.   PT403.D395
Includes bibliographical references and index.

414

Entwicklungstendenzen in der Literatur der BRD am Beginn der siebziger Jahre: Kolloquium vom 29.—30. 5. 1974 an der Sektion Sprach- und Literaturwissenschaft Universität Rostock/ verantwortlicher Redakteur, Bruno Schrage. Rostock: Universität Rostock, 1975. 180 p.   PT403.E5
Includes bibliographical references.

415

Frankfurter Anthologie: Gedichte und Interpretationen. Frankfurt am Main: Insel-Verlag, 1976–1986. v. 1–10.
         PT1155.F68 v. 1–10

416

Hahn, Ulla. Literatur in der Aktion: zur Entwicklung operativer Literaturformen in der Bundesrepublik. Wiesbaden: Akademische Verlagsgesellschaft Athenaion, 1978. 257 p.
         PT405.H25
Includes index.
Bibliography: p. 236–251.

417

Hildebrand, Alexander. Autoren, Autoren: zur literarischen Szene in Wiesbaden. Wiesbaden: Seyfried, 1974. 93 p.: ports.
         PT3807.W6 H5

418

Honsza, Norbert. Zur literarischen Situation nach 1945 in der BRD, in Österreich und in der Schweiz. Wrocław, Państwowe Wydawn: Naukowe, 1974. 239 p. (Acta Universitatis Wratislaviensis; no. 214)   PT401.H58
     Bibliography: p. 234–237.

419

Lexikon der deutschsprachigen Gegenwartsliteratur. Neu bearbeitet und herausgegeben von Herbert Wiesner. München: Nymphenburger, 1981. 568 p.   PT155.L48 1981
     Includes bibliographies.

420

Literatur und Gesellschaft in der Bundesrepublik von 1969 bis 1973: Referate und Diskussionen eines internationalen Kolloquiums in Ludwigsburg vom 14.–17. Dezember 1973: Materialien zu Deutschlandstudien/ bearbeitet von Dieter Menyesch. Ludwigsburg: Deutsch-Französisches Institut, 1975. 139 p.
     PT403.L55
     Includes bibliographical references.

421

Lyrik und Prosa vom Hohen Ufer/ Martin Anger . . . et al. Hannover: Moorburg-Verlag, 1979. 416 p.: port.
     PT3807.H46 L9
     Authors dealing with social criticism.

422

Mannack, Eberhard. Zwei deutsche Literaturen?: zu G. Grass, U. Johnson, H. Kant, U. Plenzdorf, und C. Wolf: mit einer Bibliographie der schönen Literatur in der DDR (1968–1974). Kronberg: Athenäum-Verlag, 1977. 142 p.   PT3708.M35
     Bibliography: p. 103–142.

423

Reinhold, Ursula. Herausforderung Literatur: Entwicklungsprobleme der demokratischen und sozialistischen Literatur in der BRD (1965–1974). München: Kürbiskern, 1976. 342 p.
     PT405.R442
     Includes bibliographical references and index.

424

Wiesand, Andreas Johannes. Literatur und Öffentlichkeit in der Bundesrepublik Deutschland. München: Hanser, 1976. 182 p.

PT405.W354

Bibliography: p. 181–182.

Individual Authors

425

Achternbusch, Herbert. Die Alexanderschlacht. Frankfurt am Main: Suhrkamp, 1978. 348 p.   MLCS 86/288 (P)

426

————. Die Atlantikschwimmer. Frankfurt am Main: Suhrkamp, 1978. 380 p.   MLCS 84/13584 (P)

427

————. Breitenbach. Köln: Kiepenheuer & Witsch, 1986. 130 p.: col. ill.   PT2661.C5 B74 1986

428

————. Es ist ein leichtes beim Gehen den Boden zu berühren. Frankfurt am Main: Suhrkamp, 1980. 234 p.   PT2661.C5 E7

429

————. Das Gespenst: Filmbuch bei Zweitausendeins. Frankfurt am Main: Zweitausendeins; Charlottesville, Va.: Blue Angel, 1983. 95 p.: ill.   PN1997.G438 1983

430

————. Happy: oder, Der Tag wird kommen. Frankfurt am Main: Suhrkamp, 1975. 167 p.: port.   PT2661.C5 T3 1975

First published in 1973 under the title: Der Tag wird kommen.

431

————. Das Haus am Nil. Frankfurt am Main: Suhrkamp, 1981. 185 p.: ill. (some col.).   PT2661.C5 H3 1981

432

————. Das Kamel: Tibet, Indio, Afganistan, 2. Mai 69. Frankfurt am Main: Suhrkamp, 1970. 68 p. PT2661.C5 K3

433
————. Land in Sicht. Frankfurt am Main: Suhrkamp, 1977.
158 p.: ill. PT2661.C5 L3

434
————. Das letzte Loch. Frankfurt am Main: Suhrkamp, 1982.
117 p.: ill. PN1997.L457 A25 1982

435
————. Die Macht des Löwengebrülls. Frankfurt am Main:
Suhrkamp, 1970. 98 p. PT2661.C5 M3

436
————. Der Neger Erwin: Filmbuch. Frankfurt am Main:
Suhrkamp, 1981. 99 p.: col. ill. MLCS 87/3533 (P)

437
————. Neunzehnhundertneunundsechzig. Frankfurt am Main:
Suhrkamp, 1978. 149 p. PT2661.C5 N4

438
————. Die Olympiasiegerin. Frankfurt am Main: Suhrkamp,
1982. 135 p. PT2661.C5 O4 1982

439
————. Revolten. Frankfurt am Main: Suhrkamp, 1982. 149 p.:
ill. MLCS 82/4111 (P)

440
————. Servus Bayern: Filmbuch. Frankfurt am Main:
Suhrkamp, 1983, c1978. 85 p.: col. ill. PN1997.S365 1983

441
————. Die Stunde des Todes. Frankfurt am Main: Suhrkamp,
1975. 153 p.: ill. PT2661.C5 S8

442
————. Südtyroler Gedichte und Siebdrucke. München:
Maistrassenpresse, 1966. 33 p. on double leaves.
PT2661.C5 S9

443

————. Der Tag wird kommen. Frankfurt am Main: Suhrkamp,
1973. 243 p.: ill.   PT2661.C5 T3

444

————. Weg. Frankfurt am Main: Suhrkamp, 1985. 103 p.
                                                        MLCS 87/378 (P)

445

————. Wellen. Frankfurt am Main: Suhrkamp, 1983. 319 p.:
ill. (some col.).   PT2661.C5 W4 1983

446

————. Zigarettenverkäufer. Frankfurt am Main: Suhrkamp,
1969. 38 1.   PT2661.C5 Z3

447

Herbert Achternbusch/ herausgegeben von Jörg Drews. Frankfurt
am Main: Suhrkamp, 1982. 318 p., 4 p. of plates: ill. (some col.).
                                                     PT2661.C5 Z69 1982
    Bibliography of works by and about H. Achternbusch:
p. 273–317.

448

Herbert Achternbusch/ mit Beiträgen von Wolfgang Jacobsen . . .
et al. München: Hanser, 1984. 190, 1 p.: ill.
                                                     PT2661.C5 Z69 1984
    Filmography: p. 164–173.
    Bibliography: p. 173–191.

****

449

Alexander, Elisabeth. Bums. Hamburg: Merlin-Verlag, 1971.
67 p.: ill.   PT2661.L4 B8

450

————. Damengeschichten. Heilbronn: Emigs Literatur-Betrieb,
1983. 141, 3 p.   PT2661.L4 D3 1983
    Bibliography: p. 144.

451

————. Die Frau, die lachte: bürgerliche Texte. Leverkusen: Etcetera-Literarischer Verlag, 1975. 120 p.   PT2661.L4 F7

452

————. Fritte Pomm. Leverkusen: Braun, 1976. 131 p., 12 leaves of plates: col. ill.   MLCM 86/4317 (P)

453

————. Glückspfennig: Gedichte für das ganze Jahr. Düsseldorf: Erb, 1984. 128 p.: ill.   PT2661.L4 G5 1984

454

————. Ich bin kein Pferd. Leverkusen: Literarischer Verlag Braun, 1976. 119 p.   PT2661.L4 I3

455

————. Ich hänge mich ans schwarze Brett: 43 Gedichte. Hamburg: Merlin, 1979. 64 p.   MLCM 84/5374 (P)

456

————. Ich will als Kind Kind sein. Münster: Kaktus-Verlag, 1978. 128 p.: ill.   PT2661.L4 I34

457

————. Nach einer gewissen Lebenszeit. Sankt Augustin: Steyler, 1975. 138 p.: ill.   PT2661.L4 N3

458

————. Sie hätte ihre Kinder töten sollen. Düsseldorf: Erb, 1982. 189 p.   MLCS 82/6181

459

————. Die törichte Jungfrau. Köln: Literarischer Verlag Braun, 1978. 399 p.   PT2661.L4 T6

* * * * * * * * * * * * * * * * * * *

460

Becker, Jürgen. Die Abwesenden: drei Hörspiele. Frankfurt am Main: Suhrkamp, 1983. 148 p.   PT2662.E293 A63 1983

461

————. Bilder. Frankfurt am Main: Suhrkamp, 1969. 107 p.

PT2662.E293 B5

462

————. Das Ende der Landschaftsmalerei. Frankfurt am Main:
Suhrkamp, 1974. 119 p.   PT2662.E293 E5

463

————. Erzähl mir nichts vom Krieg. Frankfurt am Main:
Suhrkamp, 1977. 108 p.   PT2662.E293 E7

464

————. Erzählen bis Ostende. Frankfurt am Main: Suhrkamp,
1981. 170 p.   MLCS 81/1939

465

————. Felder. Frankfurt am Main: Suhrkamp, 1964. 145 p.

PT2662.E293 F4

466

————. Fenster und Stimmen. Frankfurt am Main: Suhrkamp,
1982. 59 p.: ill. (some col.).   PT2662.E293 F43 1982

467

————. Gedichte 1965–1980. Frankfurt am Main: Suhrkamp,
1981. 389 p.   MLCS 81/244

468

————. Happenings. Fluxus. Pop art. Reinbek bei Hamburg:
Rowohlt, 1965. 470 p.: ill.   PN3203.B38

469

————. In der verbleibenden Zeit. Frankfurt am Main: Suhrkamp,
1979. 124 p.   PT2662.E293 I5

470

————. Odenthals Küste. Frankfurt am Main: Suhrkamp, 1986.
143 p.   MLCS 86/7018 (P)

471

————. Ränder. Frankfurt am Main: Suhrkamp, 1968. 111 p.
PT2662.E293 R3

472

————. Schnee. Berlin: Literarisches Colloquium, 1971. 38 p.
PT2662.E293 S3

473

————. Die Türe zum Meer. Frankfurt am Main: Suhrkamp,
1983. 128 p. MLCS 84/2152 (P)

474

————. Umgebungen. Frankfurt am Main: Suhrkamp, 1970.
167 p. PT2662.E293 U4

475

————. Eine Zeit ohne Wörter. Frankfurt am Main: Suhrkamp,
1971. 1 v. (chiefly illus.). TR654.B42

476

Janshen, Doris. Opfer und Subjekt des Alltäglichen: Denkstruktur
und Sprachform in den Prosatexten Jürgen Beckers. Köln, Wien:
Böhlau, 1976. 153 p. PT2662.E293 Z68
Bibliography: p. 149–153.

477

Kreutzer, Leo. Über Jürgen Becker. Frankfurt am Main:
Suhrkamp, 1972. 198 p. PT2662.E293 Z7

478

Linder, Christen. Schreiben und Leben. Köln: Kiepenheuer &
Witsch, 1974. 144 p.: ill. PT155.L53

479

Müller-Schwefe, Hans-Ulrich. Schreib'alles: zu Jürgen Beckers
„Rändern," „Feldern," „Umgebungen," anhand einer Theorie
simuliert präsentativer Texte. München: Fink, 1977. 144 p.
PT2662.E293 Z77 1977

Originally presented as the author's thesis, Hamburg, 1975.
Includes index.
Bibliography: p. 142–144.

****

480
Bieler, Manfred. Der Bär. Hamburg: Hoffmann und Campe, 1983.
444 p.   PT2662.I38 B3 1983

481
———. Drei Rosen aus Papier. München: Biederstein, 1970.
199 p.   PT2662.I38 A19 1970

482
———. Ewig und drei Tage. Hamburg: Knaus, 1980. 282 p.
MLCS 84/14877 (P)

483
———. Der Hausaufsatz. Stuttgart: Reclam. 1974. 54 p.
PT2662.I38 H3

484
———. Der junge Roth. München: Deutscher Taschenbuch-
Verlag, 1974. 185 p.   PT2662.I38 A6 1974

485
———. Der Kanal. Hamburg: Knaus, 1978. 479 p.
PT2662.I38 K3

486
———. Der Mädchenkrieg. Hamburg: Hoffman und Campe,
1975. 567 p.   PT2662.I38 M28

487
———. Märchen und Zeitungen. Berlin, Weimar: Aufbau-Verlag,
1966. 195 p.   PT2662.I38 M3

488
———. Maria Morzeck. München: Biederstein, 1969. 309 p.
PT2662.I38 M35

489

―――. Der Passagier: Erzählung. München: Biederstein, 1971.
180 p.   PT2662.I38 P3

490

―――. The sailor in the bottle. New York: Dutton, 1966, c1965.
221 p.   PZ4.B585 Sai

491

―――. The three daughters. New York: St. Martin's Press, 1978.
352 p.   PZ4.B585 Th
    Translation of: Der Mädchenkrieg.

492

―――. Vater und Lehrer. Stuttgart: Reclam, 1970. 47 p.
                                              PT2662.I38 V3

****

493

Bienek, Horst. Bakunin, an invention. London: Gollancz, 1977.
119 p.   HX915.B3 B5413 1977
    Translation of: Bakunin, eine Invention.

494

―――. Bakunin, eine Invention. München: Deutscher
Taschenbuch-Verlag, 1973. 111 p.   HX915.B3 B54 1973
    Includes bibliographical references.

495

―――. Beschreibung einer Provinz: Aufzeichnungen, Materialien, Dokumente. München: Hanser, 1983. 256 p.: ill.
                                   PT2662.I39 Z463 1983

496

―――. The cell. Santa Barbara, Calif.: Unicorn, 1972. viii, 93 p.:
port.   PZ4.B5857 Ce
    Translation of: Die Zelle.

497

―――. Erde und Feuer. München: Hanser, 1982. 325 p.
                                        MLCS 84/2147 (P)

498

————. Die erste Polka. München, Wien: Hanser, 1975. 378 p.

PT2662.I39 E7

499

————. The first polka. San Francisco: Fjord Press, 1984. 326 p.:
ill.   PT2662.I39 E713 1984
    Revised translation of: Die erste Polka.

500

————. Der Freitag der kleinen Freuden. Düsseldorf: Eremiten-
Presse, 1981. 40 p.: ill. (some col.).   PT2662.I39 F7 1981

501

————. Gleiwitzer Kindheit: Gedichte aus zwanzig Jahren.
München: Hanser, 1976. 146 p.   PT2662.I39 G6

502

————. Königswald, oder, Die letzte Geschichte. München:
Hanser, 1984. 119 p.   MLCS 86/5532 (P)

503

————. Nachtstücke. München: Deutscher Taschenbuch-Verlag,
1968. 128 p.   PT2662.I39 N3

504

————. September light. New York: Atheneum, 1987. 273 p.

PT2662.I39 S413 1987
    Translation of: Septemberlicht.

505

————. Septemberlicht. München: Hanser, 1977. 347 p.

PT2662.I39 S4

506

————. Solschenizyn und andere. München: Hanser, 1972. 102 p.

PG3016.B53

507

————. Time without bells. New York: Atheneum, 1988. 338 p.

PT2662.I39 Z2413 1988
    Translation of: Zeit ohne Glocken.

508
————. Vorgefundene Gedichte. München: Hanser, 1969. 47 p.
PT2662.I39 V6

509
————. Werkstattgespräche mit Schriftstellern. München:
Deutscher Taschenbuch-Verlag, 1976, c1962. 293 p.
PT155.B47 1976
Bibliography: p. 286–293.

510
————. Die Zeit danach. Düsseldorf: Eremiten-Presse, 1974. 37
l.: ill. (part col.). PT2662.I39 Z23

511
————. Zeit ohne Glocken. München: Hanser, 1979. 411 p.
PT2662.I39 Z24

512
————. Von Zeit und Erinnerung: Erzählungen, Gedichte, Essays.
Gütersloh: Gütersloher Verlagshaus Mohn, 1980. 95 p.
PT2662.I39 V58

513
————. Die Zelle. München: Hanser, 1968. 182 p.
PT2662.I39 Z25

514
Bienek lesen: Materialien zu seinem Werk/ herausgegeben von
Michael Krüger. München: Hanser, 1980. 255 p.
PT2662.I39 Z59
Bibliography of works by and about H. Bienek: p. 226–254.

515
Heimat: neue Erkundungen eines alten Themas. München:
Hanser, 1985. 143 p. (Dichtung und Sprache; Bd. 3)
PT405.H348 1985

****

516
Böll, Heinrich. Absent without leave: two novellas. New York:
McGraw-Hill, 1965. 148 p.   PZ4.B6713 Ab
   Translation of: Entfernung von der Truppe, and Als der Krieg
ausbrach. Als der Krieg zu Ende war.

517
————. Adam, and, The train: two novels. New York: McGraw-
Hill, 1970. 268 p.   PZ4.B6713 Act
   Translation of: Wo warst du Adam? And Der Zug war
pünktlich.

518
————. And never said a word. New York: McGraw-Hill, 1978.
197 p.   PZ4.B6713 A1
   Translation of: Und sagte kein einziges Wort.

519
————. Der Angriff: Erzählungen, 1947–1949. Köln: Kiepenheuer
& Witsch, 1983. 170 p.   PT2603.O394 A68 1983

520
————. Ansichten eines Clowns. Gütersloh: Bertelsmann; Wien:
Buchgemeinschaft Donauland, 1966. 254 p.
                                   PT2603.O394 A7 1966b

521
————. Anstoss und Ermutigung: Gustav W. Heinemann
Bundespräsident, 1969–1974. Frankfurt am Main: Suhrkamp,
1974. 443 p.   DD259.7.H33 B63
   Includes bibliographical references.

522
————. Antikommunismus in Ost und West: zwei Gespräche.
Köln: Bund-Verlag, 1982. 124 p.   HX40.B585 1982

523
————. Aufsätze, Kritiken, Reden. Köln, Berlin: Kiepenheuer &
Witsch, 1967. 510 p.   PT2603.O394 A16 1967

524

―――. Aus unseren Tagen. New York: Holt, Rinehart, and Winston, 1960. 138 p.   PT2603.O394 A85

525

―――. Berichte zur Gesinnungslage der Nation. Köln: Kiepenheuer & Witsch, 1975. 62 p.   PT2603.O394 B4

526

―――. Bilanz Klopfzeichen. Stuttgart: Reclam, 1963. 66 p.

PT2603.O394 A19 1963

527

―――. Bild, Bonn, Boenisch. Bornheim-Merten: Lamuv, 1984. 171 p.: ill.   PN5213.B64 B65 1984

528

―――. Billard um halb zehn. Köln: Kiepenheuer & Witsch, 1971, c1966. 518 p.   PT2603.O394 A15 1971

529

―――. Billards at half-past nine. New York: McGraw-Hill, 1962. 280 p.   PZ4.B6713 Bi

530

―――. Böll für Zeitgenossen. New York: Harper & Row, 1970. xxv, 259 p.: ill.   PT2603.O394 B6

531

―――. The bread of those early years. New York: McGraw-Hill, 1976. 134 p.   PZ4.B6713 Br

Translation of: Das Brot der frühen Jahre.

532

―――. Das Brot der frühen Jahre. Köln: Kiepenheuer & Witsch, 1980, c1955. 141 p.   PT2603.O394 B7 1980

533

―――. Children are civilians too. Harmondsworth, New York: Penguin, 1976. 184 p.   PZ4.B6713 Ch 1976

"These stories formed part of a volume entitled 1947 bis 1951."

534

————. The clown. New York: McGraw-Hill, 1965. 247 p.
PZ4.B6713 C1

535

————. Doktor Murkes gesammeltes Schweigen. Köln:
Kiepenheuer & Witsch, 1958. 157 p.   PT2603.O394 D6

536

————. 18 stories by Heinrich Böll. New York: McGraw-Hill,
1966. 243 p.   PZ4.H6713 Ei

537

————. Ein-und Zusprüche: Schriften, Reden und Prosa,
1981–1983. Köln: Kiepenheuer & Witsch, 1984. 246 p.
PT2603.O394 A6 1984

538

————. Einmischung erwünscht:Schriften zur Zeit. Köln: Kiepenheuer & Witsch, 1977. 402 p.   PT2603.O394 A16 1977

539

————. The end of a mission. London: Weidenfeld & Nicolson,
1968. 11, 207 p.   PZ4.B6713 En3
Translation of: Ende einer Dienstfahrt.

540

————. Ende einer Dienstfahrt. München: Deutscher
Taschenbuch-Verlag, 1969. 152 p.   PT2603.O394 E5 1969

541

————. Entfernung von der Truppe. Köln: Kiepenheuer &
Witsch, 1964. 140 p.   PT2603.O394 E6 1964

542

————. Erzählungen, 1950–1970. Köln: Kiepenheuer & Witsch,
1972. 444 p.   PT2603.O394 A15 1972

543

————. Essayistische Schriften und Reden. Köln: Kiepenheuer
& Witsch, 1979–1980. 3 v.   PT2603.O394 A6 1979
Includes bibliographical references.

544
————. Die Fähigkeit zu trauern: Schriften und Reden, 1983–1985. Bornheim-Merten: Lamuv, 1986. 318 p.

PT2603.O394 F3 1986

Illustrations on lining papers.
Bibliography: p. 309–318.

545
————. Du fährst zu oft nach Heidelberg: und andere Erzählungen. Bornheim-Merten: Lamuv, 1979. 100 p.

MLCS 84/13602 (P)

546
————. Frankfurter Vorlesungen. München: Deutscher Taschenbuch-Verlag, 1968. 121 p.   PT2603.O394 F7 1968

547
————. Frauen vor Flusslandschaft: Roman in Dialogen und Selbstgesprächen. Köln: Kiepenheuer & Witsch, 1985. 254 p.

PT2603.O394 F75 1985

548
————. Fürsorgliche Belagerung. Köln: Kiepenheuer & Witsch, 1979. 415 p.   PT2603.O394 F85

549
————. Gedichte. München: Deutscher Taschenbuch-Verlag, 1981. 58 p.: ill.   PT2603.O394 A6 1981

550
————. Group portrait with lady. New York: McGraw-Hill, 1973. 405 p.   PZ4.B6713 Gr
   Translation of: Gruppenbild mit Dame.

551
————. Gruppenbild mit Dame. Köln: Kiepenheuer & Witsch, 1971. 400 p.   PT2603.O394 G7

552
————. Haus ohne Hüter. Köln: Kiepenheuer & Witsch, 1974, c1954. 323 p.   PT2603.O394 H3 1974

553

————. Hausfriedensbruch. Köln, Berlin: Kiepenheuer & Witsch,
1969. 165 p. front.   PT2603.O394 H34

554

————. Heinrich Böll, Nobel prize for literature, 1972. Bonn-Bad
Godesberg: Inter Nationes, 1973. 27 p.   PT2603.O394 Z52
Bibliography: p. 26–27.

555

————. Irisches Tagebuch. München: Deutscher Taschenbuch-
Verlag, 1972, c1957. 137 p.   DA978.B56 1972

556

————. Irish journal. New York: McGraw-Hill, 1967. 127 p.
                                                             DA978.B58
Translation of: Irisches Tagebuch.

557

————. Der Lorbeer ist immer noch bitter: literarische Schriften.
München: Deutscher Taschenbuch-Verlag, 1976, c1973. 143 p.
                                                          PN37.B58 1976

558

————. The lost honor of Katharina Blum: how violence develops
and where it can lead. New York: McGraw-Hill, 1975. 140 p.
                                                          PZ4.B6713 Lo
Translation of: Die verlorene Ehre der Katharina Blum.

559

————. Mein trauriges Gesicht: Humoresken und Satiren.
Leipzig: Reclam, 1979. 392 p.   PT2603.O394 A6 1979b

560

————. Missing persons and other essays. New York: McGraw-
Hill, 1977. viii, 281 p.   PT2603.O394 A28

561

————. Politische Meditationen zu Glück und Vergeblichkeit.
Darmstadt, Neuwied: Luchterhand, 1973. 128 p.: ill.
                                                          PT2603.O394 P6

562
————. Querschnitte: aus Interviews, Aufsätzen und Reden. Köln: Kiepenheuer & Witsch, 1977. 216 p.: ill.

PT2603.O394 A16 1977b
Includes bibliographical references.

563
————. The safety net. Franklin Center, Pa.: Franklin Library, 1981, c1982. 368 p.: col. ill.   PT2603.O394 F8513 1982b
Translation of: Fürsorgliche Belagerung.

564
————. Die schwarzen Schafe: Erzählungen, 1950–1952. Köln: Kiepenheuer & Witsch, 1983. 211 p.   PT2603.O394 S4 1983

565
————. A soldier's legacy. New York, N.Y.: Penguin Books, 1986. 131 p.   PT2603.O394 V4713 1986
Translation of: Das Vermächtnis.

566
————. The train was on time. London: Secker and Warburg, 1973. 7, 110 p.   PZ4.B6713 Tr6
Translation of: Der Zug war pünktlich.

567
————. Und sagte kein einziges Wort. Köln: Kiepenheuer & Witsch, 1953. 214 p.   PT2603.O394 U5

568
————. Die verlorene Ehre der Katharina Blum: oder, Wie Gewalt entstehen und wohin sie führen kann. Köln: Kiepenheuer & Witsch, 1974. 188 p.   PT2603.O394 V4

569
————. Das Vermächtnis. Bornheim: Lamuv, 1982. 158 p.

PT2603.O394 V47 1982

570
————. Vermintes Gelände: essayistische Schriften, 1977–1981. Köln: Kiepenheuer & Witsch, 1982. 274 p.

PT2603.O394 A16 1982

,,Quellenverzeichnis, Erstveröffentlichungen der Arbeiten in diesem Band'': p. 270-274.

571

Die Verwundung und andere frühe Erzählungen. Bornheim: Lamuv, 1983. 303 p.: 2 ill.   PT2602.O394 V48 1983
,,Die 22 Erzählungen, die hier zum ersten Mal veröffentlicht werden, sind zwischen 1946 und 1952 entstanden.''
Illustrations on lining papers.

572

————. Warum haben wir aufeinander geschossen? Bornheim-Merten: Lamuv, 1981. 222 p.: ill.   PT2603.O394 Z583 1981
Includes interviews by K. Bednarz, contributions by F. Burda, et al., and Die Flugblätter des Majors Lew Kopelew.
Includes some text in Russian with German translation.
Bibliography: p. 220-222.

573

————. Was soll aus dem Jungen bloss werden?, oder, Irgendwas mit Büchern. Bornheim: Lamuv, 1981. 96 p.
                                                PT2603.O394 Z476

574

————. Werke: Romane und Erzählungen. Köln, Middelhauve: Kiepenheuer & Witsch, 1977. 5 v.   PT2603.O394 A6 1977
CONTENTS: 1. 1947-1951/ 2. 1951-1954/ 3. 1954-1959/ 4. 1961-1970/ 5. 1971-1977.

575

————. What's to become of the boy?, or, Something to do with books. New York, N.Y.: Penguin Books, 1985. 82 p.: port.
                                                PT2603.O394 Z47613 1985
Translation of: Was soll aus dem Jungen bloss werden?

———————————————

576

Bruhn, Peter. Heinrich Böll in der Sowjetunion: 1952-1979: Einführung in die sowjetische Böll-Rezeption und Bibliographie der in der UdSSR in russischer Sprache erschienenen Schriften

von und über Heinrich Böll. Berlin: Schmidt, 1980. 176 p.: 15
ill.   PT2603.O394 Z588
   Includes indexes.

577

Burns, Robert A. The theme of non-conformism in the work of
Heinrich Böll. Coventry: University of Warwick, Department
of German Studies, 1973. 87 p. (University of Warwick.
Department of German Studies. Occasional papers in German
studies; no. 3)   PT2603.O394 Z59
   Includes bibliographical references.

578

Conard, Robert C. Heinrich Böll. Boston: Twayne, 1981. 228 p.:
port.   PT2603.O394 Z596
   Includes index.
   Bibliography: p. 217–225.

579

Friedrichsmeyer, Erhard. Die satirische Kurzprosa Heinrich Bölls.
Chapel Hill: University of North Carolina Press, 1981. 221 p.
(University of North Carolina studies in Germanic languages
and literatures; 97)   PT2603.O394 Z64
   Includes index.
   Bibliography: 211–217.

580

Heinrich Böll, on his death: selected obituaries and the last
interview. Bonn: Inter Nationes, 1985. 63 p.: ill.
                                       PT2603.O394 Z6915 1985

581

Hoffmann, Gabriele. Heinrich Böll. Bornheim-Merten: Lamuv,
   1986. 288 p.: ports.   PT2603.O394 Z6952 1986
   Includes material by H. Böll.
   Bibliography of works by and about H. Böll: p. 287–288.

582

Kilborn, R. W. Whose lost honour?: a study of the film adaptation
of Böll's "The lost honour of Katharina Blum." Glasgow:

Scottish Papers in Germanic Studies, 1984. 73 p., 6 p. of plates:
ill. (Scottish papers in Germanic studies; vol. 4)
                                                    PN1997.V473 K55 1984
          Bibliography: p. 71-73.

583
Lehnardt, Eberhard. Urchristentum und Wohlstandsgesellschaft:
    das Romanwerk Heinrich Bölls von „Haus ohne Hüter" bis
    „Gruppenbild mit Dame." Bern, New York: Lang, 1984. 355 p.
    (Europäische Hochschulschriften. Reihe I, Deutsche Sprache und
    Literatur; Bd. 720)   PT2603.O394 Z7227 1984
          Bibliography: p. 349-355.

584
Linder, Christian. Heinrich Böll: Leben & Schreiben, 1917-1985.
    Köln: Kiepenheuer & Witsch, 1986. 256 p.: ill.
                                            PT2603.O394 Z7238 1986
          Bibliography: p. 233-243.

585
Martin, Werner. Heinrich Böll: eine Bibliographie seiner Werke.
    Hildesheim, New York: Olms, 1975. 236 p. (Bibliographien zur
    deutschen Literatur; 2)   Z8106.28.M37

586
Reich-Ranicki, Marcel. Mehr als ein Dichter: über Heinrich Böll.
    Köln: Kiepenheuer & Witsch, 1986. 122 p.
                                            PT2603.O394 Z729 1986

587
Reid, J. H. (J. Hamish). Heinrich Böll, a German for his time.
    Leamington Spa, Warwickshire, New York: Berg, Distributed
    exclusively in the US and Canada by St. Martin's Press, 1987.
    n.p.   PT2603.O394 Z7297 1987
          Includes index.
          Bibliography.

588
Silen, Ulla Grandell. Marie, Leni, Katharina und ihre Schwestern:
    eine Analyse des Frauenbilds in drei Werken von Heinrich Böll.
    Stockholm: Stockholms universitet, Tyska institutionen, 1982.

36 p. (Schriften des Deutschen Instituts, Universität Stockholm;
13)   PT2603.O394 Z765 1982
    Bibliography: p. 36.

589

White, Ray Lewis. Heinrich Böll in America, 1954–1970.
Hildesheim, New York: Olms, 1979. 170 p. (Germanistische
Texte und Studien; Bd. 8)   PT2603.O394 Z796
"Books about Heinrich Böll in English": p. 170.

590

Ziltener, Walter. Die Literaturtheorie Heinrich Bölls. Bern: Lang,
1980. ii, 247 p. (Europäische Hochschulschriften. Reihe I,
Deutsche Sprache und Literatur; Bd. 369)
                              PT2603.O394 Z98 1980
    Originally presented as the author's thesis (doctoral)—Zürich,
1978.
    Bibliography: p. 230–247.

* * * * * * * * * * * * * * * * * * *

591

Born, Nicolas. Das Auge des Entdeckers. Reinbek bei Hamburg:
Rowohlt, 1972. 114 p.: ill.   PT2662.O7 A95

592

———. The deception. Boston: Little, Brown, 1983. 238 p.
                              PT2662.O7 F313 1983
    Translation of: Die Fälschung.

593

———. Die erdabgewandte Seite der Geschichte. Reinbek bei
Hamburg: Rowohlt, 1976. 250 p.   PT2662.O7 E7

594

———. Die Fälschung. Reinbek bei Hamburg: Rowohlt, 1979.
316 p.   MLCS 84/11727 (P)

595

———. Gedichte: 1967–1978. Reinbek bei Hamburg: Rowohlt,
1978. 232 p.   PT2662.O7 A17 1978

596
————. Marktlage. Köln, Berlin: Kiepenheuer & Witsch, 1967.
66 p.   PT2662.O7 M3

597
————. Täterskizzen. Reinbek bei Hamburg: Rowohlt, 1983.
243 p.   MLCS 84/7215 (P)

598
————. Die Welt der Maschine: Aufsätze und Reden. Reinbek
bei Hamburg: Rowohlt, 1980. 220 p.   PN774.B67 1980

599
————. Wo mir der Kopf steht. Köln, Berlin: Kiepenheuer &
Witsch, 1970. 60 p.: ill., front.   PT2662.O7 W6

600
————. Der zweite Tag. Köln, Berlin: Kiepenheuer & Witsch,
1965. 214 p.   PT2662.O7 Z48

601
Die Literatur und die Wissenschaften/ herausgegeben von Nicolas
Born und Heinz Schlaffer. Reinbek bei Hamburg: Rowohlt,
1976. 253 p.   PT1141.L54
Includes bibliographical references.

602
Der Neue Irrationalismus/ Redaktion: Nicolas Born, Jürgen
Manthey, Delf Schmidt. Reinbek bei Hamburg: Rowohlt, 1978.
336 p.   PT1141.N38
Includes bibliographical references.

603
Die Phantasie an die Macht: Literatur als Utopie/ herausgegeben
von Nicolas Born. Reinbek bei Hamburg: Rowohlt, 1975. 290 p.
                                                PN6034.P5

604

Schreiben oder Literatur/ Redaktion: Nicolas Born, Jürgen Manthey, Delf Schmidt. Reinbek bei Hamburg: Rowohlt, 1979. 388 p.   PN45.S254
  Bibliography: p. 150–151.

605

Die Sprache des grossen Bruders: gibt es ein ost-westliches Kartell der Unterdrückung?/ herausgegeben von Nicolas Born und Jürgen Manthey. Reinbek bei Hamburg: Rowohlt, 1977. 315 p.
                                          PT1141.S64
  Includes bibliographical references.

****

606

Dittberner, Hugo. Der Biss ins Gras. Köln: Palmenpresse, 1976. 42 p.   PT2664.I8 B5
  Bibliography of the author's works: p. 42.

607

———. Draussen im Dorf. Reinbek bei Hamburg: Rowohlt, 1978. 218 p.   PT2664.I8 D7

608

———. Drei Tage Unordnung. Bielefeld: Pendragon-Verlag, 1983. 60 p.   PT2664.I8 D76 1983

609

———. Die gebratenen Tauben. Reinbek bei Hamburg: Rowohlt, 1981. 214 p.   MLCS 87/3535 (P)

610

———. Heinrich Mann: eine kritische Einführung in die Forschung. Frankfurt am Main: Athenäum Fischer Taschenbuch Verlag, 1974. 232 p.   PT2625.A43 Z64
  Bibliography: p. 211–225.

611

———. Das Internat: Papiere vom Kaffeetisch. Darmstadt: Luchterhand, 1974. 180 p.   PT2664.I8 I5

612

————. Kurzurlaub: eine Reiseerzählung. Darmstadt:
Luchterhand, 1976. 145 p.   PT2664.I8 K8

613

————. Ruhe hinter Gardinen: Gedichte, 1971–1980. Reinbek bei
Hamburg: Rowohlt, 1980. 106 p.   PT2664.I8 R8 1980

614

————. Wie man Provinzen erobert. Reinbek bei Hamburg:
Rowohlt, 1986. 177 p.   MLCS 86/3618 (P)

****

615

Domin, Hilde. Abel steh auf: Gedichte, Prosa, Theorie. Stuttgart:
Reclam, 1979. 96 p.   PT2664.O53 A63
    Includes bibliographical references.

616

————. Aber die Hoffnung: Autobiographisches aus und über
Deutschland. München: Piper, 1982. 208, 2 p.
                            PT2664.O53 Z462 1982
    Bibliography of the author's works: p. 210.

617

————. Die andalusische Katze. Stierstadt im Taunus: Eremiten-
Presse, 1971. 26 l.   PT2664.O53 A8

618

————. Doppelinterpretationen. Frankfurt am Main, Bonn:
Athenäum, 1966. 365 p.   PT552.D6

619

————. Hier. Frankfurt am Main: Fischer, 1964. 61 p.
                            PT2664.O53 H5

620

————. Höhlenbilder: Gedichte, 1951–1952. Duisburg:
Hildebrandt, 1968. 15 l.   PT2664.O53 H6 (Rare Bk Coll)

621

————. Ich will dich. München: Piper, 1970. 46 p.

PT2664.O53 I24

622

————. Nachkrieg und Unfrieden. Darmstadt: Luchterhand, 1970. 192 p. PT1221.D6 1970

623

————. Nur eine Rose als Stütze. Frankfurt am Main: Fischer, 1959. 83 p. PT2664.O53 N8

624

————. Rückkehr der Schiffe. Frankfurt am Main: Fischer, 1965, c1962. 61 p. PT2664.O53 R8 1965

625

————. Von der Natur nicht vorgesehen: Autobiographisches. München: Piper, 1974. 157 p. PT2664.O53 Z528

626

————. Wozu Lyrik heute: Dichtung und Leser in der gesteuerten Gesellschaft. München: Piper, 1968. 201 p. PN1274.D6

627

————. Das zweite Paradies. München: Piper, 1968. 199 p.

PT2664.O53 Z43

* * * * * * * * * * * * * * * * * *

628

Drewitz, Ingeborg. Auch so ein Leben: die fünfziger Jahre in Erzählungen. Göttingen: Herodot, 1985. 156 p.

PT2664.R4 A96 1985

629

————. Berliner Salons: Gesellschaft und Literatur zwischen Aufklärung und Industriezeitalter. Berlin: Haude und Spener, 1979. 112 p.: ill. (Berlinische Reminizenzen; 7)

PT3807.B3 D7

Includes index.
Bibliography: p. 107–109.

630

————. Bettine von Arnim: Romantik, Revolution, Utopie: eine Biographie. Düsseldorf: Claassen, 1984. 319 p., 8 p. of plates: ill.   PT1808.A4 D7 1984

    Includes index.

    Bibliography: p. 290–297.

631

————. Der eine, der andere. Stuttgart: Gebühr, 1976. 190 p.

PT2664.R4 E36

632

————. Eingeschlossen. Düsseldorf: Claassen, 1986. 238 p.

MLCS 86/3590 (P)

633

————. Eis auf der Elbe. Düsseldorf: Claassen, 1982. 206 p.

MLCS 84/2247 (P)

634

————. Eine fremde Braut. München: Claudis Verlag, 1968. 79 p.

PT2664.R4 F7

635

————. Gestern war heute: 100 Jahre Gegenwart. Düsseldorf: Claassen, 1978. 382 p.   PT2664.R4 G4

636

————. Hinterm Fenster die Stadt: aus einem Familienalbum. Düsseldorf: Claassen, 1985. 94 p.: ill.   PT2664.R4 Z464 1985

637

————. Das Hochhaus. Stuttgart: Gebühr, 1975. 246 p.

PT2664.R4 H6

    Bibliography: p. 246–247.

638

————. Kurz vor 1984: Literatur und Politik: Essays. Stuttgart: Radius-Verlag, 1981. 214 p.   PT2664.R4 K8

639

———. Leben und Werk von Adam Kuckhoff, deutscher Schriftsteller und Widerstandskämpfer, hingerichtet durch den Strang in Berlin-Plötzensee am 5. August 1943. Berlin: Friedenauer Presse, 1968. 14 p.   PT2621.U13 Z6

640

———. Die Literatur und ihre Medien. Positionsbestimmungen. Düsseldorf: Diederichs, 1972. 250 p.   PN45.5.D7

641

———. Mit Sätzen Mauern eindrücken: Briefwechsel mit einem Strafgefangenen. Düsseldorf: Claassen, 1979. 208 p.
                                    SHV6248.B767 D73

642

———. Oktoberlicht, oder, Ein Tag im Herbst. Düsseldorf: Claassen, 1981. 175 p.   PT2664.R4 O3 1981

643

———. Die Samtvorhänge: Erzählungen, Szenen, Berichte. Gütersloh: Gütersloher Verlagshaus Mohn, 1978. 122 p.
                                    SPT2664.R4 S2

644

———. Schrittweise Erkundung der Welt. Wien: Europaverlag, 1982. 205 p.   G465.D73 1982

645

———. Städte 1945: Berichte und Bekenntnisse. Düsseldorf, Köln: Diederichs, 1970. 206 p.: ill.   DD991.D73

646

———. Unter meiner Zeitlupe: Porträts und Panoramen. Wien: Europa Verlag, 1984. 214 p.   PT105.D74 1984
  List of the author's works: p. 211–213.

647

———. Wer verteidigt Katrin Lambert? Stuttgart: Gebühr, 1974. 174 p.   PT2663.R4 W4

648

————. Wuppertal: Porträt einer Stadt. Wuppertal: Hammer,
1973. 51 p.: ill.   DD901.W98 D73

649

————. Zeitverdichtung: Essays, Kritiken, Portraits: gesammelt
aus zwei Jahrzehnten. Wien, München, Zürich: Europaverlag,
1980. 392 p.   PT2664.R4 A16 1980

650

————. Die zerstörte Kontinuität: Exilliteratur und Literatur des
Widerstandes. Wien: Europaverlag, 1981. 206 p.
                                                PT3808.D7 1981
    Includes bibliographical references.

———————————————

651

Ingeborg Drewitz: Materialien zu Werk und Wirken/ unter
    Mitarbeit von Christa Melchinger und Bernhard Drewitz,
    herausgegeben von Titus Haussermann. Stuttgart: Radius-
    Verlag, 1983. 160 p.   PT2664.R4 Z72 1983
    Bibliography: p. 125–160.

652

So wächst die Mauer zwischen Mensch und Mensch: Stimmen aus
    dem Knast und zum Strafvollzug/ herausgegeben von Ingeborg
    Drewitz und Johann P. Tammen. Bremerhaven: Wirtschafts-
    verlag NW, 1980. 196 p.: ill.   MCLS 87/209 (P)

653

Standortzuweisung: linksliberal, kommunistische Tarnorganisation/
    herausgegeben von Ingeborg Drewitz. München: PDI-Konkret,
    1977. 94 p.: ill.   JN3971.A3 1977 .S69

654

Strauss ohne Kreide: ein Kandidat mit historischer Bedeutung/
    herausgegeben von Ingeborg Drewitz. Reinbek bei Hamburg:
    Rowohlt, 1980. 214 p.   DD259.7.S7 S685
    Includes bibliographical references.

* * * * * * * * * * * * * * * * * * * *

655
Enzensberger, Hans Magnus. Beschreibung eines Dickichts. Berlin:
Volk und Welt, 1979. 224 p.   PT2609.N9 B4

656
————. Blindenschrift. Frankfurt am Main: Suhrkamp, 1967.
96 p.   PT2609.N9 B5 1967

657
————. Brentanos Poetik. München: Hanser, 1961. 157 p.
                                         PT1825.Z5 E5 1961

658
————. The consciousness industry: on literature, politics and the
media. New York: Seabury Press, 1974. 184 p.   PT2609.N9 C6
Includes bibliographical references.

659
————. Critical essays. New York: Continuum, 1982. xvi, 250 p.
                                         PT2609.N9 A24 1982
Includes bibliographical references.

660
————. Deutschland, Deutschland unter anderm. Frankfurt am
Main: Suhrkamp, 1967. 177 p.   JA78.E5

661
————. Einzelheiten. Frankfurt am Main: Suhrkamp, 1962.
364 p.   PT2609.N9 E5

662
————. Einzelheiten II: Poesie und Politik. Frankfurt am Main:
Suhrkamp, 1962–1963. 142 p.   MLCS 85/9082 (P)

663
————. Falter. Köln: Hake, 1965. 22 l.   PT2609.N9 F3

664
————. Die Furie des Verschwindens. Frankfurt am Main:
Suhrkamp, 1980. 86 p.: port.   PT2609.N9 F8

665

————. Gespräche mit Marx und Engels. Frankfurt am Main:
Insel, 1973. 768 p.   HX39.5.E59

666

————. The Havana inquiry. New York: Holt, Rinehart and
Winston, 1974. xxiv, 229 p.   PT2609.N9 V3813
Translation of: Das Verhör von Habana.
Bibliography: p. 227–228.

667

————. Der kurze Sommer der Anarchie: Buenaventura Durrutis
Leben und Tod. Frankfurt am Main: Suhrkamp, 1972. 299, 1 p.
                                                PT2609.N9 K8

668

————. Landessprache. Frankfurt am Main: Suhrkamp, 1969.
97 p.   PT2609.N9 L3

669

————. Mausoleum: 37 Balladen aus der Geschichte des
Fortschritts. Frankfurt am Main: Suhrkamp, 1975. 125 p.
                                                PT2609.N9 M3
Includes index.

670

————. Mausoleum: thirty-seven ballads from the history of
progress. New York: Urizen, 1976. 155 p.   PT2609.N9 M313
Includes index.

671

————. Der Menschenfreund. Frankfurt am Main: Suhrkamp,
1984. 144 p.   MLCS 86/5367 (P)

672

————. Museum der modernen Poesie. München: Deutscher
Taschenbuch-Verlag, 1969, c1960. 398 p.   PN6104.E6 1969

673

————. Palaver: politischer Überlegungen (1967–1973). Frankfurt
am Main: Suhrkamp, 1974. 231 p.   AC35.E65

674

————. Poems for people who don't read poems. London: Secker & Warburg, 1968. 7, 179 p.   PT2609.N9 P59 1968b
Parallel German text, English translation.

675

————. Politics and crime. New York: Seabury Press, 1974. 215 p.
PT2609.N9 A27

676

————. Politik und Verbrechen: neun Beiträge. Frankfurt am Main: Suhrkamp, 1964. 395, 3 p.   HV6187.E5

677

————. Raids and reconstructions: essays on politics, crime, and culture. London: Pluto Press, 1976. 312 p.   H35.E613 1976
Includes bibliographical references and index.

678

————. The sinking of the Titanic: a poem. Boston: Houghton Mifflin, 1980. viii, 98 p.   PT2609.N9 U513
Translation of: Der Untergang der Titanic.

679

————. Der Untergang der Titanic. Frankfurt am Main: Suhrkamp, 1978. 114 p.   PT2609.N9 U5
Epic poem.

680

————. Verteidigung der Wölfe. Frankfurt am Main: Suhrkamp, 1957. 91 p.   PT2609.N9 V4

681

Dietschreit, Frank. Hans Magnus Enzensberger. Stuttgart: Metzler, 1986. viii, 174 p.   PT2609.N9 Z64 1986
Includes index.
Bibliography: p. 148–169.

682

Eggers, Ingrid. Veränderungen des Literaturbegriffs im Werk von
Hans Magnus Enzensberger. Frankfurt am Main, Bern: Lang,
1981. 152 p. (Europäische Hochschulschriften. Reihe I, Deutsche
Sprache und Literatur; Bd. 388)   PT2609.N9 Z65
   Bibliography of works by and about H. M. Enzensberger:
   p. 145–149.
   Bibliography: p. 149–152.

683

Falkenstein, Henning. Hans Magnus Enzensberger. Berlin: Colloquium Verlag, 1977. 86 p. (Köpfe des XX. Jahrhunderts; Bd.
86)   PT2665.N93 Z65
   Bibliography of works by and about H. M. Enzensberger:
   p. 83–84.
   Includes bibliographical references.

684

Grimm, Reinhold. Texturen: Essays und anderes zu Hans Magnus
Enzensberger. New York: Lang, 1984. 236 p.: port. (New York
University Ottendorfer series; n.F., Bd. 19)
                                           PT2609.N9 Z67 1984
      Bibliography: p. 235–236.

685

Hans Magnus Enzensberger/ herausgegeben von Reinhold Grimm.
Frankfurt am Main: Suhrkamp, 1984. 436 p.
                                           PT2609.N9 Z69 1984
      Bibliography: p. 346–435.

686

Zimmermann, Arthur. Hans Magnus Enzensberger: die Gedichte
und ihre literaturkritische Rezeption. Bonn: Bouvier, 1977.
230 p. (Abhandlungen zur Kunst-, Musik- und Literaturwissenschaft; Bd. 227)   PT2609.N9 Z98 1977
   Includes bibliographical references.

****

687

Fels, Ludwig. Alles geht weiter. Darmstadt: Luchterhand, 1977.
   80 p.   PT2666.E397 A77

688
———. Der Anfang der Vergangenheit. München: Piper, 1984. 118 p.   MLCS 86/5217 (P)

689
———. Anläufe. Darmstadt: Luchterhand, 1973. 84 p.   PT2666.E397 A8

690
———. Ernüchterung. Erlangen, Berlin: Renner, 1975. 42 p.   PT2666.E397 E7

691
———. Ich war nicht in Amerika. Erlangen: Renner, 1978. 67 p.: port.   PT2666.E397 I2

692
———. Kanakenfauna: fünfzehn Berichte. Darmstadt: Luchterhand, 1982. 180 p.   PT2666.E397 K3 1982

693
———. Lammermann. Frankfurt am Main: Verlag der Autoren, 1983. 95 p.   MLCS 84/2234 (P)

694
———. Mein Land. Darmstadt, Neuwied: Luchterhand, 1978. 136 p.   PT2666.E397 M4

695
———. Platzangst. Darmstadt: Luchterhand. 1974. 78 p.   PT2666.E397 P5

696
———. Die Sünden der Armut. Darmstadt, Neuwied: Luchterhand, 1975. 134 p.   PT2666.E397 S9

697
———. Ein Unding der Liebe. Darmstadt, Neuwied: Luchterhand, 1981. 338 p.   MLCS 81/486

698
————. Vom Gesang der Bäuche. Darmstadt: Luchterhand, 1980.
150 p.   PT2666.E397 V6 1980

****

699
Grass, Günter. Ach Butt, dein Märchen geht böse aus: Gedichte
und Radierungen. Darmstadt: Luchterhand, 1983. 111 p.: ill.
MLCS 84/8574 (P)

700
————. Aufsätze zur Literatur. Darmstadt: Luchterhand, 1980.
168 p.   PT2613.R338 A7

701
————. Aus dem Tagebuch einer Schnecke. Neuwied:
Luchterhand, 1972. 368 p.   PT2613.R338 A88

702
————. Ausgefragt. Gedichte und Zeichnungen. Neuwied, Berlin:
Luchterhand, 1967. 105 p.   PT2613.R338 A9

703
————. Die Ballerina. Berlin: Friedenauer Presse, 1969. 13 p.
GV1795.G79 1969
Limited ed. of 400 copies.

704
————. Die Blechtrommel. Neuwied: Luchterhand, 1968, c1959.
555 p.: ill. (part col.).   PT2613.R338 B55 1968

705
————. Briefe über die Grenze. Hamburg: Wegner, 1968. 118 p.:
ill.   HX44.G67

706
————. Der Bürger und seine Stimme: Reden, Aufsätze, Kom-
mentare. Darmstadt, Neuwied: Luchterhand, 1974. 270 p.
DD259.4.G64

707
————. Der Butt. Darmstadt, Neuwied: Luchterhand, 1977. 693 p.   PT2613.R338 B8

708
————. Cat and mouse. Harmondsworth: Penguin Books, 1966. 137 p.   PZ4.G774 Cat 3

709
————. The Danzig Trilogy. Orlando, Fla.: Harcourt Brace Jovanovich, 1987. 1,030 p.   PT2613.R338 D2713 1987
Translation of: Danziger Trilogie.

710
————. Danziger Trilogie. Darmstadt, Neuwied: Luchterhand, 1980. 1,157 p.   PT2613.R338 D27

711
————. Davor: ein Stück in 13 Szenen. New York: Harcourt Brace Jovanovich, 1973. 182 p.   PT2613.R338 D3 1973

712
————. Denkzettel: politische Reden und Aufsätze. Darmstadt: Luchterhand, 1978. 232 p.   PT2613.R338 A3

713
————. Dich singe ich, Demokratie. Neuwied, Berlin: Luchterhand, 1965. 6 v.   DD259.4.G65

714
————. Dog years. New York: Harcourt Brace & World, 1965. 570 p.   PZ4.G774 Do

715
————. Der Fall Axel C. Springer am Beispiel Arnold Zweig: eine Rede, ihr Anlass und die Folgen. Berlin: Voltaire Verlag, 1967. 76 p.: ill.   AC30.V58 Nr. 15

716
————. The flounder. New York: Harcourt Brace Jovanovich, 1978. xi, 547 p.   PZ4.G774 F1
Translation of: Der Butt.

717
————. Four plays. New York: Harcourt Brace & World, 1967.
xiii, 289 p.   PT2613.R338 F6

718
————. From the diary of a snail. New York: Harcourt Brace
Jovanovich, 1976, c1973. 310 p.   PZ4.G774 Fr5
Translation of: Aus dem Tagebuch einer Schnecke.

719
————. Gesammelte Gedichte. Neuwied: Luchterhand, 1971.
261 p.   PT2613.R338 A17 1971

720
————. Geschenkte Freiheit: Rede zum 8. Mai 1945. Berlin:
Akademie der Künste, 1985. 23 p. (Anmerkungen zur Zeit; 24)
                                         PT2613.R338 Z647 1985
„Rede aus Anlass des 40. Jahrestages der deutschen
Kapitulation am 8. Mai 1945, gehalten am 5. Mai 1985 im
Studio der Akademie der Künste Berlin.''

721
————. Graphics and writing. San Diego: Harcourt Brace
Jovanovich, 1983–1985. 2 v.: ill.   NX550.Z9 G725 1983
Translation of: Zeichnen und Schreiben.

722
————. Headbirths, or, The Germans are dying out. New York:
Harcourt Brace Jovanovich, 1982. 136 p.   PT2613.R338 K613
Translation of: Kopfgeburten.

723
————. Hochwasser, and Noch zehn Minuten bis Buffalo. New
York: Appleton-Century-Crofts, 1967. vii, 108 p.: port.
                                         PT2613.R339 H62

724
————. Hundejahre. Neuwied am Rhein: Luchterhand, 1963.
682 p.   PT2613.R338 H8 1963

725

————. In the egg and other poems. New York: Harcourt Brace Jovanovich, 1977. xi, 143 p.   PT2613.R338 A24 1977

726

————. Inmarypraise. New York: Harcourt Brace Jovanovich, 1973. 87 p.: ill. (part col.).   NC251.G63 R3513
Translation of: Mariazuehren.
Poem in English and German.

727

————. Katz und Maus. London: Heinemann, 1971. xxxi, 5–244 p.: col. maps (on lining papers).   PT2613.R338 K3 1971
German text, English introduction and notes.

728

————. Kopfgeburten: oder, Die Deutschen sterben aus. Darmstadt: Luchterhand, 1980. 180 p.   PT2613.R338 K6

729

————. Local anaesthetic. New York: Harcourt Brace & World, 1970. 284 p.   PZ4.G774 Lo
Translation of: Örtlich betäubt.

730

————. Mariazuehren. München: Bruckmann, 1973. 88 p.: of ill. (part col.).   NC251.G63 R35

731

————. Max: a play. New York: Harcourt Brace Jovanovich, 1972. 122 p.   PT2613.R338 D313
Translation of: Davor, originally published in the author's Theaterspiele, 1970.

732

————. The meeting at Telgte. New York: Harcourt Brace Jovanovich, 1981. 147 p.   PT2613.R338 T713
Translation of: Das Treffen in Telgte.

733

——. Örtlich betäubt. Neuwied: Luchterhand, 1969. 358 p.
                                                      PT2613.R338 O3

734

——. On writing and politics, 1967–1983. San Diego: Harcourt
Brace Jovanovich, 1985. xv, 157 p.   PT2613.R338 A25 1985
Includes bibliographical references.

735

——. The plebeians rehearse the uprising: a German tragedy;
with an introductory address by the author. London: Secker &
Warburg, 1967. xxxvi, 122 p.   PT2613.R338 P53 1967
Originally published in Germany as Die Plebejer proben den
Aufstand.
Bibliographical footnotes.

736

——. Die Plebejer proben den Aufstand. London: Heinemann,
1971. xlii, 5–186 p.   PT2613.R338 P5 1971
German text, English introduction and notes.
Bibliography: p. 159–163.

737

——. Poems of Günter Grass. Harmondsworth: Penguin, 1969.
88 p.   PT2613.R338 A24

738

——. The rat. San Diego: Harcourt Brace Jovanovich, 1987.
371 p.   PT2613.R338 R313 1987
Translation of: Die Rattin.

739

——. Die Rattin. Darmstadt: Luchterhand, 1986. 504 p.
                                                      PT2613.R338 R3 1986

740

——. Der Schriftsteller als Bürger—eine Siebenjahresbilanz.
Wien: Dr.-Karl-Renner-Institut, 1973. 61 p.
                                                      PT2667.R348 Z527

741

————. Speak out: speeches, open letters, commentaries. New York: Harcourt Brace & World, 1969. xii, 142 p.

DD259.4.G653

Mainly selected from the author's Über das Selbstverständliche, published in 1968.

742

————. Theaterspiele. Reinbek bei Hamburg: Rowohlt, 1975. 301 p. PT2613.R338 T5

743

————. The tin drum. New York: Pantheon Books, 1963, c1962. 591 p. PZ4.G774 Ti2

744

————. Das Treffen in Telgte: eine Erzählung. Leipzig: Reclam, 1984, c1979. 118 p. MLCS 86/5485 (P)

745

————. Über das Selbstverständliche. München: Deutscher Taschenbuch-Verlag, 1969. 208 p. PT2613.R338 A6 1969

746

————. Über meinen Lehrer Alfred Döblin. Olten: Walter, 1977. xxxi, 502 p. PT2607.035 Z714

747

————. Die Vorzüge der Windhühner. Berlin: Luchterhand, 1967. 64 p.: ill. PT2613.R338 V6 1967

748

————. Werkverzeichnis der Radierungen. Berlin: G. Grass, Auslieferung, Galerie André-A. Dreher, 1979–80. 295 p.: ill. NE2050.5.G72 A4 1979

749

————. Widerstand lernen: politische Gegenreden 1980–1983. Darmstadt: Luchterhand, 1984. 107 p.

PT2613.R338 Z65 1984

Bibliography: p. 107.

750

————. Zeichnen und Schreiben: das bildnerische Werk des
Schriftstellers Günter Grass. Darmstadt: Luchterhand, 1982.
148 p.: ill.   NX550.Z9 G725 1982 (fol) Bd. 2
    CONTENTS: Bd. 2. Radierungen und Texte 1972–1982.

751

————. Zeichnungen und Texte 1954–1977. Darmstadt: Luchterhand, 1982. 133 p.: ill.   NX550.Z9 G725 1982 (fol) Bd. 1

——————

752

Adventures of a flounder: critical essays on Günter Grass Der Butt/
edited by Gertrud Bauer Pickar. München: Fink, 1982. v, 118 p.,
12 p. of plates: ill.   PT2613.R338 A67 1982
    English and German.
    Includes bibliographical references.

753

„Die Blechtrommel": Attraktion und Ärgernis: ein Kapitel
deutscher Literaturkritik/ herausgegeben von Franz Josef Görtz.
Darmstadt: Luchterhand, 1984. 161 p.
                                PT2613.R338 B54 1984
    Includes bibliographical references.

754

Brode, Hanspeter. Günter Grass. München: Beck, Edition Text +
Kritik, 1979. 225 p.   PT2613.R338 Z578
    Includes index.
    Bibliography of G. Grass' works: p. 217–220.
    Bibliography: p. 220–222.

755

————. Die Zeitgeschichte im erzählenden Werk von Günter
Grass: Versuch einer Deutung der „Blechtrommel" und der
„Danziger Trilogie." Frankfurt: Lang, 1977. 174 p. (Regens-
burger Beiträge zur deutschen Sprach- und Literaturwissenschaft.
Reihe B, Untersuchungen; Bd. 11)   PT2613.R338 Z58
    Includes indexes.
    Bibliography of G. Grass' works: p. 161.
    Bibliography: p. 162–167.

756

Cepl-Kaufmann, Gertrude. Günter Grass: eine Analyse des Gesamtwerkes unter dem Aspekt von Literatur und Politik. Kronberg/Ts.: Scriptor, 1975. 305 p.   PT2613.R338 Z59
    Bibliography: p. 290–294.

757

Critical essays on Günter Grass/ edited by Patrick O'Neill. Boston, Mass.: Hall, 1987. vi, 230 p.   PT2613.R338 Z597 1987
    Includes index.
    Bibliography: p. 225–227.

758

Diller, Edward. A mythic journey: Günter Grass's Tin drum. Lexington: University Press, 1974. viii, 216 p.: front.
                                   PT2613.R338 B5533
    Bibliography: p. 197–209.

759

Elsner Hunt, Irmgard. Mutter und Muttermythos in Günter Grass' Roman Der Butt. Frankfurt am Main: Lang, 1983. iv, 226 p. (Europäische Hochschulschriften. Reihe I, Deutsche Sprache und Literatur; Bd. 647)   PT2613.R338 B833 1983
    Bibliography: p. 222–226.

760

Everett, George A. A select bibliography of Günter Grass (from 1956 to 1973) including the works, editions, translations, and critical literature. New York: Franklin, 1974. vi, 89 p.: ill.
                                        Z8366.48.E93

761

Gerstenberg, Renate. Zur Erzähltechnik von Günter Grass. Heidelberg: Winter, 1980. 194 p. (Beiträge zur neueren Literaturgeschichte: 3. Folge; Bd. 47)   PT2613.R338 Z63
    Preface in English.
    Bibliography: p. 185–194.

762

Günter Grass: ein Materialienbuch/ herausgegeben von Rolf Geissler. Darmstadt: Luchterhand, 1976. 187 p.
                               PT2613.R338 Z648 1976

Bibliography of G. Grass' works: 179–180.
Bibliography: p. 180–186.

763
Hayman, Ronald. Günter Grass. London, New York: Methuen, 1985. 80 p.   PT2613.R338 Z664 1985
Bibliography: p. 77–80.

764
Hollington, Michael. Günter Grass, the writer in a pluralist society. London, New York: Boyars, 1987, c1980. 186 p.
PT2613.R338 Z67 1987
Includes index.
Bibliography: p. 176–182.

765
Krumme, Detlef. Günter Grass, Die Blechtrommel. München: Hanser, 1986. 160 p.   PT2613.R338 B55357 1986
Includes index.
Bibliography: 155–158.

766
Lawson, Richard H. Günter Grass. New York: Ungar, 1985. xvii, 176 p.   PT2613.R338 Z69 1985
Includes index.
Bibliography: p. 160–169.

767
Mason, Ann L. The skeptical muse: a study of Günter Grass' conception of the artist. Bern, Frankfurt am Main: Lang, 1974. 138 p. (Stanford German studies; v. 5)   PT2613.R338 Z75
English or German.
Bibliography: p. 130–138.

768
Neuhaus, Volker. Günter Grass, Die Blechtrommel: Interpretation. München: Oldenbourg, 1982. 135 p.
PT2613.R338 B55365 1982
Bibliography: p. 132–135.

769

O'Neill, Patrick. Günter Grass: a bibliography, 1955–1975.
Toronto, Buffalo: University of Toronto Press, 1976. viii, 108 p.
Z8366.48.O53
Includes index.

770

Reed, Donna K. The novel and the Nazi past. New York: Lang,
1985. x, 216 p. (American university studies. Series I, Germanic
languages and literature; v. 28)   PT772.R38 1985
Revision of thesis (Ph.D.)—Harvard University.
Includes index.
Bibliography: p. 173–207.

771

Richter, Frank. Günter Grass: die Vergangenheitsbewältigung in
der Danzig-Trilogie. Bonn: Bouvier, 1979. 169 p. (Abhandlungen zur Kunst-, Musik- und Literaturwissenschaft; Bd. 244)
PT2613.R338 Z79
Bibliography: p. 165–169.

772

Schlondorff, Volker. „Die Blechtrommel": Tagebuch einer
Verfilmung. Darmstadt, Neuwied: Luchterhand, 1979. 160 p.:
ill.   PT2613.R338 Z827 1979
Includes bibliographical references.

773

Schneider, Irmela. Kritische Rezeption: die Blechtrommel als
Modell. Frankfurt am Main: Lang, 1975. 197 p. (Europäische
Hochschulschriften: Reihe 1, Deutsche Literatur und
Germanistik; Bd. 123)   PT2613.R338 B5539 1975
Originally presented as the author's thesis, Frankfurt am
Main, 1974.
Bibliography: p. 182–196.

774

Schröder, Susanne. Erzählerfiguren und Erzählperspektive in
Günter Grass' „Danziger Trilogie." Frankfurt am Main, New
York: Lang, 1986. 145 p. (Europäische Hochschulschriften.
Reihe I, Deutsche Sprache und Literatur; Bd. 784)
PT2613.R338 D2737 1986
Bibliography: p. 140–145.

775
Thomas, Noel. The narrative works of Günter Grass: a critical interpretation. Amsterdam, Philadelphia: Benjamins, 1982. 370 p. (German language and literature monographs; v. 12)
PT2613.R338 Z894 1982
Includes bibliographical references.

776
Vormweg, Heinrich. Günter Grass: mit Selbstzeugnissen und Bilddokumenten. Reinbek bei Hamburg: Rowohlt, 1986. 143 p.: ill.   PT2613.R338 Z897 1986
Bibliography: p. 137–142.

777
White, Ray Lewis. Günter Grass in America: the early years. Hildesheim, New York: Olms, 1981. ix, 158, 1 p. (Germanistische Texte und Studien; Bd. 12)   PT2613.R338 Z93 1981
Bibliography: p. 159.

778
Willson, Amos Leslie. Die doppelspitzige Feder von Günter Grass. Mainz: Akademie der Wissenschaften und der Literatur; Wiesbaden: Steiner, 1983. 40 p.: ill. (Abhandlungen der Klasse der Literatur; Jahrg. 1983, Nr. 1)   NX550.Z9 G738 1983
Includes bibliographical references.

****

779
Grün, Max von der. Am Tresen gehn die Lichter aus. Stierstadt im Taunus: Eremiten-Presse, 1972. 56 p.   PT2667.R83 A8

780
———. Etwas ausserhalb der Legalität und andere Erzählungen. Darmstadt, Neuwied: Luchterhand, 1980. 212 p.
MLCS 81/295

781
———. Fahrtunterbrechung und andere Erzählungen. Frankfurt am Main: Europäische Verlagsanstalt, 1965. 230 p.
PT2667.R83 F3

782

————. Feierabend. Recklinghausen: Paulus, 1968. 79 p.: front.
PN1992.77.G7

783

————. Flächenbrand. Darmstadt: Luchterhand, 1979. 361 p.
MLCS 84/12610 (P)

784

————. Flug über Zechen und Wälder. Braunschweig: Westermann, 1970. 117 p.: col. plates. DD801.N6 G75

785

————. Howl like the wolves: growing up in Nazi Germany. New York: Morrow, 1980. 285 p.: ill. PT2667.R83 Z52413
Translation of: Wie war das eigentlich?
Includes index.
Bibliography: p. 273–276.

786

————. Irrlicht und Feuer. London: Harrap, 1974. xxvi, 205 p.: ill., map, port. PT2667.R83 I7 1974
Bibliography of the author's works: p. 1.
Includes bibliographical references.

787

————. Klassengespräche: Aufsätze, Reden, Kommentare. Darmstadt: Luchterhand, 1981. 228 p. PT2667.R83 A6 1981

788

————. Die Lawine. Darmstadt: Luchterhand, 1986. 363 p.
MLCS 86/5840 (P)

789

————. Leben im gelobten Land: Gastarbeiterporträts. Darmstadt: Luchterhand, 1975. 117 p. HD8458.A2 G76

790

————. Männer in zweifacher Nacht. Bergisch-Gladbach: Bastei-Lübbe, 1973, c1963. 158 p. PT2667.R83 M3 1973

791

————. Reisen in die Gegenwart: vier Erzählungen. Düsseldorf:
Eremiten-Presse, 1976. 89 p.: 12 ill.   PT2667.R83 R4

792

————. Späte Liebe. Darmstadt: Luchterhand, 1982. 172 p.
                                                           MLCS 82/6180

793

————. Ein Tag wie jeder andere: Reisen in die Gegenwart; Nach
Sudiler und zurück. München: Deutscher Taschenbuch-Verlag,
1978, c1976. 114 p.   PT2667.R83 A6 1978

794

————. Unser schönes Nordrhein-Westfalen: von Menschen und
Natur, von Kohle und Kultur. Frankfurt am Main: Umschau,
1983. 127 p.: chiefly col. ill.   DD801.N6 G76 1983
Dutch, English, French, and German.

795

————. Unterwegs in Deutschland. Düsseldorf: Eremiten-Presse,
1979. 100 p.: ill.   PT2667.R83 U57

796

————. Urlaub am Plattensee. Stierstadt: Eremiten-Presse, 1970.
36 p.: col. ill.   PT2667.R83 U7

797

————. Vorstadtkrokodil: eine Geschichte vom Aufpassen.
München: Bertelsmann, 1976. 109 p.: ill.   PZ33.G846

798

————. Wenn der tote Rabe vom Baum fällt. München,
Gütersloh, Wien: Bertelsmann, 1975. 204 p.   PT2667.R83 Z52

799

————. Wie war das eigentlich?: Kindheit und Jugend im Dritten
Reich. Darmstadt: Luchterhand, 1979. 263 p.: ill.
                                        PT2667.R83 Z524 1979
Includes bibliographies and index.

800

Max von der Grün. München: Edition Text + Kritik, 1975. 53 p.

PT2667.R83 Z78

,,Bibliographie und Filmographie zu Max von der Grün'':
p. 42-52.

801

Max von der Grün: Auskunft für Leser/ herausgegeben von
Stephan Reinhardt. Darmstadt: Luchterhand, 1986. 281 p.: ill.

PT2667.R83 Z7815 1986

Bibliography: p. 269-281.

802

Max von der Grün: Materialienbuch/ herausgegeben von Stephan
Reinhardt. Darmstadt: Luchterhand, 1978. 189 p.: ill.

PT2667.R83 Z782

Bibliography: p. 181-190.

803

Schönauer, Franz. Max von der Grün. München: Beck, Edition
Text + Kritik, 1978. 169 p.   PT2667.R83 Z88

Bibliography by and about M. v. d. Grün: p. 167-169.

****

804

Hahn, Ulla. Freudenfeuer. Stuttgart: Deutsche Verlags-Anstalt,
1985. 103 p.   MLCS 86/1132 (P)

805

————. Günter Wallraff. München: Beck, Edition Text + Kritik,
1979. 125 p. (Autorenbücher; 14)   PN5213.W3 H3

Includes bibliographical references.

806

————. Herz über Kopf. Stuttgart: Deutsche Verlags-Anstalt,
1981. 87 p.   MLCS 81/2523

807

————. Literatur in der Aktion: zur Entwicklung operativer
Literaturformen in der Bundesrepublik. Wiesbaden:

Akademische Verlagsgesellschaft Athenaion, 1978. 257 p.

PT405.H25

Includes index.

Bibliography: p. 236–251.

808

————. Spielende. Stuttgart: Deutsche Verlags-Anstalt, 1983.
102 p.   PT2668.A4223 S65 1983

****

809

Harig, Ludwig. Allseitige Beschreibung der Welt zur Heimkehr
des Menschen in eine schönere Zukunft. München: Hanser,
1974. 303 p.   CB358.H37

810

————. Ein Blumenstück. Wiesbaden: Limes, 1969. 246 p.

PT2668.A68 B5

811

————. Das Fussballspiel: ein stereophones Hörspiel. Stuttgart:
Edition Mayer, 1967. 40 p. (on double leaves).

PT2668.A68 F8

812

————. Das Geräusch. Neuwied, Berlin: Luchterhand, 1965. 31 p.

PT2668.A68 G4

813

————. Heilige Kühe der Deutschen: eine feuilletonistische
Anatomie. München: Hanser, 1981. 114 p.

PT2668.A68 H4 1981

814

————. Heimweh: ein Saarländer auf Reisen. München, Wien:
Hanser, 1979. 207 p.: ill.   PT2668.A68 Z52

Includes bibliographical references.

815

————. Im men see. Berlin: Fietkau, 1969. 34 p.

PT2668.A68 I4

816

————. Der kleine Brixius. München: Hanser, 1980. 121 p.

PT2668.A68 K5 1980

817

————. Logbuch eines Luftkutschers: mit einer autobiographischen Einleitung. Stuttgart: Reclam, 1981. 103 p.

PT2668.A68 L6

Bibliography: p. 99–102.

818

————. Netzer kam aus der Tiefe des Raumes. München: Hanser, 1974. 187 p.

GV943.2.H28

819

————. Ordnung ist das ganze Leben: Roman meines Vaters. München: Hanser, 1986. 498 p.

MLCS 86/7024 (P)

820

————. Permutationen, Wiederholungen in Konstellationsvarianten: dargestellt an zwei Beispielen. Mainz: Akademie der Wissenschaften und der Literatur; Wiesbaden: Steiner, 1984. 17 p. (Abhandlungen der Klasse der Literatur, Akademie der Wissenschaften und der Literatur; Jahrg. 1984, Nr. 3)

PT2668.A68 P4 1984

821

————. Reise nach Bordeaux. Wiesbaden: Limes, 1965. 100 p.

PT2668.A68 R4

822

————. Rousseau: der Roman vom Ursprung der Natur im Gehirn. München, Wien: Hanser, 1978. 353 p.

PT2668.A68 R6

823

————. Die saarländische Freude: ein Lesebuch über die gute Art zu denken und zu leben. München: Hanser, 1977. 173 p.: ill.

PT2668.A68 S2

824

―――. Sprechstunden für die deutsch-französische Verständigung und die Mitglieder des Gemeinsamen Marktes, ein Familienroman. München: Hanser, 1971. 231 p.: ill.

PT2668.A68 S6

825

―――. Trierer Spaziergänge. München: Hanser, 1983. 247 p.: ill.

DD901.T81 H37 1983

826

―――. Und sie fliegen über die Berge, weit durch die Welt. München: Hanser, 1972. 133 p.: ill.   PT1354.H37

827

―――. Wie kommt Leopold Bloom auf die Bleibtreustrasse. Berlin: Literarisches Colloquium, 1975. 52 p.: ill.

PT2668.A68 W5

828

―――. Zum Schauen bestellt: Deidesheimer Tagebuch. Landau/Pfalz: Pfälzische Verlagsanstalt, 1984. 183 p.: ill.

PT2668.A68 Z478 1984

829

―――. Zustand und Veränderungen. Wiesbaden: Limes, 1963. 67 p.   PT2668.A68 Z48

****

830

Heissenbüttel, Helmut. Briefwechsel über Literatur. Neuwied: Luchterhand, 1969. 97 p.   PN45.H39

831

―――. Das Durchhauen des Kohlhaupts: dreizehn Lehrgedichte: Projekt Nr. 2. Darmstadt: Luchterhand, 1974. 233 p.

PT2668.E393 D8 1974

832

―――. Eichendorffs Untergang und andere Märchen: Projekt 3/1. Stuttgart: Klett-Cotta, 1978. 188 p.   PT2668.E393 E3

833

————. Das Ende der Alternative: einfache Geschichten: Projekt 3/3. Stuttgart: Klett-Cotta, 1980. 176 p.   PT2668.E393 E5

834

————. Die Erfindung der Libido: das deutsche Epos in der zweiten Hälfte des 19. Jahrhunderts. Mainz: Akademie der Wissenschaften und Literatur; Wiesbaden: Steiner, 1981. 16 p. (Abhandlungen der Klasse der Literatur; Jahrg. 1981/82, Nr. 1)
MLCS 82/2855

835

————. Der fliegende Frosch und das unverhoffte Krokodil: Wilhelm Busch als Dichter. Mainz: Akademie der Wissenschaften und der Literatur; Wiesbaden: Steiner, 1976. 16 p. (Abhandlungen der Klasse der Literatur; Jahrg. 1976, Nr. 1)
PT2603.U8 Z67
,,Vorgetragen in der Plenarsitzung am 12. April 1975.''

836

————. Die Freuden des Alterns. Duisburg: Hildebrandt, 1971. 14 1. col. ill.   PT2668.E393 F7 (Rare Bk Coll)

837

————. Geiger. Stuttgart: Hatje, 1972. 57, 6 p.: ill. (part col.).
N6888.G43 H4

838

————. Gelegenheitsgedichte und Klappentexte. Darmstadt: Luchterhand, 1973. 142 p.   PT2668.E393 G4

839

————. Die goldene Kuppel des Comes Arbogast: oder, Lichtenberg in Hamburg: fast eine einfache Geschichte. Stuttgart: Klett-Cotta, 1980. 104 p.: col. ill.   PT2668.E393 G64

840

————. Mümmelmann oder die Hasendämmerung. Mainz: Akademie der Wissenschaften und der Literatur; Wiesbaden: Steiner, 1978. 15 p. (Abhandlungen der Klasse der Literatur; Jahrg. 1978, Nr. 1)   PT2623.O36 M834
,,Vorgetragen in der Plenarsitzung am 29. April 1977.''

841
————. Neue Abhandlungen über den menschlichen Verstand.
Neuwied, Berlin: Luchterhand, 1967. 45 p.   PT2668.E393 N4

842
————. Ödipuskomplex made in Germany: Gelegenheitsgedichte,
Totentage, Landschaften, 1965–1980. Stuttgart: Klett-Cotta,
1981. 105 p.   MLCM 87/1631 (P)

843
————. Der Philosoph. Zürich: Verlag 3, 1983. 43 p.: ill.
                                    PT2668.E393 P47 1983
Includes English translation.

844
————. Das Textbuch. Neuwied, Berlin: Luchterhand, 1970.
282 p.   PT2668.E393 T4 1970

845
————. Textbuch 8: 1981–1985. Stuttgart: Klett-Cotta, 1985.
93 p.   MLCS 86/3595 (P)

846
————. Textbuch 10: von Liebeskunst. Stuttgart: Klett-Cotta,
1986. 79 p.   MLCS 86/5842 (P)

847
————. Texts. London: Boyars, 1977. 119 p.
                                        PT2668.E393 A24
Translated from the German.

848
————. Über Literatur. Olten, Freiburg i. Br.: Walter, 1966.
247 p.   PN774.H4

849
————. Versuch über die Lautsonate von Kurt Schwitters. Mainz:
Akademie der Wissenschaften und der Literatur; Wiesbaden:
Steiner, 1983. 18 p. (Abhandlungen der Klasse der Literatur;
Jahrg. 1983, Nr. 6)   PT2638.W896 Z7 1983

850

———. Von der Lehrbarkeit des Poetischen, oder, Jeder kann Gedichte schreiben. Mainz: Akademie der Wissenschaften und der Literatur; Wiesbaden: Steiner, 1981. 17 p. (Abhandlungen der Klasse der Literatur; Jahrg. 1981/82, Nr. 4)

MLCM 82/2856

851

———. Von fliegenden Fröschen, libidinösen Epen, vaterländischen Romanen, Sprechblasen und Ohrwürmern: dreizehn Essays. Stuttgart: Klett-Cotta, 1982. 189 p.

PT2668.E393 V6 1982

852

———. Was ist das Konkrete an einem Gedicht? Itzehoe: Hansen, 1969. 120 p. PN1031.H4 1969

853

———. Der Wassermaler: Das Dilemma auf dem Trockenen zu sitzen. Zürich: Verlag 3, 1976. vi, 33 p.: ill.

PT2668.E393 W3

Edition of 100 numbered copies signed by the author and the artist. This is no. 63.

854

———. Wenn Adolf Hitler den Krieg nicht gewonnen hätte: historische Novellen und wahre Begebenheiten: Projekt 3/2. Stuttgart: Klett-Cotta, 1979. 188 p. PT2668.E393 W4

855

———. Zur Tradition der Moderne. Aufsätze und Anmerkungen 1964–1971. Neuwied, Berlin West: Luchterhand, 1972. 394 p.

PN774.H42

856

Amery, Jean. Der integrale Humanismus: zwischen Philosophie und Literatur: Aufsätze und Kritiken eines Lesers, 1966–1978. Stuttgart: Klett-Cotta, 1985. 280 p. B793.A55 1985

857

Burns, Robert A. Commitment, language and reality: an
introduction to the work of Helmut Heissenbüttel. Coventry:
University of Warwick, Department of German Studies, 1975.
48 p. (Occasional papers in German studies; no. 7)

PT2668.E393 Z6

Bibliography: p. 48.

858

Köhler, Karl Heinz. Reduktion als Erzählverfahren in
Heissenbüttels Textbüchern: Anspruch, theoretische Begründung
und erzählerische Leistung von Heissenbüttels Reduktions-
formen. Frankfurt am Main: Haag und Herchen, 1978. 188 p.

PT2668.E393 Z7 1978

Originally presented as the author's thesis, Heidelberg, 1977.
Bibliography: p. 160–188.

859

Rumold, Rainer. Sprachliches Experiment und literarische Tradition: zu den Texten Helmut Heissenbüttels. Bern, Frankfurt am
Main: Lang, 1975. 151 p. (Stanford German studies; vol. 9)

PT2668.E393 Z86

Bibliography H. Heissenbüttel: p. 145–147.
Bibliography: p. 149–151.

****

860

Herburger, Günter. Die amerikanische Tochter. Darmstadt:
Luchterhand, 1973. 319 p.   PT2668.E7 A8

861

————. Die Augen der Kämpfer. Darmstadt: Luchterhand, 1980.
408 p.   PT2668.E7 A95

862

————. Birne brennt durch: sechsundzwanzig Abenteuer-
geschichten für Kinder und Erwachsene. Darmstadt: Luchterhand, 1975. 112 p.: ill.   PZ34.9.H397

863

————. Birne kann alles. Neuwied: Luchterhand, 1971. 100 p.:
ill.   PZ34.9.H4

864

————. Birne kann noch mehr. Neuwied, Berlin: Luchterhand,
1971. 112 p.: ill.   PZ33.H238

865

————. Blick aus dem Paradies: Thuja: zwei Spiele eines Themas.
Darmstadt: Luchterhand, 1981. 104 p.   PT2668.E7 B5 1981

866

————. Capri: die Geschichte eines Diebs. Darmstadt: Luchterhand, 1984. 185 p.   MLCS 86/7475 (P)

867

————. Die Eroberung der Zitadelle: Erzählungen. Darmstadt:
Luchterhand, 1972. 331 p.   PT2669.E7 E7

868

————. Das Flackern des Feuers im Land: Beschreibungen.
Darmstadt: Luchterhand, 1983. 188 p.   PT2668.E7 A16 1983

869

————. Flug ins Herz. Darmstadt: Luchterhand, 1977. 2 v.: 687 p.
                                                      PT2668.E7 F6

870

————. Eine gleichmässige Landschaft. Neuwied: Luchterhand,
1972, c1964. 255 p.   PT2668.E7 G55 1972

871

————. Hauptlehrer Höfer. Ein Fall von Pfingsten: zwei Erzählungen. Darmstadt, Neuwied: Luchterhand, 1975. 94 p.
                                                      PT2668.E7 H3

872

————. Jesus in Osaka: Zukunftsroman. Neuwied: Luchterhand,
1970. 327 p.   PT2668.E7 J4

873
————. Makadam: Gedichte. Darmstadt: Luchterhand, 1982.
134 p.   MLCS 82/6433

874
————. Die Messe. Neuwied: Luchterhand, 1969. 484 p.
PT2668.E7 M4

875
————. A monotonous landscape. London: Calder & Boyars,
1969. 5, 184 p.   PZ4.H537 Mo3

876
————. Nüssen und andere Erzählungen. Berlin, Weimar:
Aufbau-Verlag, 1975. 363 p.   PT2668.E7 N8

877
————. Operette: Gedichte. Darmstadt: Luchterhand, 1973.
135 p.   PT2668.E7 O6

878
————. Orchidee: Gedichte. Darmstadt, Neuwied: Luchterhand,
1979. 112 p.   PT2668.E7 O63

879
————. Training: Gedichte. Neuwied, Berlin: Luchterhand, 1970.
55 p.   PT2668.E7 T7

880
————. Ventile: Gedichte. Köln: Kiepenheuer & Witsch, 1966.
53 p.   PT2668.E7 V4

881
————. Ziele. Reinbek bei Hamburg: Rowohlt, 1977. 166 p.
PT2668.E7 Z3

* * * * * * * * * * * * * * * * * * *

882
Hochhuth, Rolf. Ärztinnen: fünf Akte. Reinbek bei Hamburg:
Rowohlt, 1980. 190 p.   PT2668.O3 A89 1980

883

————. Die Berliner Antigone: Prosa und Verse. Reinbek bei
Hamburg: Rowohlt, 1975. 124 p.   PT2668.O3 B4

884

————. The deputy. New York: Grove Press, 1964. 352 p.
                                        PT2668.O3 S813
Includes the author's "Sidelights on history": p. 287-352.
Bibliographical references included in footnotes.

885

————. Dramen. Reinbek bei Hamburg: Rowohlt, 1972. 669 p.:
ill.   PT2668.O3 A19 1972

886

————. A German love story. Boston: Little, Brown, 1980. 269 p.
                                        PZ4.H68525 Ge 1980

887

————. Die grossen Meister. Köln: Kiepenheuer & Witsch, 1966.
2 v.   PN6065.G4 H6 1966

888

————. Guerillas: Tragödie in fünf Akten. Reinbek bei Hamburg:
Rowohlt, 1970. 219 p.   PT2668.O3 G8

889

————. Die Hebamme. Reinbek bei Hamburg: Rowohlt, 1974,
c1971. 183 p.   PT2668.O3 H4 1974

890

————. Judith. Reinbek bei Hamburg: Rowohlt, 1984. 263 p.
                                        MLCS 86/5675 (P)

891

————. Juristen: drei Akte für sieben Spieler. Reinbek bei
Hamburg: Rowohlt, 1979. 205 p.   PT2668.O3 J8

892

————. Krieg und Klassenkieg. Reinbek bei Hamburg: Rowohlt,
1971. 254 p.   HN18.H635

893
———. Eine Liebe in Deutschland. Reinbek bei Hamburg:
Rowohlt, 1978. 318 p.   PT2668.O3 L5

894
———. Lysistrate und die NATO. Reinbek bei Hamburg:
Rowohlt, 1973. 235 p.   PT2668.O3 L9

895
———. Räuber-Rede: drei deutsche Vorwürfe: Schiller, Lessing,
Geschwister Scholl. Reinbek bei Hamburg: Rowohlt, 1982.
222 p.   PT2496.P6 H62 1982
Includes bibliographical references.

896
———. Soldaten. Nekrolog auf Genf: Tragödie. Reinbek bei
Hamburg: Rowohlt, 1967. 191 p.: ill., front.   PT2668.O3 S6

897
———. Soldiers: an obituary for Geneva. New York: Grove Press,
1968. 255 p.   PT2668.O3 S613
Translation of: Soldaten.

898
———. Der Stellvertreter: ein christliches Trauerspiel. Reinbek
bei Hamburg: Rowohlt, 1967. 295 p.   PT2668.O3 S8 1967

899
———. Tell 38. Boston: Little, Brown, 1984. vi, 158 p.
                                         PT2668.O3 Z47613 1984
Translation of: Tell 38.

900
———. Tod eines Jägers. St. Pölten: Niederösterreichisches Pressehaus, 1979. 43 p.: port.   PT2668.O3 T62

901
———. Zwischenspiel in Baden-Baden. Reinbek bei Hamburg:
Rowohlt, 1974. 158 p.: ill.   PT2668.P3 Z45

902

Bentley, Eric Russell. The storm over the deputy. New York: Grove
Press, 1964. 254 p.   PT2668.O3 S824

903

Berg, Jan. Hochhuths „Stellvertreter" und die Stellvertreter-
Debatte: Vergangenheitsbewältigung in Theater und Presse der
sechziger Jahre. Kronberg/Ts.: Scriptor, 1977. ix, 234 p.
                                       PT2668.O3 S832
Bibliography p. 228-234.

904

Rolf Hochhuth. München: Edition Text + Kritik, 197& 67 p.
                                       PN4.T45 Heft 58
Bibliography: p. 62-65.

905

Rolf Hochhuth: Dokumente zur politischen Wirkung/
herausgegeben und eingeleitet von Reinhart Hoffmeister.
München: Kindler, 1980. 339 p.   PT2668.O3 Z85
Includes bibliographical references.

906

Rolf Hochhuth, Eingriff in die Zeitgeschichte: Essays zum Werk/
herausgegeben von Walter Hinck. Reinbek bei Hamburg:
Rowohlt, 1981. 285, 2 p.   PT2668.O3 Z853 1981
„Auswahlbibliographie zu Rolf Hochhuth von Andreas F.
Kelletat": p. 271-286.
Bibliography: p. 287.

907

Ruhm und Ehre: die Nobelpreisträger für Literatur. Gütersloh:
Bertelsmann, 1970. 991 p.: ill., ports.   PN6034.R8
Rolf Hochhuth was awarded the Nobel Prize for Literature.

908

Taeni, Rainer. Rolf Hochhuth. München: Beck, Edition Text +
Kritik, 1977. 130 p. (Autorenbücher; 5)   PT2668.O3 Z9
Includes bibliographical references.

****

909
Johnson, Uwe. An absence. London: Cape, 1969. 61 p.

PZ4.J717 Ab
Originally published as Eine Reise wegwohin, in Karsch, und andere Prosa.

910
————. Anniversaries: from the life of Gesine Cresspahl. New York: Harcourt Brace Jovanovich, 1975. 504 p.

PT2670.O36 J3213 1975
Translation based on v. 1 and part of v. 2 of Jahrestage.

911
————. Anniversaries II: from the life of Gesine Cresspahl. San Diego: Harcourt Brace Jovanovich, 1987. x, 644 p.

PT2670.O36 J3212 1987

912
————. Begleitumstände: Frankfurter Vorlesungen. Frankfurt am Main: Suhrkamp, 1980. 457 p.: ill.   PT2670.O36 B39

913
————. Berliner Sachen. Frankfurt am Main: Suhrkamp, 1975. 111 p.   PT2670.O36 B4
Two essays also in English.

914
————. Ingrid Babendererde: Reifeprüfung 1953. Frankfurt am Main: Suhrkamp. 1985. 263 p.   PT2670.O36 I53 1985

915
————. Karsch, und andere Prosa. Frankfurt am Main: Suhrkamp, 1966. 102 p.   PT2670.O36 K3 1966

916
————. Mutmassungen über Jakob. Frankfurt am Main: Suhrkamp, 1981, c1959. 307 p.   PT2670.O36 M8 1981

917
————. Eine Reise nach Klagenfurt. Frankfurt am Main: Suhrkamp, 1974. 108 p.   PT2670.O36 R4
Includes bibliographical references and index.

918

————. Speculations about Jacob. New York: Grove Press, 1963. 240 p.   PZ4.J717 Sp

919

————. The third book about Achim. New York: Harcourt Brace & World, 1967. 246 p.   PZ4.J717 Th
Translation of: Das dritte Buch über Achim.

920

————. Zwei Ansichten. Frankfurt am Main: Suhrkamp, 1976. 242 p.   PT2670.O36 Z48 1976

921

Boulby, Mark. Uwe Johnson. New York: Ungar, 1974. vii, 136 p.
                                                                                PT2670.O36 Z65
Bibliography: p. 127–129.

922

Fahlke, Eberhard. Die „Wirklichkeit'' der Mutmassungen: eine politische Lesart der „Mutmassungen über Jakob'' von Uwe Johnson. Frankfurt am Main: Lang, 1982. 323 p. (Europäische Hochschulschriften. Reihe I, Deutsche Sprache und Literatur; Bd. 424)   PT2670.O36 M834 1982
Originally presented as the author's thesis (doctoral).
Bibliography: p. 313–323.

923

Fickert, Kurt J. Neither left nor right: the politics of individualism in Uwe Johnson's work. New York: Lang, 1987. 182 p. (American university studies. Series I, Germanic languages and literature; vol. 59)   PT2670.O36 Z67 1987
Includes index.
Bibliography: p. 163–169.

924

Johnsons „Jahrestage''/ herausgegeben von Michael Bengel. Frankfurt am Main: Suhrkamp, 1985. 395, 1 p.: ill.
                                                                          PT2670.O36 J335 1985
Bibliography: p. 371–396.

925

Neumann, Bernd. Utopie und Mimesis: zum Verhältnis von Ästhetik, Gesellschaftsphilosophie und Politik in den Romanen Uwe Johnsons. Kronberg/Ts.: Athenäum, 1978. ix. 352 p.

PT2670.O36 Z78

Includes index.

Habilitationsschrift—Freie Universität, Berlin, 1976.

Bibliography: p. 342-347.

926

Riedel, Nicolai. Uwe Johnson, Bibliographie 1959-1980. 2., völlig neu bearbeitete Aufl. Bonn: Bouvier, 1981. 326 p. (Abhandlungen zur Kunst-, Musik- und Literaturwissenschaft; Bd. 200)

Z8455.88.R54 1981

Includes index.

927

Schmitz, Walter. Uwe Johnson. München: Beck, Edition Text + Kritik, 1984. 139 p.: ill. (Autorenbücher; 43)

PT2670.O36 Z86 1984

Bibliography: p. 130-139.

928

Uwe Johnson/ herausgegeben von Rainer Gerlach und Matthias Richter. Frankfurt am Main: Suhrkamp, 1984. 345 p.

PT2670.O36 Z9 1984

Bibliography: p. 330-340.

****

929

Kempowski, Walter. Alle unter einem Hut. Bayreuth: Loewe, 1976. 125 p.: ill.   PZ33.K424124

930

————. Aus grosser Zeit. Hamburg: Knaus, 1978. 447 p.

PT2671.E43 A94

931

————. Days of greatness. New York: Knopf, 1981. 399 p.

PT2671.E43 A9413 1981

Translation of: Aus grosser Zeit.

932

―――. Did you ever see Hitler?: German answers. New York:
Avon Books, 1975. 140 p.: ill.   DD247.H5 K4413
Translation of: Haben Sie Hitler gesehen?

933

―――. Haben Sie davon gewusst?: deutsche Antworten. Hamburg:
Knaus, 1979. 148 p.: map.   D810.J4 H324

934

―――. Haben Sie Hitler gesehen? München: Hanser, 1973.
118 p.   DD247.H5 K44

935

―――. Herzlich willkommen. München: Knaus, 1984. 351 p.
MLCS 87/375 (P)

936

―――. Im Block. Frankfurt am Main: Fischer-Taschenbuch-
Verlag, 1972. 255 p.   PT2671.E43 I4 1972

937

―――. Immer so durchgemogelt: Erinnerungen an unsere
Schulzeit. München: Hanser, 1974. 255 p.: ill.   LA23.K45

938

―――. Ein Kapitel für sich. München: Hanser, 1975. 387 p.
PT2671.E43 K3

939

―――. Mein Lesebuch. Frankfurt am Main: Fischer, 1980. 225 p.
PT1105.M45

940

―――. Schöne Aussicht. Hamburg: Knaus, 1981. 541 p.
MLCS 81/1926

941

―――. Tadelloser & Wolff. München: Goldmann, 1980, c1978.
476 p.   MLCS 84/11070 (P)

942
————. Uns geht's ja noch gold. München: Hanser, 1972. 371 p.
PT2671.E43 U5

943
————. Unser Herr Bockelmann. Hamburg: Knaus, 1979. 96 p.
MLCM 87/2102 (P)

944
Alfs, Günter. „Genauso war es—'': Kempowskis Familienge-
schichte „Tadelloser & Wolff'' im Urteil des Publikums.
Oldenburg: Holzberg, 1982. 157 p. (Schriftenreihe der
Universität Oldenburg)   PT2671.E43 T332 1982
Bibliography: p. 146–156.

945
Dierks, Manfred. Walter Kempowski. München: Beck, Edition
Text + Kritik, 1984. 138 p.   PT2671.E43 Z63 1984
Includes bibliographical references.

946
Neumann, Michael. Kempowski der Schulmeister. Braunschweig:
Westermann, 1980. 134 p.: ill. (some col.).
LA2375.G32 K345

947
Westphal, Hansgerhard. Schnoor: Bremen zwischen Stavendamm
und Balge/ fotographiert von Hansgerhard Westphal; mit einem
Text von Walter Kempowski. Bremen: Schmalfeldt, 1978. 95 p.:
chiefly ill.   DD901.B74 W47

****

948
Kipphardt, Heinar. Angelsbrücker Notizen. München: Bertelsmann,
1977. 219 p.: 10 ill.   PT2671.I6 A8

949

―――. Aus Liebe zu Deutschland: Satiren zu Franz Josef Strauss.
München: Verlag Autoren-Edition, 1980. 224 p.: ill.

DD259.7.S7 A9 1980

Includes quotations of F. J. Strauss.

950

―――. Bruder Eichmann. Reinbek bei Hamburg: Rowohlt, 1983.
160 p. MLCS 84/7662 (P)

951

―――. Die Ganovenfresse. München: Rütten + Loening, 1964.
184 p. PT2671.I6 G3

952

―――. In der Sache J. Robert Oppenheimer: ein szenischer
Bericht. Frankfurt am Main: Suhrkamp, 1966, c1964. 125 p.

PT2671.I6 I5 1966

953

―――. Joel Brand. Die Geschichte eines Geschäfts. Frankfurt am
Main: Suhrkamp, 1965. 141 p. PT2671.I6 J6

954

―――. Leben des schizophrenen Dichters Alexander M.: ein
Film. Berlin: Wagenbach, 1976. 92 p.: ill. PT2671.I6 L4

955

―――. Der Mann des Tages und andere Erzählungen. München:
Bertelsmann, 1977. 221 p. PT2671.I6 M35

956

―――. März. München: Bertelsmann, 1976. 252 p.

PT2671.I6 M3

957

―――. März: ein Künstlerleben: Schauspiel. Köln: Kiepenheuer
& Witsch, 1980. 115 p. PT2671.I6 M33 1980

958

―――. Die Soldaten. Frankfurt am Main: Suhrkamp, 1968. 94 p.

PT2671.I6 S6

959
————. Stücke. Frankfurt am Main: Suhrkamp, 1973–1974. 2 v.
PT2671.I6 S8

960
————. Theaterstücke. Köln: Kiepenheuer & Witsch, 1978. 358 p.
PT2671.I6 A19 1978

961
————. Traumprotokolle. München: Verlag Autoren Edition,
1981. 244 p.   MLCS 82/2413

962
————. Zwei Film-Komödien. Königstein/Ts.: Verlag Autoren
Edition, Athenäum, 1979. 153 p.   MLCS 86/7603 (P)

————————————

963
Ingen, Ferdinand van. Heinar Kipphardt, In der Sache J. Robert
Oppenheimer. Frankfurt am Main, Berlin, München:
Diesterweg, 1978. 69 p. (Grundlagen zum Verständnis des
Dramas)   PT2671.I6 I535
    Bibliography: p. 68–69.

****

964
Krechel, Ursula. Information und Wertung: Untersuchungen zum
theater- und filmkritischen Werk von Herbert Ihering. Köln:
1972. 380 p.   PN1708.I3 K65 1972

965
————. Nach Mainz. Darmstadt: Luchterhand, 1977. 71 p.
PT2671.R383 N3

966
————. Rohschnitt: Gedicht in sechzig Sequenzen. Darmstadt:
Luchterhand, 1983. 102 p.   PT2671.R383 R6 1983

967

————. Selbsterfahrung und Fremdbestimmung: Bericht aus der neuen Frauenbewegung. 3.überarb. Aufl. Darmstadt, Neuwied: Luchterhand, 1978. 166 p.   HQ1154.K73 1978
,,Frauengruppen in der Bundesrepublik . . . und in West-Berlin'': p. 163–166.
Includes bibliographical references.

968

————. Verwundbar wie in den besten Zeiten. Darmstadt, Neuwied: Luchterhand, 1979. 83 p.   PT2671.R383 V4

969

————. Vom Feuer lernen. Darmstadt: Luchterhand, 1985. 89 p.
MLCM 86/43 (P)

970

————. Zweite Natur: Szenen eines Romans. Darmstadt: Luchterhand, 1981. 208 p.   PT2671.R383 Z4 1981

****

971

Kroetz, Franz Xaver. Bauern sterben: Materialien zum Stück. Reinbek bei Hamburg: Rowohlt, 1985. 189 p.: ill. (Programmbücher des Deutschen Schauspielhauses Hamburg)PT2671.R59 B38 1985
,,Premiere am 1. Dezember 1985 im Deutschen Schauspielhaus in Hamburg''— p. 55.

972

————. Chiemgauer Gschichten: Bayrische Menschen erzählen . . . Köln: Kiepenheuer & Witsch, 1977. 292 p.
CT1069.K76

973

————. Farmyard, and four other plays. New York: Urizen, 1976. 132 p.   PT2671.R59 A25

974

————. Frühe Prosa, frühe Stücke. Frankfurt am Main: Suhrkamp, 1983. 181 p.: ill.   MLCS 84/8645 (P)

975

————. Furcht und Hoffnung der BRD: das Stück, das Material, das Tagebuch. Frankfurt am Main: Suhrkamp, 1984. 297 p.
PT2671.R59 F8 1984

976

————. Gesammelte Stücke. Frankfurt am Main: Suhrkamp, 1975. 503 p.   PT2671.R59 1975

977

————. Heimarbeit; Hartnäckig; Männersache: drei Stücke. Frankfurt am Main: Suhrkamp, 1971. 97 p.   PT2671.R59 H4

978

————. Mensch Meier; Der stramme Max; Wer durchs Laub geht . . . : drei neue Stücke. Frankfurt am Main: Suhrkamp, 1979. 201 p.   PT2671.R59 M4

979

————. Der Mondscheinknecht; Fortsetzung. Frankfurt am Main: Suhrkamp, 1983. 170 p.   MLCS 84/2533 (P)

980

————. Nicaragua Tagebuch. Hamburg: Konkret Literatur Verlag, 1985. 197 p.: ill.   MLCS 86/5828 (P)

981

————. Nicht Fisch, nicht Fleisch; Verfassungsfeinde; Jumbo-Track: drei Stücke. Frankfurt am Main: Suhrkamp, 1981. 144 p.
PT2671.R59 N5 1981

982

————. Oberösterreich: Dolomitenstadt Lienz; Maria Magdalena; Münchner Kindl. Frankfurt am Main: Suhrkamp, 1972. 303 p.
PT2671.R59 O3

983

————. Reise ins Glück; Wunschkonzert; Weitere Aussichten: drei Stücke. Wien, München: Sessler, 1976. 55 p.: port.
PT2671.R59 R39

Bibliography of the author's works: p. 2-4.

984

————. Stallerhof; Geisterbahn; Lieber Fritz; Wunschkonzert: vier Stücke. Frankfurt am Main: Suhrkamp, 1972. 110 p.

PT2671.R59 A6 1972

985

————. Stücke. Berlin: Henschelverlag, 1981. 606 p.

PT2671.R59 A19 1981

986

————. Weitere Aussichten . . . : neue Texte: Texte für Filme: Hörspiele, Stücke: DDR-Report, Aufsätze. Interviews. Berlin: Henschelverlag, 1976. 626 p., 8 leaves of plates: 22 ill.

PT2671.R59 W4 1976b

Bibliography of the author's works: p. 619–621.

987

————. Wildwechsel. Wollerau: Lentz, 1973. 60 p.

PT2671.R59 W5

988

Blevins, Richard W. Franz Xaver Kroetz: the emergence of a political playwright. New York: Lang, 1983. 295 p. (New York University Ottendorfer series; n.F., Bd. 18)

PT2671.R59 Z57 1983

Bibliography: p. 279–295.

989

Carl, Rolf-Peter. Franz Xaver Kroetz. München: Beck, Edition Text + Kritik, 1978. 171 p. (Autorenbücher; 10)

PT2671.R59 Z6

Bibliography: p. 163–166.

990

Hein, Jürgen. Franz Xaver Kroetz: Oberösterreich, Mensch Meier. Frankfurt am Main: Diesterweg, 1986. 127 p.

PT2671.R59 Z72 1986

Bibliography: p. 124–127.

991

Hoffmeister, Donna L. The theater of confinement: language and survival in the milieu plays of Marieluise Fleisser and Franz Xaver Kroetz. Columbia, S.C.: Camden House, 1983. 176 p.: 2 ports. (Studies in German literature, linguistics, and culture; v. 11)   PT668.H58 1983

Revision of the author's thesis (Ph.D.)—Brown University, 1979.

Includes index.

Bibliography: p. 167–173.

992

Panzner, Evalouise. Franz Xaver Kroetz und seine Rezeption: die Intentionen eines Stückeschreibers und seine Aufnahme durch die Kritik. Stuttgart: Klett, 1976. 117 p. (Literaturwissenschaft, Gesellschaftswissenschaft; 23)   PT2671.R59 Z82

Bibliography: p. 69–81.

993

Schregel, Ursula. Neue deutsche Stücke im Spielplan: am Beispiel von Franz Xaver Kroetz. Berlin: Spiess, 1980. 394 p. (Hochschul-Skripten. Literaturwissenschaft; 3)

PT2671.R59 Z87

Bibliography: p. 190–213.

****

994

Krolow, Karl. Alltägliche Gedichte. Frankfurt am Main: Suhrkamp, 1968. 95 p.   PT2621.R695 A7

995

———. Das andere Leben: eine Erzählung. Frankfurt am Main: Suhrkamp, 1979. 178 p.   PT2621.R695 A83

996

———. Ausgewählte Gedichte. Frankfurt am Main: Suhrkamp, 1963, c1962. 96, 3 p.   PT2621.R695 A6 1963

997

———. Bürgerliche Gedichte. Hamburg: Merlin, 1970. 45 p.: ill.
PT2671.R597 B8

998

————. Deutschland deine Niedersachsen. Hamburg: Hoffmann und Campe, 1972. 210 p.: ill.   DD801.N4 K75

999

————. Der Einfachheit halber: Gedichte. Frankfurt am Main: Suhrkamp, 1977. 88 p.   PT2621.R695 E37

1000

————. Flug über Heide, Moor und grüne Berge. Braunschweig: Westermann, 1969. 118 p.: col. plates.

    DD801.N4 K76

1001

————. Foreign bodies. Athens: Ohio University Press, 1969. xiii, 189 p.   PT2621.R695 F7 1969
    Poems.
    English and German.
    Translation of: Fremde Körper.

1002

————. Fremde Körper. Frankfurt am Main: Suhrkamp, 1966. 104 p.   PT2621.R695 F7 1966

1003

————. Ein Gedicht entsteht. Frankfurt am Main: Suhrkamp, 1973. 202 p.   PT2621.R695 G4

1004

————. Gedichte. Frankfurt am Main: Suhrkamp, 1980. 91 p.

    PT2621.R695 A6 1980

1005

————. Herbstsonett mit Hegel. Frankfurt am Main: Suhrkamp, 1981. 65 p.   MLCS 81/1947

1006

————. Im Gehen. Frankfurt am Main: Suhrkamp, 1981. 86 p.

    PT2621.R695 I4 1981

1007

————. Invisible hands: poems. London: Cape Goliard, 1969. 70 p.   PT2621.R695 I5

1008

————. Landschaften für mich. Frankfurt am Main: Suhrkamp,
1966. 107 p.   PT2621.R695 L3

1009

————. Ein Lesebuch. Frankfurt am Main: Suhrkamp, 1975.
284 p.   PT2621.R695 L4

1010

————. Melanie: Geschichte eines Namens. München: Nymphenburger, 1983. 158 p.   PT2621.R695 M4 1983

1011

————. Minuten-Aufzeichnungen. Frankfurt am Main:
Suhrkamp, 1968. 155 p.   PT2621.R695 M5

1012

————. Nichts weiter als Leben: neue Gedichte mit einem Anhang
„Über ein eigenes Gedicht." Frankfurt am Main: Suhrkamp,
1970. 115 p.   PT2621.R695 N5

1013

————. On account of: selected poems. Oberlin, Ohio: Oberlin
College, 1985. 117 p.   PT2621.R695 A24 1985

1014

————. Poems against death: selected poems. Washington:
Charioteer Press, 1969. xi, 41 p.   PT2621.R695 A27

1015

————. Poetisches Tagebuch. Frankfurt am Main: Suhrkamp,
1966. 139 p.   PT2621.R695 P6

1016

————. Das Problem des langen und kurzen Gedichts—heute.
Mainz: Verlag der Akademie der Wissenschaften und der
Literatur; Wiesbaden: Steiner, 1966. 18 p.   PN1031.K72

1017

————. Die Rolle des Autors im experimentellen Gedicht. Mainz:
Akademie der Wissenschaften und der Literatur; Wiesbaden:
Steiner, 1962. 18 p.   PN1974.K7

1018

————. Schattengefecht. Frankfurt am Main: Suhrkamp, 1964. 124 p.   PN1031.K73

1019

————. Schönen Dank und vorüber: Gedichte. Frankfurt am Main: Suhrkamp, 1984. 102 p.   MLCS 84/9242 (P)

1020

————. Spanische Gedichte des XX. Jahrhunderts. Frankfurt am Main: Insel-Verlag, 1962. 66 p.   PQ6187.K7

1021

————. Unsichtbare Hände: Gedichte, 1959–1962. Frankfurt am Main: Suhrkamp, 1962. 70 p.   PT2621.R695 U5

1022

————. Unter uns Lesern. Darmstadt: Roether, 1967. 126 p.   PT2621.R695 A16 1967

1023

————. Unumwunden. Schöndorf: Babel, 1985. 14 leaves: ill.   MLCS 86/7598 (P)

1024

————. Wind und Zeit: Gedichte, 1950–1954. Stuttgart: Deutsche Verlags-Anstalt, 1954. 82 p.   PT2621.R695 W5

1025

————. Zeitvergehen. Frankfurt am Main: Suhrkamp, 1972. 111 p.   PT2621.R695 Z25

1026

————. Zu des Rheins gestreckten Hügeln: Goethereise 1972. Troisdorf: Grote, 1972. 57 p.: ill.   PT2130.R45 K7

1027

————. Zwischen Null und Unendlich: Gedichte. Frankfurt am Main: Suhrkamp, 1982. 72 p.   MLCS 82/6426

1028

Daemmrich, Horst S. Messer und Himmelsleiter: eine Einführung
in das Werk Karl Krolows. Heidelberg: Groos, 1980. 94 p.
                                                    PT2621.R695 Z62
Bibliography: p. 91–94.

1029

Kolter, Gerhard. Die Rezeption westdeutscher Nachkriegslyrik am
Beispiel Karl Krolows: zu Theorie und Praxis literarischer
Kommunikation. Bonn: Bouvier, 1977. 446 p. (Abhandlungen
zur Kunst-, Musik- und Literaturwissenschaft; Bd. 242)
                                            PT2621.R695 Z74 1977
Includes index.
A slightly revised ed., with additions to the bibliography of
the author's thesis, Mannheim.
Bibliography: p. 235–422.

1030

Massoud, Fatma. Epochengeschichtliche Aspekte in der Lyrik Karl
Krolows. Frankfurt am Main: Lang, 1981. 224 p. (Europäische
Hochschulschriften. Reihe I, Deutsche Sprache und Literatur;
Bd. 405)   PT2621.R695 Z77 1981
Originally presented as the author's thesis (doctoral)—
Universität Marburg.
Includes indexes.
Bibliography: p. 186–198.

1031

Paulus, Rolf. Karl-Krolow-Bibliographie. Frankfurt am Main:
Athenäum, 1972. viii, 86 p.   Z8467.82.P3

1032

Paulus, Rolf. Der Lyriker Karl Krolow: Biographie-
Werkentwicklung-Gedichtinterpretation-Bibliographie. Bonn:
Bouvier, 1983. 132 p: ill., ports. (Abhandlungen zur Kunst-,
Musik- und Literaturwissenschaft; Bd. 333)
                                            PT2621.R695 Z853 1983
Includes bibliographical references.

1033

Rummler, Artur. Die Entwicklung der Metaphorik in der Lyrik
Karl Krolows (1942–1962). Die Beziehung zu deutschen,

französischen und spanischen Lyrikern. Bern: Lang, 1972. 286 p. (Europäische Hochschulschriften. Reihe I, Deutsche Literatur und Germanistik; Bd. 66)   PT2621.R695 Z86 1972
  Originally presented as the author's thesis, Mainz.
  Bibliography: p. 271–286.

* * * * * * * * * * * * * * * * * *

1034
Kuhn, Dieter. Auf der Zeitachse: vier Konzepte. Frankfurt am Main: Suhrkamp, 1980. 258 p.   PT2671.U324 A87

1035
————. Ausflüge im Fesselballon. Frankfurt am Main: Suhrkamp, 1977. 138 p.   PT2671.U324 A9 1977

1036
————. Bettines letzte Liebschaften. Frankfurt am Main: Insel, 1986. 115 p.   PT2671.U324 B48 1986

1037
————. Festspiel für Rothäute. Frankfurt am Main: Suhrkamp, 1974. 97 p.   PT2671.U324 F4

1038
————. Galaktisches Rauschen: 6 Hörspiele. Frankfurt am Main: Fischer, 1980. 184 p.: 3 ill.   PT2671.,U324 G3 1980

1039
————. Goldberg-Variationen: Hörspieltexte mit Materialien. Frankfurt am Main: Suhrkamp, 1976. 157 p.
      PT2671.U324 G6

1040
————. Der Herr der fliegenden Fische: ein Märchen. Frankfurt am Main: Insel, 1979. 103 p.: ill.   PZ33.K7789

1041
————. Ich Wolkenstein: eine Biographie. Frankfurt am Main: Insel, 1980. 620 p: 16 ill.   PT1695.W4 K8 1980
  Includes index.
  Bibliography: p. 599–609.

1042

————. Josephine: aus der öffentlichen Biografie der Josephine
Baker. Frankfurt am Main: Suhrkamp, 1976. 159 p.: ill.
                                                    GV1785.B3 K83

1043

————. Die Kammer des schwarzen Lichts. Frankfurt am Main:
Suhrkamp, 1984. 366 p.   MLCS 86/5510 (P)

1044

————. Löwenmusik: Essays. Frankfurt am Main: Suhrkamp,
1979. 137 p.   ML60.K976 L6

1045

————. Ludwigslust: Erzählungen. Frankfurt am Main: Suhrkamp, 1977. 100 p.   PT2671.U324 L8

1046

————. Luftkrieg als Abenteuer: Kampfschrift. München: Hanser,
1975. 129 p.   PT772.K8

1047

————. Mit dem Zauberpferd nach London: Kinderroman.
Darmstadt: Luchterhand, 1973. 157 p.   PZ33.K779

1048

————. Schnee und Schwefel: Gedichte. Frankfurt am Main:
Suhrkamp, 1982. 93 p.   MLCS 84/5945 (P)

1049

————. Stanislaw der Schweiger. Frankfurt am Main: Suhrkamp,
1975. 157 p.   PT2671.U324 S8

1050

————. Und der Sultan von Oman: Erzählung. Frankfurt am
Main: Suhrkamp, 1979. 234 p.   MLCS 84/10624 (P)

****

1051

Lenz, Siegfried. Der Anfang von etwas. 2., erw. Aufl. Leipzig:
Reclam, 1986. 236 p.   MLCS 87/3115 (P)

1052
———. Die Augenbinde: Schauspiel. Reinbek bei Hamburg:
Rowohlt, 1969. 149 p.   PT2623.E583 A9

1053
———. Beziehungen: Ansichten und Bekenntnisse zur Literatur.
Hamburg: Hoffmann und Campe, 1970. 296 p.
                                        PT2623.E583 B4

1054
———. Brot und Spiele. Hamburg: Hoffmann und Campe, 1959.
280 p.   PT2623.E583 B7

1055
———. Deutschstunde. Hamburg: Hoffmann und Campe, 1968.
559 p.   PT2623.E583 D4

1056
———. Drei Stücke. Hamburg: Hoffmann und Campe, 1980.
296 p.   PT2623.E583 A6 1980

1057
———. Elfenbeinturm und Barrikade: Erfahrungen am
Schreibtisch. Hamburg: Hoffmann und Campe, 1983. 252, 1 p.
                                        PT2623.E583 Z74 1983
„Dieser Band enthält Aufsätze, Reden und Kritiken aus den
letzten zehn Jahren.''

1058
———. Es waren Habichte in der Luft. München: Deutscher
Taschenbuch-Verlag, 1969. 166 p.   PT2623.E583 E8 1969

1059
———. An exemplary life. New York: Hill and Wang, 1976.
423 p.   PZ4.L575 Ex 3
Translation of: Das Vorbild.

1060
———. Exerzierplatz. Hamburg: Hoffmann und Campe, 1985.
459 p.   MLCS 86/1441 (P)

1061

————. Das Feuerschiff. Hamburg: Hoffmann und Campe, 1971,
c1960. 160 p.   PT2623.E583 F4 1971

1062

————. Flug über Land und Meer. Nordsee—Schleswig-
Holstein—Ostsee. Braunschweig: Westermann, 1967. 117 p.:
ill.   DD724.L46

1063

————. Die frühen Romane. Hamburg: Hoffmann und Campe,
1976. 776 p.   PT2623.E583 F7

1064

————. Der Geist der Mirabelle: Geschichten aus Bollerup.
Hamburg: Hoffmann und Campe, 1975. 125 p.
                                                      PT2623.E583 G38

1065

————. The German lesson. New York, N.Y.: New Directions,
1986. 470 p.   PT2623.E583 D413 1986
Translation of: Deutschstunde.

1066

————. Gesammelte Erzählungen. Hamburg: Hoffmann und
Campe, 1970. 632 p.   PT2623.E583 A6 1970

1067

————. Das Gesicht. Hamburg: Hoffmann und Campe, 1970,
c1964. 91 p.   PT2623.E583 G4 1970

1068

————. Heimatmuseum. Hamburg: Hoffman und Campe, 1978.
654 p.   PT2623.E583 H4

1069

————. The heritage. New York: Hill and Wang, 1981. 458 p.
                                                      PT2623.E583 H413 1981
Translation of: Heimatmuseum.

1070

―――. Jäger des Spotts, und andere Erzählungen. New York: Norton, 1965. x, 83 p. PT2623.E583 J3

1071

―――. Ein Kriegsende. Hamburg: Hoffmann und Campe, 1984. 62 p. D810.S45 B355 1984

1072

―――. Lehmanns Erzählungen. Hamburg: Hoffmann und Campe, 1966, c1964. 125 p.: ill. PT2623.E583 L4 1966

1073

―――. Leute von Hamburg. Hamburg: Hoffmann und Campe, 1969, c1968. 71 p. DD901.H28 L38

1074

―――. The lightship. New York: Hill and Wang, 1962. 125 p. PZ4.L575 Li

1075

―――. Der Mann im Strom. Hamburg: Hoffmann und Campe, 1969. 221 p. PT2623.E583 M3 1969

1076

―――. Das schönste Fest der Welt. Haussuchung. Stuttgart: Reclam, 1968. 86 p. PT2623.E583 S3

1077

―――. So war das mit dem Zirkus: fünf Geschichten aus Suleyken. Hamburg: Hoffmann und Campe, 1971. 47 p.: col. ill. PZ33.L45

1078

―――. So zärtlich war Suleyken: masurische Geschichten. Frankfurt am Main: Fischer, 1971. 117 p. PT2623.E583 S6 1971

1079

―――. Der Spielverderber. München: Deutscher Taschenbuch-Verlag, 1969. 161 p. PT2623.E583 S63 1969

1080

————. Stadtgespräch. München: Deutscher Taschenbuch-Verlag,
1976, c1963. 201 p.   PT2623.E583 S85 1976

1081

————. Stimmungen der See. Stuttgart: Reclam, 1962. 78 p.
                                                       PT2623.E583 S87

1082

————. Der Verlust. Hamburg: Hoffmann und Campe, 1981.
223 p.   PT2623.E583 V4

1083

————. Das Vorbild. Hamburg: Hoffmann und Campe, 1973.
526 p.   PT2623.E583 V6

1084

————. Das Wrack, and other stories. London: Heinemann, 1967.
5, 156 p.: front. port.   PT2672.E54 W7
   Bibliography: p. 152.

1085

————. Die Wracks von Hamburg. Oldenburg, Hamburg:
Stalling, 1978. 144 p.: numerous ill.   PT2623.E583 W7

1086

————. Zeit der Schuldlosen. Zeit der Schuldigen. Zwei Hörspiele.
New York: Appleton-Century-Crofts, 1967. 152 p.: ill., port.
                                                 PT2623.E583 Z4 1967

1087

Bassmann, Winfried. Siegfried Lenz: sein Werk als Beispiel für
   Weg und Standort der Literatur in der Bundesrepublik
   Deutschland. Bonn: Bouvier, 1976. 221 p. (Abhandlungen zur
   Kunst-, Musik- und Literaturwissenschaft; Bd. 222)
                                                 PT2623.E583 Z55
      Bibliography: p. 215–221.

1088

Elm, Theo. Siegfried Lenz, Deutschstunde: Engagement und Realismus im Gegenwartsroman. München: Fink, 1974. 143 p.

PT2623.E583 D435

1089

Meyerhoff, Hagen. Die Figur des Alten im Werk von Siegfried Lenz. Frankfurt am Main: Lang, 1979. 286 p. (Europäische Hochschulschriften. Reihe I, Deutsche Literatur und Germanistik; Bd. 327)   PT2623.E583 Z78 1979

Originally presented as the author's thesis (doctoral)— Gesamthochschule Wuppertal.

Bibliography: p. 259–286.

1090

Reber, Trudis E. Siegfried Lenz. 2., erg. Aufl. Berlin: Colloquium, 1976. 96 p. (Köpfe des XX. Jahrhunderts; Bd. 74)

PT2623.E583 Z83 1976

Bibliography: p. 91.

1091

Siegfried Lenz. München: Edition Text + Kritik, 1976. 54 p. (Text + Kritik; 52)   PN4.T45 v. 52

„Kommentierte Auswahlbibliographie zu Siegfried Lenz, Hartmut Patzold": p. 44–53.

Includes bibliographical references.

1092

Siegfried Lenz: Werk und Wirkung/ herausgegeben von Rudolf Wolff. Bonn: Bouvier, 1985. 155 p.: ill. (Sammlung Profile; Bd. 15)   PT2623.E583 Z93 1985

Bibliography: p. 138–155.

1093

Wagener, Hans. Siegfried Lenz. München: Beck, Edition Text + Kritik, 1985, c1976. 166 p.   PT2623.E583 Z95 1985

Bibliography: p. 164–166.

****

1094

Meckel, Christoph. Amüsierpapiere oder Bilder aus Phantasus' Bauchladen. München: Ellermann, 1969. 40 p.

NC251.M4 A42

1095

———. Anabasis. München: Hanser, 1982. 114 leaves of plates: chiefly ill.   NE2050.5.M39 1982

„Anabasis ist der dritte und umfangreichste Zyklus einer gezeichneten Weltkomödie, die vor 25 Jahren begonnen wurde und mehrere hundert Blätter umfasst."

1096

———. Ausgewählte Gedichte, 1955-1978. Königstein/Ts.: Athenäum, 1979. vii, 104 p.   PT2673.E28 A17 1979

1097

———. Die Balladen des Thomas Balkan. Berlin: Stollenwerk, 1969. 89 p.   PT2673.E28 B3

1098

———. Bei Lebzeiten zu singen. Berlin: Wagenbach, 1967. 79 p.

PT2673.E28 B4

1099

———. Bericht zur Entstehung einer Weltkomödie. München: Hanser, 1985. 126 p.: ill.   PT2673.E28 B44 1985

1100

———. Bockshorn. München: Nymphenburger Verlagshandlung, 1973. 263 p.   PT2673.E28 B6

1101

———. Christoph Meckel: Zeichnungen, Radierungen: Hans Thoma-Gesellschaft, Reutlingen, Spendhaus, 8. April—20. Mai 1984. Reutlingen: Die Gesellschaft, 1984. 87 p.: ill. (some col.).

NC251.M4 A4 1984

Bibliography: p. 80-81.

1102

———. The figure on the boundary line: selected prose. Manchester: Carcanet Press, 1983. 178 p.: ill.   PT2673.E28 A6 1983

1103

————. Flaschenpost für eine Sintflut: Lyrik, Prosa, Graphik. Berlin, Weimar: Aufbau-Verlag, 1975. 367 p., 10 leaves of plates: ill.   PT2673.E28 F6

1104

————. Die Geschichte der Geschichten. München: Ellermann, 1971. 24 p.: col. ill.   PZ33.M382

1105

————. Die Gestalt am Ende des Grundstücks: mit 8 Miniaturen des Autors. Düsseldorf: Eremiten-Presse, 1975. 93 p.: 8 ill.
                    PT2673.E28 G4

1106

————. Hotel für Schlafwandler. Stierstadt im Taunus: Eremiten-Presse, 1971. 91 l. with col. ill.   PT2673.E28 H6

1107

————. Im Land der Umbramauten. Köln: Literarischer Verlag Braun, 1977. 168 p.   MLCS 86/3715 (P)

1108

————. In der Tinte. Mit 10 mehrfarbigen Zeichnungen und einem Titelholzschnitt. Berlin: Neue Rabenpresse, 1968. 14 p. (on double leaves).   NC1145.M397 A46

1109

————. Jahreszeiten. Berlin: Verlag für Zeitgenössische Kunst, 1984. 116 p.: ill. (all col.).   NC251.M4 A4 1984a

1110

————. Jasnandos Nachtlied: Gedichte und 5 Linolschnitte. Freiburg im Breisgau: Syrinx Presse, 1969. 1 v. (unpaged) col. plates.   PT2673.E28 J3

1111

————. Kranich. Düsseldorf: Eremiten-Presse, 1973. 75 p. (on double leaves): ill.   PT2673.E28 K68

1112

————. Kraut und Gehilfe. Berlin: Friedenauer Presse, 1970.
12 p.: ill.   PT2673.E28 K7

1113

————. Licht. München: Nymphenburger Verlagshandlung,
1978. 159 p.   PT2673.E28 L48

1114

——Lieder aus dem Dreckloch. Stierstadt im Taunus: Eremiten-
Presse, 1972. 44 p. (on double leaves): ill.   PT2673.E28 L5

1115

————. Lyrik. München: Unverhau, 1965. 81 p. (p. 33–61 ill.):
front.   NE654.M46 U59

1116

————. Manifest der Toten. Stierstadt im Taunus: Eremiten-
Presse, 1971. 57 p. (on double leaves): ill.   PT2673.E28 M3

1117

————. Das Meer. München: Ellermann, 1965. 61 l. of ill.
           NE654.M46 A44 (fol.)

1118

————. Moel. Hamburg: Ellermann, 1959. 1 v. of ill. (unpaged).
           NE654.M46 A45

1119

————. Nachricht für Baratynski. München, Wien: Hanser, 1981.
157 p.: 1 ill.   MLCS 81/1864

1120

————. Nachtessen. Berlin: Literarisches Colloquium, 1975. 35 p.:
ill.   PT2673.E28 N3

1121

————. Nebelhörner. Leverkusen: Braun, 1977. 71 p.
           PT2673.E28 N4

1122

———. Die Noticen des Feuerwerkers Christopher Magalan. Berlin: Wagenbach, 1966. 68 p.: ill.   NE654.M3 M4

1123

———. Plunder. München: Hanser, 1986. 131 p.
PT2673.E28 P58 1986

1124

———. Ein roter Faden: gesammelte Erzählungen. München: Hanser, 1983. 385 p.: ill.   MLCS 84/2026 (P)

1125

———. Säure: mit einer Grafik des Autors. Düsseldorf: Claassen, 1979. 61 p.: ill.   MLCS 84/12179 (P)

1126

———. Eine Seite aus dem Paradiesbuch: ein Hörspiel. Berlin: Wagenbach, 1969. 64 p.: ill.   PT2673.E28 S4

1127

———. Souterrain. München: Hanser, 1984. 79 p.: ill.
MLCM 86/3089 (P)

1128

———. Die Stadt. Hamburg: Ellermann, 1960. 1 v. (chiefly ill.).
NE654.M46 A55

1129

———. Suchbild: über meinen Vater; mit einer Grafik des Autors. Düsseldorf: Claassen, 1980. 190 p.: 1 ill.
PT2625.E18 S9

1130

———. Tunifers Erinnerungen und andere Erzählungen. Frankfurt am Main: Fischer, 1980. 124 p.: ill.
PT2673.E28 T9 1980

1131

———. Der Turm. Hamburg: Ellermann, 1961. 1 v. (chiefly ill.).
NE654.M46 A56

1132

————. Verschiedene Tätigkeiten. Stuttgart: Reclam, 1972. 84 p.:
ill.   PT2673.E28 A6 1972

1133

————. Wen es angeht. Mit Graphiken des Autors. Düsseldorf:
Eremiten-Presse, 1974. 52 p. (on double leaves): ill.
                                                        PT2673.E28 W4

1134

————. Werkauswahl. München: Nymphenburger Verlagshandlung, 1971. 259 p.: ill.   PT2673.E28 A6 1971

1135

————. You're welcome. Berlin: Atelier F. Siebrasse, 1969. 1
portfolio (2 l., 8 plates, part col.).
                                          NE2415.M4 A58 (Rare Bk Coll)

1136

Aue, Walter. Worte, die Worte, die Bilder: Texte hinter der
Wirklichkeit. Graphiken von Christoph Meckel. Köln: Hake,
1963. 43 p. (on double leaves): ill.   PT2661.U3 W6

****

1137

Novak, Helga M. Aufenthalt in einem irren Haus. Neuwied:
Luchterhand, 1971. 212 p.   PT2674.O88 A95 1971

1138

————. Ballade von der reisenden Anna. Neuwied, Berlin: Luchterhand, 1965. 82 p.   PT2674.O88 B3

1139

————. Balladen vom kurzen Prozess. Berlin: Rotbuch-Verlag,
1975. 71 p.   PT2674.O88 B33

1140

————. Colloquium mit vier Häuten. Neuwied, Berlin: Luchterhand, 1967. 77 p.   PT2674.O88 C6

1141
———. Eines Tages hat sich die Sprechpuppe nicht mehr ausziehen lassen. München, Gütersloh, Wien: Bertelsmann, 1972. 323 p.   HQ1627.N68

1142
———. Die Eisheiligen. Darmstadt: Luchterhand, 1979. 362 p.
                                            MLCS 84/13649 (P)

1143
———. Geselliges Beisammensein. Darmstadt: Luchterhand, 1968. 135 p.   PT2674.O88 G4

1144
———. Grünheide, Grünheide: Gedichte, 1955–1980. Darmstadt: Luchterhand, 1983. 128 p.   MLCS 84/8650 (P)

1145
———. Die Landnahme von Torre Bela. Berlin: Rotbuch-Verlag, 1976. 71 p.   PT2674.O88 L3

1146
———. Margarete mit dem Schrank. Berlin: Rotbuch-Verlag, 1978. 77 p.   PT 2674.O88 M3

1147
———. Palisaden: Erzählungen 1967–1975. Darmstadt, Neuwied: Luchterhand, 1980. 172 p.   PT2674.O88 P34

1148
———. Seltsamer Bericht aus einer alter Stadt. Hannover: Fackelträger-Verlag, 1973. 28 p.: ill. (part col.).   PZ33.N767

1149
———. Vogel federlos. Darmstadt: Luchterhand, 1982. 289 p.
                                            PT2674.O88 V6 1982

1150
———. Wohnhaft im Westend: Dokumente, Berichte, Konversation. Neuwied, Berlin: Luchterhand, 1970. 85 p.
                                            PT2674.O88 W6

****

1151
Reinig, Christa. Das Aquarium. Stuttgart: Reclam, 1969. 46 p.
PT2678.E347. A8

1152
———. Drei Schiffe. Frankfurt am Main: Fischer, 1965. 144 p.
PT2678.E347 D7

1153
———. Entmannung: die Geschichte Ottos und seiner vier
Frauen. Düsseldorf: Eremiten-Presse, 1976. 257 p.: ill.
PT2678.E347 E5

1154
———. Die ewige Schule. München: Frauenoffensive, 1982.
114 p.   MLCS 84/7656 (P)

1155
———. Gedichte. Frankfurt am Main: Fischer, 1963. 52 p.
PT2678.E347 G4

1156
———. Das grosse Bechterew-Tantra. Exzentrische Anatomie.
Stierstadt im Taunus: Eremiten-Presse, 1970. 90 p. (on double
leaves): ill. (part col.).   PT2678.E347 G7

1157
———. Hantipanti: zwölf Kindergeschichten zum Nachdenken
und ein Nachwort. Weinheim: Beltz & Gelberg, 1972. 63 p.:
col. ill., insert. (in pocket).   PZ33.R425

1158
———. Die himmlische und die irdische Geometrie. Düsseldorf:
Eremiten-Presse, 1975. 219 p.: ill.   PT2678.E347 H5

1159
———. Der Hund mit dem Schlüssel. Düsseldorf: Eremiten-
Presse, 1976. 22 p. (on double leaves): ill.   PT2678.E347 H8

1160
———. Mädchen ohne Uniform. Düsseldorf: Eremiten-Presse,
1981. 46 p.: ill.   MLCS 81/2330

1161

————. Mein Herz ist eine gelbe Blume. Düsseldorf: Eremiten-Presse, 1978. 36 p.   PT2678.E347 Z47

1162

————. Müssiggang ist aller Liebe Anfang. Düsseldorf: Eremiten-Presse, 1979. 126 p. (on double fold): ill.
          PT2678.E347 M8

1163

————. Papantscha-Vielerlei. Exotische Produkte Altindiens. Eine Anthologie. Stierstadt im Taunus: Eremiten-Presse, 1971. 57 p. (on double leaves): ill.   PT2678.E374 P3

1164

————. Orion trat aus dem Haus. Stierstadt im Taunus: Eremiten-Presse, 1968. 118 p. (on double leaves).   PT2678.E347 O7

1165

————. Die Prüfung des Lächlers: Gesammelte Gedichte. München: Deutscher Taschenbuch-Verlag, 1980, c1974. 125 p.
          MLCS 86/5258 (P)

1166

————. Schwabinger Marterln: nebst zwei preussischen Marterln. Stierstadt im Taunus: Eremiten-Presse, 1968. 30 p. (on double leaves).   PT2678.E347 S3

1167

————. Schwalbe von Olevano: neue Gedichte. Stierstadt im Taunus: Eremiten-Presse, 1969. 42 p. (on double leaves): ill.
          PT2678.E347 S33

1168

————. Die Steine von Finisterre. Düsseldorf: Eremiten-Presse, 1974. 75 p.: ill. (col.).   PT2678.E347 S8

1169

————. Der Traum meiner Verkommenheit. Berlin: Fietkau, 1968, c1961. 30 p.   PT2678.E347 T7 1968

1170

————. Der Wolf und die Witwen: Erzählungen und Essays.
Düsseldorf: Eremiten-Presse, 1980. 77 p.

MLCS '87.2239 (P)

————————

1171

Gratuliere: Wort- und Bildgeschenke zum 50. Geburtstag von
Christa Reinig am 6. August 1976: 50 Jahre Christa Reinig/
gesammelt von Dieter Hülsmanns und Friedolin Reske.
Düsseldorf: Eremiten-Presse, 1976. 92 p.: ill.

PT1231.R4 G7

Bibliography: p. 89–91.

****

1172

Rinser, Luise. Baustelle: eine Art Tagebuch, 1967–70. Frankfurt
am Main: Fischer, 1970. 390 p.: facsim.   PT2635.I68 Z5

1173

————. Bruder Feuer. Stuttgart: Thienemann, 1976, c1975.
143 p.   PT2635.I68 B7 1976

1174

————. Ein Bündel weisser Narzissen. Frankfurt am Main:
Fischer, 1967, c1956. 263 p.   PT2635.I68 B8 1967

1175

————. Dem Tode geweiht?: Lepra ist heilbar. Percha am Starnberger See; Kempfenhausen am Starnberger See: Schulz, 1974.
230 p., 24 leaves of plates: 24 ill. (some col.).   RC154.R5

1176

————. Den Wolf umarmen. Frankfurt am Main: Fischer, 1981.
413 p.   MLCS 87/1419 (P)

1177

————. Gefängnis Tagebuch. Frankfurt am Main: Fischer, 1963,
c1946. 185 p.   PT2635.I68 G4 1963

1178

———. Geschichten aus der Löwengrube: acht Erzählungen. Frankfurt am Main: Fischer, 1986. 162 p.

MLCS 86/5852 (P)

1179

———. Gespräch von Mensch zu Mensch. Würzburg: Echter-Verlag, 1974, c1967. 135 p. PT2678.I55 G4 1974

1180

———. Gespräche über Lebensfragen. Würzburg: Echter-Verlag, 1966. 131 p. PT2635.I68 G45 1966

1181

———. Grenzübergänge: Tagebuch-Notizen. Frankfurt am Main: Fischer, 1972. 348 p. PT2635.I68 G7

1182

———. Hat beten einen Sinn? Zürich: Verlag der Arche, 1966. 61 p. BV213.R53

1183

———. Hochebene. Frankfurt am Main: Fischer, 1976. 169 p. PT2635.I68 H6 1976

1184

———. Hochzeit der Widersprüche. Kempfenhausen am Starnberger See: Schulz, 1973. 262 p. BJ1548.R56

1185

———. Ich bin Tobias. Frankfurt am Main: Fischer, 1966. 314 p. PT2635.I68 I3

1186

———. Im Dunkeln singen, 1982 bis 1985. Frankfurt am Main: Fischer, 1985. 249 p. PT2635.I68 I5 1985

1187

———. Jan Lobel aus Warschau: Erzählungen. Mit einem autobiographischen Nachwort. Stuttgart: Reclam, 1966. 76 p. PT2635.I68 J3

1188

————. Jugend unserer Zeit. Würzburg: Echter-Verlag, 1967.
153 p.: ill.   HQ796.R546

1189

————. Khomeini und der islamische Gottesstaat: eine grosse Idee,
ein grosser Irrtum? Percha am Starnberger See: Schulz, 1979.
228 p., 4 leaves of plates: ill.   DS318.R56
Bibliography: p. 225–228.

1190

————. Kriegsspielzeug: Tagebuch 1972–1978. Frankfurt am
Main: Fischer, 1978. 267 p.   PT2635.I68 Z78

1191

————. Laie, nicht ferngesteuert. Zürich: Verlag der Arche, 1967.
61 p.   BX1920.R5

1192

————. Leiden, sterben, auferstehen. Würzburg: Echter Verlag,
1975. 77 p.   BT732.7.R55 1975

1193

————. Mein Lesebuch. Frankfurt am Main: Fischer, 1980. 190 p.
                                                    PT2635.I68 Z79
Includes bibliographical references.

1194

————. Mirjam. Frankfurt am Main: Fischer, 1983. 331 p.
                                                    MLCS 84/2082 (P)

1195

————. Mit wem reden. Stuttgart: Thienemann, 1980. 129 p.
                                                    MLCS 87/1716 (B)

1196

————. Mitte des Lebens. Frankfurt am Main: Fischer, 1952,
c1950. 350 p.   PT2635.I68 M5

1197

————. Nach seinem Bild. Zürich: NZN Buchverlag; Würzburg:
Echter, 1969. 36 p., 115 p.: ill.   TR654.R5

1198

————. Nina: Mitte des Lebens. Abenteuer der Tugend. Berlin, Frankfurt am Main: Fischer, 1968. 472 p.   PT2635.I68 N5

1199

————. Pestalozzi und wir: der Mensch und das Werk. Stuttgart: Günther, 1947. 39 p.   LB629.R5

1200

————. Rings of glass. Chicago: Regnery, 1958. 176 p.

PZ3.R477 Ri

1201

————. Der schwarze Esel. Frankfurt am Main: Fischer, 1974. 270 p.   PT2635.I68 S3

1202

————. Der Schwerpunkt. Frankfurt am Main: Fischer, 1960. 212 p.   PT403.R5

1203

————. Septembertag. Frankfurt am Main: Fischer, 1965, c1964. 142 p.   PT2635.I68 S4

1204

————. Silberschuld. Frankfurt am Main: Fischer, 1987. 232 p.

MLCS 87/3613 (P)

1205

————. Das Squirrel. Stuttgart: Thienemann, 1985. 125 p.: ill.

MLCS 86/1225 (P)

1206

————. Der Sündenbock. Frankfurt am Main: Fischer, 1955. 201 p.   PT2635.I68 S8

1207

————. Unterentwickeltes Land Frau. Würzburg: Echter; Zürich: NZN Buchverlag, 1970. 100 p.   HQ1122.R53

1208
———. Die vollkommene Freude. Frankfurt am Main: Fischer,
1963, c1962. 329 p.   PT2635.I68 V6

1209
———. Von der Unmöglichkeit und der Möglichkeit heute Priester
zu sein. Würzburg: Echter, 1968. 58 p.   BX1912.R6

1210
———. Weihnachts-Triptychon. Zürich: Verlag der Arche, 1963.
46 p.: ill. (part col.).   PT2635.I68 W4

1211
———. Wenn die Wale kämpfen: Porträt eines Landes, Süd-
Korea. Percha: Schulz, 1976. 231 p., 4 leaves of plates: ill.
                                                    DS902.R47
    Bibliography: p. 225.

1212
———. Wer wirft den Stein?: Zigeuner sein in Deutschland: eine
Anklage. Stuttgart: Weitbrecht, 1985. 160 p.   DX229.R56 1985

1213
———. Wie, wenn wir ärmer würden: oder, die Heimkehr des
verlorenen Sohnes. Percha am Starnberger See: Schultz, 1974.
125 p.   PT2635.I68 W5

1214
———. Winterfrühling, 1979–1982. Frankfurt am Main: Fischer,
1982. 236 p.   MLCS 84/2801 (P)

1215
———. Zölibat und Frau. Würzburg: Echter, 1968. 45 p.
                                                  BV4390.R5 1968

———————————

1216
Materialien zu Leben und Werk/ herausgegeben von Hans-Rüdiger
Schwab. Frankfurt am Main: Fischer, 1986. 308 p.
                                              PT2635.I68 Z47 1986
    Biography of Luise Rinser.
    Bibliography: p. 284–308.

1217

Scholz, Albert August. Luise Rinsers Leben und Werk: eine Einführung. Syracuse, N.Y.: Peerless Press, 1968. viii, 123 p.: port.   PT2635.I68 Z8

****

1218

Rühmkorf, Peter. Agar Agar, Zaurzaurim: zur Naturgeschichte des Reims und der menschlichen Anklangsnerven. Reinbek bei Hamburg: Rowohlt, 1981. 156 p.: ill.   PN1059.R5 R83 1981

1219

―――. Bleib erschütterbar und widersteh: Aufsätze, Reden, Selbstgespräche. Reinbek bei Hamburg: Rowohlt, 1984. 260 p.: ill.   PT2678.U363 B6 1984
    Bibliography: p. 259–260.

1220

―――. Dintemann und Schindemann: Aufgeklärte Märchen. Leipzig: Reclam, 1985, c1983. 197 p.   MLCS 86/3172 (P)

1221

―――. Es muss doch noch einen zweiten Weg ums Gehirn rum geben. Köln: Internationale Literaturfabrik im Bund-Verlag, 1981. 129 p.   MLCS 87/2140 (P)

1222

―――. Gemischtes Doppel. Köln: Hake, 1967. 20 l.: ill.
    PT2678.U363 G4

1223

―――. Gesammelte Gedichte. Reinbek bei Hamburg: Rowohlt, 1976. 134 p.   PT2678.U363 A17 1976

1224

―――. Haltbar bis Ende 1999. Reinbek bei Hamburg: Rowohlt, 1979. 119 p.   PT2678.U363 H28

1225

―――. Die Handwerker kommen: ein Familiendrama. Berlin: Wagenbach, 1974. 66 p.: ill.   PT2678.U363 H3

1226

————. Hunderteinunddreissig expressionistische Gedichte.
Berlin: Wagenbach, 1976. 158 p.: ill.   PT1174.H8

1227

————. Der Hüter des Misthaufens: aufgeklärte Märchen.
Reinbek bei Hamburg: Rowohlt, 1983. 279 p.
                                            MLCS 84/2391 (P)

1228

————. Die Jahre, die ihr kennt: Anfälle und Erinnerungen.
Reinbek bei Hamburg: Rowohlt, 1972. 251 p.
                                            PT2678.U363 J3

1229

————. Kleine Fleckenkunde. Zürich: Haffmans, 1982. 111 p.:
ill.   MLCS 84/7242 (P)

1230

————. Lombard gibt den Letzten: ein Schauspiel. Berlin:
Wagenbach, 1972. 81 p.: front.   PT2678.U363 L6

1231

————. Phönix voran. Dreieich: Pawel-Pan-Presse, 1977. 14 p.
(on double leaves): numerous ill.   PT2678.U363 P4
    This copy is no. 159, signed by the artist.

1232

————. Strömungslehre. Reinbek bei Hamburg: Rowohlt, 1978.
299 p.   PT403.R8

1233

————. Über das Volksvermögen. Exkurse in den literarischen
Untergrund. Reinbek bei Hamburg: Rowohlt, 1967. 288 p.
                                            PF5981.R8

1234

————. Walther von der Vogelweide; Klopstock und ich. Reinbek
bei Hamburg: Rowohlt, 1976. 189 p.   PT1673.R8
    Includes poems by W. v. d. Vogelweide and F. G. Klopstock.
    Includes bibliographies.

1235

Bekes, Peter. Peter Rühmkorf. München: Beck, Edition Text +
Kritik, 1982. 174 p. (Autorenbücher; 32)

PT2678.U363 Z57 1982

Bibliography: p. 168–171.

1236

Brunner, Sabine. Rühmkorfs Engagement für die Kunst. Essen:
Verlag die Blaue Eule, 1985. 222 p.   PT2678.U363 Z64 1985

Bibliography: p. 219–222.

1237

Ihekweazu, Edith. Peter Rühmkorf: Bibliografie, Essay zur Poetik.
Frankfurt am Main, New York: Lang, 1984. 172 p., 1 leaf of
plates: port. (Europäische Hochschulschriften. Reihe I, Deutsche
Sprache und Literatur; Bd. 746)   Z8763.89.I38 1984

Bibliography: p. 159–172.

1238

Uerlings, Herbert. Die Gedichte Peter Rühmkorfs: Subjektivität
und Wirklichkeitserfahrung in der Lyrik. Bonn: Bouvier, 1984.
445 p. (Literatur und Wirklichkeit; Bd. 24)

PT2678.U363 Z88 1984

Bibliography: p. 414–445.

1239

Verweyen, Theodor. Eine Theorie der Parodie: am Beispiel Peter
Rühmkorfs. München: Fink, 1973. 137 p.   PT2678.U363 Z9

****

1240

Schmidt, Arno. Abend mit Goldrand: eine Märchenposse. Frankfurt am Main: Fischer, 1975. 215 p.: ill.   PT2638.M453 A77

1241

————. Alexander: oder, Was ist Wahrheit: 3 Erzählungen. Frankfurt am Main: Fischer, 1975. 136 p.   PT2638.M453 A79

1242

————. Aus dem Leben eines Fauns. Frankfurt am Main: Fischer,
1973. 165 p.   PT2638.M453 A9 1973

1243

————. Aus julianischen Tagen. Frankfurt am Main: Fischer, 1979. 256 p.: ill.   PT2638.M453 A93

1244

————. Belphegor: Nachrichten von Büchern und Menschen. Karlsruhe: Stahlberg, 1961. 453 p.   PT2638.M453 B46 1961

1245

————. Brand's Haide. Frankfurt am Main: Fischer, 1974. 151 p.
                                                    PT2638.M453 B7
Sequel to: Aus dem Leben eines Fauns.

1246

————. Deutsches Elend: 13 Erklärungen zur Lage der Nationen. Zürich: Arno Schmidt Stiftung im Haffmans Verlag, 1984. 119 p.   DD61.3.S275 1984

1247

————. The Egghead republic: a short novel from the Horse latitudes. London, Boston: Boyars, 1979. 8, 164 p.
                                          PT2638.M453 G413 1979
Translation of: Die Gelehrtenrepublik.
Includes bibliographical references.

1248

————. Evening edged in gold. New York: Harcourt Brace Jovanovich, 1980. 215 p.: ill.   PT2638.M453 A7713
Translation of: Abend mit Goldrand.

1249

————. Fouqué und einige seiner Zeitgenossen. Karlsruhe: Stahlberg, 1958. 587 p.: port.   PT2389.Z5 S28

1250

————. Die Gelehrtenrepublik. Frankfurt am Main, Hamburg: Fischer, 1971. 150 p.: map.   PT2638.M453 G4 1971

1251

————. Julia, oder, Die Gemälde. Zürich: Arno Schmidt Stiftung im Haffmans Verlag, 1983. 100 p.: ill.   PT2638.M453 J8 1983

1252

————. Kaff auch Mare Crisium. Karlsruhe: Stahlberg, 1960.
346 p.   PT2638.M453 K3

1253

————. Krakatau. Stuttgart: Reclam, 1975. 67 p.
                          PT2638.M453 K7

1254

————. Kühe in Halbtrauer. Karlsruhe: Stahlberg, 1964. 347 p.
                          PT2638.M453 K8

1255

————. Leviathan und Schwarze Spiegel. Frankfurt am Main:
Fischer, 1974. 141 p.   PT2638.M453 L44 1974

1256

————. Nachrichten aus dem Leben eines Lords: sechs Nachtpro-
gramme. Frankfurt am Main: Fischer, 1975. 319 p.
                          PT2638.M453 N33 1975

1257

————. Nachrichten von Büchern und Menschen. Frankfurt am
Main, Hamburg: Fischer, 1971. 2 v.   PT287.S4

1258

————. Die Ritter vom Geist. Karlsruhe: Stahlberg, 1965. 316 p.
                          PT2638.M453 R5

1259

————. Die Schule der Atheisten: Novellen-Comödie in 6 Aufzügen.
Frankfurt am Main: Fischer, 1972. 271 p.   PT2638.M453 S3

1260

————. Seelandschaft mit Pocahontas. Frankfurt am Main,
Hamburg: Fischer, 1966. 150 p.   PT2638.M453 S4

1261

————. Sommermeteor: 23 Kurzgeschichten. Frankfurt am Main,
Hamburg: Fischer, 1969. 126 p.   PT2638.M453 T712 1969

1262

———. Das steinerne Herz: historischer Roman aus dem Jahre
1954. Karlsruhe: Stahlberg, 1964, c1956. 286 p.
                                        PT2638.M453 S8 1964

1263

———. Tina oder über die Unsterblichkeit. Frankfurt am Main,
Hamburg: Fischer, 1966. 175 p.   PT2638.M453 T5

1264

———. Der Triton mit dem Sonnenschirm. Karlsruhe: Stahlberg,
1969. 426 p.   PR96.S35

1265

———. Die Umsiedler. Frankfurt am Main: Frankfurter Verlags-
anstalt, 1953. 71 p.   PT2638.M453 U6

1266

———. Zettels Traum: 1963-69; Studienausgabe in 8 Heften.
Frankfurt am Main: Fischer, 1973. 8 v. 1330 p.: ill.
                                        PT2638.M453 Z25 1973

1267

Barczaitis, Rainer. Kein simpel-biedrer Sprachferge: Arno Schmidt
als Übersetzer. Frankfurt am Main: Bangert & Metzler, 1985.
311 p.   PT2638.M453 Z54 1985
   Originally presented as the author's thesis (doctoral)—
Göttingen.
   Bibliography: p. 294–311.

1268

Kuhn, Dieter. Kommentierendes Handbuch zu Arno Schmidts
Roman „Aus dem Leben eines Fauns.'' München: Edition
Text + Kritik, 1986. 272 p.   PT2638.M453 A9235 1986
   Includes index.
   Bibliography: p. 261.

1269

————. Das Missverständnis: polemische Überlegungen zum politischen Standort Arno Schmidts. München: Editon Text + Kritik, 1982. 68 p.   JC263.S275 K84 1982
Bibliography: p. 65–68.

1270

Rosenberg, Leibl. Das Hausgespenst: ein begleitendes Handbuch zu Arno Schmidts „Die Schule der Atheisten": Ergänzungsband. München: Edition Text + Kritik, 1979. 317 p.
PT2638.M453 S337 1979
Includes indexes.

1271

Stundel, Dieter. Register zu Zettels Traum: eine Annäherung. München: Edition Text + Kritik, Boorberg, 1974. ix, 538 p.
PT2638.M453 Z2538 1974
Bibliography: p. 536–538.

****

1272

Schneider, Peter. Atempause: Versuch, meine Gedanken über Literatur und Kunst zu ordnen. Reinbek bei Hamburg: Rowohlt, 1977. 233 p.   PT403.S26
Articles originally published 1964–1976.
Includes bibliographical references.

1273

————. Die Botschaft des Pferdekopfs und andere Essais aus einem friedlichen Jahrzehnt. Darmstadt: Luchterhand, 1981. 252 p.
PT2680.N37 B67 1981
Includes bibliographical references.

1274

————. Lenz: eine Erzählung. Berlin, Rotbuch Verlag, 1974, c1973. 90 p.   PT2680.N37 L4 1974

1275

————. Der Mauerspringer. Darmstadt: Luchterhand, 1982. 135 p.   MLCS 82/4544

1276
———. Messer im Kopf. Berlin: Rotbuch Verlag, 1979. 107 p.
                                        MLCS 86/2371 (N)

1277
———. Schon bist du ein Verfassungsfeind: das unerwartete
Anschwellen der Personalakte des Lehrers Kleff. Berlin: Rotbuch
Verlag, 1976, c1975. 109 p.   PT2680.N37 S3
    Includes bibliographical references.

1278
———. Totoloque: das Geiseldrama von Mexiko-Tenochtitlan:
Stück in drei Spielen. Darmstadt: Luchterhand, 1985. 94 p.:
ill.   MLCS 87/628 (P)

1279
———. The wall jumper. New York: Pantheon Books, 1983.
139 p.   PT2680.N37 M313 1983
    Translation of: Der Mauerspringer.

1280
———. Die Wette. Berlin: Rotbuch Verlag, 1978. 111 p.
                                         PT2680.N37 W4
    Bibliography of the author's works: p. 111.

                    ****

1281
Sperr, Martin. Bayrische Trilogie. Frankfurt am Main: Suhrkamp,
1972. 170 p.   PT2681.P48 A19 1972

1282
———. Jagd auf Aussenseiter. Jagdszenen aus Niederbayern.
München: Weismann, 1971. 111 p.: ill.   PT2681.P48 J3

1283
———. Koralle Meier. Die Geschichte der Privaten. Frankfurt
am Main: Verlag der Autoren, 1970. 108 p.   PT2681.P48 K6

1284
———. Die Spitzeder. Frankfurt am Main: Verlag der Autoren,
1977. 57 p.   PT2681.P48 S6
    Play.

1285

————. Tales from Landshut. London: Methuen, 1969. 76 p.

PT2681.P48 L33

Translation of: Landshuter Erzählungen.

1286

————. Willst du Giraffen ohrfeigen, musst du ihr Niveau haben. München: Huber & Klenner, 1979. 104 leaves: ill.

MLCM 87/2282 (P)

****

1287

Strauss, Botho. Big and little: scenes. New York: Farrar, Straus, Giroux, 1979. 179 p.   PT2681.T6898 G713 1979

Translation of: Gross und klein.

1288

————. Devotion. New York: Farrar, Straus and Giroux, 1979. 120 p.   PZ4.S9132 De 1979

Translation of: Die Widmung.

1289

————. Diese Erinnerung an einen, der nur einen Tag zu Gast war. München: Hanser, 1985. 73 p.   MLCS 86/1130 (P)

1290

————. Die Fremdenführerin: Stück in zwei Akten. München: Hanser, 1986. 76 p.   MLCS 86/3570 (P)

1291

————. Gross und klein: Szenen. München, Wien: Hanser, 1978. 139 p.   PT2681.T6898 G7

1292

————. Die Hypochonder: Bekannte Gesichter, gemischte Gefühle. Zwei Theaterstücke. München, Wien: Hanser, 1979. 125 p.

PT2681.T6898 H9 1979

1293

————. Der junge Mann. München: Hanser, 1984. 387 p.

MLCS 87/933 (P)

1294

————. Kalldewey: Farce. München: Hanser, 1981. 121 p.

MLCS 82/6166

1295

————. Marlenes Schwester: zwei Erzählungen. München: Hanser, 1975. 104 p.   PT2681.T6898 M3

1296

————. Paare, Passanten. München: Hanser, 1981. 204 p.

MLCS 82/2623

1297

————. Der Park. München: Hanser, 1983. 127 p.

MLCS 84/2155 (P)

1298

————. Rumor. München, Wien: Hanser, 1980. 232 p.

PT2681.T6898 R85

1299

————. Schützenehre. Düsseldorf: Eremiten-Presse, 1975. 16 p. (on double leaves): col. ill.   PT2681.T6898 S3
Limited ed. of 500 copies signed by the author and the artist. This is no. 145.

1300

————. Trilogie des Wiedersehens. München, Wien: Hanser, 1976. 121 p.   PT2681.T6898 T7

1301

————. Tumult. Manchester: Carcanet Press, 1984. 136 p.

PT2681.T6898 R8513 1984
Translation of: Rumor.

1302

————. Die Widmung: eine Erzählung. München: Hanser, 1977. 144 p.   PT2681.T6898 W5

1303

Adelson, Leslie A. Crisis of subjectivity: Botho Strauss's challenge to West German prose of the 1970's. Amsterdam: Rodopi, 1984. iv, 273 p. (Amsterdamer Publikationen zur Sprache und Literatur; Bd. 56)   PT2681.T6898 Z54 1984
  Bibliography: p. 250-273.

1304

DeMeritt, Linda C. New subjectivity and prose forms of alienation: Peter Handke and Botho Strauss. New York: Lang, 1987. n.p. (Studies in modern German literature; v. 5)   PT735.D 1987
  Includes index.
  Bibliography.

1305

Herwig, Henriette. Verwünschte Beziehungen, verwebte Bezüge: Zerfall und Verwandlung des Dialogs bei Botho Strauss. Tübingen: Stauffenburg, 1986. 248 p.
                         PT2681.T6898 Z69 1986
  Originally presented as the author's thesis (doctoral)— Gesamthochschule Kassel/ Universität des Landes Hessen, 1985.
  Bibliography: p. 217-248.

1306

Sandhack, Monika. Jenseits des Rätsels: Versuch einer Spurensicherung im dramatischen Werk von Botho Strauss. Frankfurt am Main, New York: Lang, 1986. 221 p. (Europäische Hochschulschriften. Reihe I, Deutsche Sprache und Literatur, Bd. 905)   PT2681.T6898 Z85 1986
  Bibliography: p. 192-221.

****

1307

Struck, Karin. Finale: Geschichte eines unentdeckten Pferdes. Hamburg: Knaus, 1984. 477 p.   MLCS 84/11002 (P)

1308

————. Glut und Asche: eine Liebesgeschichte. München: Knaus, 1985. 207 p.   MLCS 86/3155 (P)

1309

————. Die Herberge. Pfaffenweiler: Pfaffenweiler Presse, 1981.
35 p.: ill.   MLCM 83/3147 (P)

1310

————. Kindheits Ende: Journal einer Krise. Frankfurt am Main:
Suhrkamp, 1982. 547 p.: ill.   PT2681.T699 Z47 1982

1311

————. Klassenliebe. Frankfurt am Main: Suhrkamp, 1973.
281 p.   PT2681.T699 K5

1312

————. Lieben. Frankfurt am Main: Suhrkamp, 1977. 450 p.
                                                      PT2681.T699 L5

1313

————. Die liebenswerte Greisin. Pfaffenweiler: Pfaffenweiler
Presse, 1977. 27 p. on folded leaves: ill.
                                                PT2681.T699 L54 1977

1314

————. Die Mutter. Frankfurt am Main: Suhrkamp, 1975. 385 p.
                                                      PT2681.T699 M8

1315

————. Trennung. Frankfurt am Main: Suhrkamp, 1978. 149 p.
                                                      PT2681.T699 T7

1316

————. Zwei Frauen. Münster: Tende, 1982. 165 p.: ill.
                                                JX1963.S8387 1982

———————————

1317

Karin Struck/ herausgegeben von Hans Adler und Hans Joachim
Schrimpf. Frankfurt am Main: Suhrkamp, 1984. 402 p.
                                                PT2681.T699 Z74 1984
Bibliography: p. 383–402.

1318
Jürgensen, Manfred. Karin Struck: eine Einführung. Bern, New
York: Lang, 1985. 190 p.: ill.   PT2681.T699 Z73 1985
  Bibliography: p. 189-190.

****

1319
Theobaldy, Jürgen. Blaue Flecken. Reinbek bei Hamburg:
Rowohlt, 1974. 90 p.: ill.   PT2682.H35 B5

1320
———. Drinks: Gedichte aus Rom. Heidelberg: Wunderhorn,
1979. 47 p.: ill.   PT2682.H35 D7 1979

1321
———. Das Festival im Hof: sechs Erzählungen. Berlin: Rotbuch
Verlag, 1985. 154 p.   MLCS 86/3931 (P)

1322
———. Midlands: Gedichte. Heidelberg: Wunderhorn, 1984.
 94 p.: ill.   MLCS 87/626 (P)

1323
———. Schwere Erde, Rauch: Gedichte. Reinbek bei Hamburg:
Rowohlt, 1980. 85 p.   MLCS 87/1646 (P)

1324
———. Die Sommertour: Gedichte. Reinbek bei Hamburg:
Rowohlt, 1983. 89 p.   MLCS 84/8646 (P)

1325
———. Sonntags Kino. Berlin: Rotbuch Verlag, 1978. 155 p.
      PT2682.H35 S57

1326
———. Spanische Wände. Reinbek bei Hamburg: Rowohlt, 1984,
 c1981. 181 p.   MLCS 87/513 (P)

1327

———. Sperrsitz: Gedichte. Köln: Palmenpresse, 1973. 49 p.: ill.

PT2682.H35 S6

1328

·———. Veränderung der Lyrik: über westdeutsche Gedichte seit 1965. München: Edition Text + Kritik, 1976. 183 p.: ill.

PT552.T5

Includes index.
Bibliography: p. 182–183.

1329

———. Zweiter Klasse: Gedichte. Berlin: Rotbuch Verlag, 1976. 78 p.   PT2682.H35 Z45

****

1330

Wallraff, Günter. Aufdeckung einer Verschwörung: die Spinola-Aktion. Köln: Kiepenheuer & Witsch, 1976. 174 p.: ill., facsims., maps.   DP680.5.W34

1331

———. Der Aufmacher: der Mann, der bei BILD Hans Esser war. Köln: Kiepenheuer & Witsch, 1977. 240 p.: ill.

PN5213.W3 A32

1332

———. Das BILD-Handbuch bis zum Bildausfall. Hamburg: Konkret Literatur, 1981. 238 p.: ill.   PN5220.B5 W33 1981

1333

———. Dreizehn unerwünschte Reportagen. + Anhang: Verbotene Aufrüstung, Giftgas für die Bundeswehr. Reinbek bei Hamburg: Rowohlt, 1976, c1969. 199 p.

HN445.5.W325 1976

1334

———. Predigt von unten. Göttingen: Steidl, 1986. 94 p.: ill.

MLCS 86/5582 (B)

1335

―――. Die Reportagen. Köln: Kiepenheuer & Witsch, 1976.
607 p.   HN445.5.W344

1336

―――. Unser Faschismus nebenan: Griechenland gestern, ein
Lehrstück für morgen. Köln: Kiepenheuer & Witsch, 1975.
223 p.: ill., facsims.   DF852.W33

1337

―――. The Wallraff reports. Woodstock, N. Y.: Overlook Press,
1979. 180 p.   HN17.5.W34
A collection and translation of some of the author's articles
originally published in German.

1338

―――. Wallraff, the undesirable journalist. London: Pluto Press,
1978. 5, 180 p.   PT2685.A475 A23
Translated selections from the writings of G. Wallraff.

1339

―――. Wie hätten wir's denn gerne?: Unternehmerstrategen
proben den Klassenkampf. Wuppertal: Hammer, 1975. 75 p.
(Schriftenreihe des Pressedienst Demokratische Initiative, Bd.
25)   HF5549.2.G3 W34

1340

―――. Zeugen der Anklage die ,,BILD''-beschreibung wird
fortgesetzt. Köln: Kiepenheuer & Witsch, 1979. 218 p.: ill.
                                          PN5220.B5 W34

―――――――――

1341

Bessermann, Hans. Der Fall Günter Wallraff. Mainz: Hase und
Koehler, 1979. 176 p.: ill.   PT2685.A475 Z59
Includes bibliographical references.

1342

Dithmar, Reinhard. Günter Wallraffs Industriereportagen.
Kronberg: Scriptor Verlag, 1973. 206 p.   PN5213.W3 D5
Bibliography: p. 106–109.

1343

Hahn, Ulla. Günter Wallraff. München: Beck, Edition Text + Kritik, 1979. 125 p. (Autorenbücher; 14)   PN5213.W3 H3
Includes bibliographical references.

1344

In Sachen Wallraff: Berichte, Analysen, Meinungen und Dokumente/ herausgegeben von Christian Linder. Reinbek bei Hamburg: Rowohlt, 1977. 204 p.   PT2685.A475 Z7 1977
Includes bibliographical references.

****

1345

Walser, Martin. Der Abstecher. Frankfurt am Main: Suhrkamp, 1967. 149 p.   PT2685.A48 A63

1346

————. Die Alternative: oder, Brauchen wir eine neue Regierung? Reinbek bei Hamburg: Rowohlt, 1961. 158 p.
                                                        JN3971.A91 W3

1347

————. Aus dem Wortschatz unserer Kämpfe. Stierstadt i. Ts.: Eremiten-Presse, 1971. 75 p. (on double leaves): ill.
                                                        PT2685.A48 A9

1348

————. Beschreibung einer Form. München: Hanser, 1968, c1961. 156 p.   PT2621.A26 Z983 1968

1349

————. Brandung. Frankfurt am Main: Suhrkamp, 1985. 318 p.
                                                   PT2685.A48 B7 1985

1350

————. Breakers. New York: Holt, 1987. 305 p.
                                             PT2685.A48 B713 1987
Translation of: Brandung.

1351

————. Brief an Lord Liszt. Frankfurt am Main: Suhrkamp, 1982.
152 p.   MLCS 84/5946 (P)

1352

————. Dorle und Wolf. Frankfurt am Main: Suhrkamp, 1987.
176 p.   MLCS 8/4147 (P)

1353

————. Ehen in Philippsburg. Reinbek: Rowohlt, 1970, c1957.
226 p.   PT2685.A48 E34 1970

1354

————. Eiche und Angora. Frankfurt am Main: Suhrkamp, 1966.
114 p.   PT2685.A48 E37 1966

1355

————. Das Einhorn. Frankfurt: Suhrkamp, 1966. 488 p.
                         PT2685.A48 E4

1356

————. Erfahrungen und Leseerfahrungen. Frankfurt am Main:
Suhrkamp, 1969, c1965. 161 p.   PT2685.A48 E7 1969

1357

————. Ein fliehendes Pferd: Theaterstück. Frankfurt am Main:
Suhrkamp, 1985. 78 p.   MLCS 86/5594 (P)

1358

————. Ein fliehendes Pferd: Novelle. Frankfurt am Main:
Suhrkamp, 1978. 150 p.   PT2685.A48 F48

1359

————. Fiction. Frankfurt am Main: Suhrkamp, 1970. 82 p.
                         PT2685.A48 F45

1360

————. Ein Flugzeug über dem Haus und andere Geschichten.
Frankfurt am Main: Suhrkamp, 1966. 119 p.
                         PT2685.A48 F5 1966

1361

————. The Gadarene Club. London: Longmans, 1960, c1959.
273 p.   PZ4.W222 Gad

1362

————. Die Gallistl'sche Krankheit. Frankfurt am Main: Suhrkamp, 1972. 127 p.   PT 2685.A48 G3

1363

————. Gesammelte Geschichten. Frankfurt am Main: Suhrkamp,
1983. 318 p.   PT2685.A48 A6 1983

1364

————. Gesammelte Stücke. Frankfurt am Main: Suhrkamp,
1971. 349 p.   PT2685.A48 A19 1971

1365

————. Goethes Anziehungskraft: Vortrag gehalten am 31. Januar
1983 anlässlich der Verleihung der Ehrendoktorwürde: mit einer
Ansprache des Rektors der Universität Konstanz, Horst Sund,
und einer Laudatio des Dekans der philosophischen Fakultät,
Ulrich Gaier. Konstanz: Universitätsverlag, 1983. 54 p.: ill.
(Konstanzer Universitätsreden: 146)   PT2178.W35 1983
Includes bibliographies.

1366

————. Der Grund zur Freude: 99 Sprüche zur Erbauung des
Bewusstseins. Düsseldorf: Eremiten-Presse, 1978. 84 p. (on
double leaves).   PT2685.A48 G7

1367

————. Halbzeit. München: Droemer Knaur, 1971. 618 p.
                                                        PT2685.A48 H3 1971

1368

————. Heilige Brocken: Aufsätze, Prosa, Gedichte. Weingarten:
Drumlin Verlag, 1986. 129 p.: ill. (some col.).
                                                        MLCS 86/5507 (P)

1369

————. Heimatkunde: Aufsätze und Reden. Frankfurt am Main:
Suhrkamp, 1968. 125, 2 p.   PT2685.A48 H4

1370

————. Heines Tränen: Essay. Düsseldorf: Eremiten-Presse, 1981.
47 p.: ill.   MLCS 82/2508

1371

————. Hölderlin zu entsprechen. Biberach an der Riss: K.
Thomae, 1970. 29 p.   PT2359.H2 W34

1372

————. In Goethes Hand: Szenen aus dem 19. Jahrhundert.
Frankfurt am Main: Suhrkamp, 1982. 170 p.
                                    PT2685.A48 I5 1982

1373

————. The inner man. New York: Holt, Rinehart and Winston,
1985, c1984. 276 p.   PT2685.A48 S413 1985
Translation of: Seelenarbeit.

1374

————. Jenseits der Liebe. Frankfurt am Main: Suhrkamp, 1976.
175 p.   PT2685.A48 J4

1375

————. Ein Kinderspiel: Stück in zwei Akten. 2. überarbeitete.
Aufl. Frankfurt am Main: Suhrkamp, 1975, c1970. 71 p.
                                    MLCS 84/14969 (P)

1376

————. Letter to Lord Liszt: a novel. New York: Holt, Rinehart
and Winston, 1985. 149 p.   PT2685.A48 B7513 1985
Translation of: Brief an Lord Liszt.

1377

————. Liebeserklärungen. Frankfurt am Main: Suhrkamp, 1983.
258 p.   PT2685.A48 Z94 1983

1378

————. Lügengeschichten. Frankfurt am Main: Suhrkamp, 1964.
121 p.   PT2685.A48 L8

1379

————. Marriage in Philippsburg. Norfolk. Conn.: New Directions, 1961. 319 p.   PZ4.W222 Mar

1380

————. Messmers Gedanken. Frankfurt am Main: Suhrkamp, 1985. 106 p.   MLCS 87/4793 (P)

1381

————. Runaway horse. New York: Holt, Rinehart, Winston, 1980. 109 p.   PZ4.W222 Ru
Translation of: Ein fliehendes Pferd.

1382

————. Santis. Stuttgart: Radius-Verlag, 1986. 62 p.
                                                       MLCS 86/5873 (P)

1383

————. Das Sauspiel: Szenen aus dem 16. Jahrhundert. Frankfurt am Main: Suhrkamp, 1978. 527 p.: ill.
                                                       PT2685.A48 S2 1978
Bibliography: p. 521–526.

1384

————. Das Schwanenhaus. Frankfurt am Main: Suhrkamp, 1980. 232 p.   MLCS 87/1759 (P)

1385

————. Seelenarbeit. Frankfurt am Main: Suhrkamp, 1979. 294 p.
                                                       PT2685.A48 S4

1386

————. Selbstbewusstsein und Ironie: Frankfurter Vorlesungen. Frankfurt am Main: Suhrkamp, 1981. 211 p.: ports.
                                                       PT134.I7 W3
Includes bibliographical references.

1387

————. Der Sturz. Frankfurt am Main: Suhrkamp, 1973. 359 p.
                                                       PT2685.A48 S8
Sequel to: Das Einhorn.

1388

————. The Swan Villa. New York: Holt, Rinehart and Winston, 1982. 247 p.   PT2685.A48 S2713 1982
Translation of: Das Schwanenhaus.

1389

————. Über Ernst Bloch. Frankfurt am Main: Suhrkamp, 1968. 150 p.   B3209.B78 U3

1390

————. The Unicorn. London: Calder and Boyars, 1971. 283 p.
      PZ4.W222 Un
Translation of: Das Einhorn.

1391

————. Variationen eines Würgegriffs: Bericht über Trinidad und Tobago. Stuttgart: Radius-Verlag, 1985. 86 p.
      PT2685.A48 Z477 1985

1392

————. Was zu bezweifeln war: Aufsätze und Reden 1958–1975. Berlin: Aufbau-Verlag, 1976. 371 p.   PT2685.A48 W3
Includes bibliographical references.

1393

————. Wer ist ein Schriftsteller?: Aufsätze und Reden. Frankfurt am Main: Suhrkamp, 1979. 108 p.   PT2685.A48 W4
Includes bibliographical references.

1394

————. Wie und wovon handelt Literatur. Frankfurt am Main: Suhrkamp, 1973. 145 p.   PT2685.A48 W5

1395

Beckermann, Thomas. Martin Walser: oder, Die Zerstörung eines Musters: literatursoziologischer Versuch über Halbzeit. Bonn: Bouvier, 1972. 217 p. (Abhandlungen zur Kunst-, Musik- und Literaturwissenschaft; Bd. 114)   PT2685.A48 H334
Bibliography: p. 211–217.

1396

Brandle, Werner. Die dramatischen Stücke Martin Walsers: Variationen über das Elend des bürgerlichen Subjekts. Stuttgart: Heinz, 1978. 248 p. (Stuttgarter Arbeiten zur Germanistik; Nr. 45)   PT2685.A48 Z59 1978
  Originally presented as the author's thesis, Tübingen, 1975.
  Summary also in English.
  Bibliography: p. 226–246.

1397

Doane, Heike. Gesellschaftspolitische Aspekte in Martin Walsers Kristlein-Trilogie: Halbzeit, Das Einhorn, Der Sturz. Bonn: Bouvier, 1978. 217 p. (Studien zur Germanistik, Anglistik und Komparatistik; Bd. 67)   PT2685.A48 Z6
  Bibliography: p. 208–217.

1398

Hick, Ulrike. Martin Walsers Prosa: Möglichkeiten des zeitgenössischen Romans unter Berücksichtigung des Realismusanspruchs: Anhang, Gespräch mit Martin Walser 4.5.1977. Stuttgart: Heinz, 1983. 303 p. (Stuttgarter Arbeiten zur Germanistik; Nr. 126)   PT2685.A48 Z67 1983
  ,,Marburger Dissertation.''
  Summary in English.
  Bibliography: p. 267–288.

1399

Martin Walser: international perspectives/ edited by Jürgen E. Schlunk and Armand E. Singer. New York: Lang, 1987. xviii, 219 p. (American university studies. Series I, Germanic languages and literature; v. 64)   PT2685.A48 Z784 1987
  English and German.
  Papers presented at the International Martin Walser Symposium, sponsored by and held at the West Virginia University, Morgantown Campus, Apr. 11–13, 1985.

1400

Rooney, Kathryn. Wife and mistress: women in Martin Walser's Anselm Kristlein trilogy. Coventry: Department of German Studies, University of Warwick, 1975. 1, 46 p. (Occasional papers in German studies; no. 6)   PT2685.A48 Z85
  Bibliography: p. 46.

1401

Waine, Anthony Edward. Martin Walser. München: Beck, Edition Text + Kritik, 1980. 187, 1 p. (Autorenbücher; 18)

PT2685.A4454 Z955

Bibliography: p. 185–188.

1402

————. Martin Walser: the development as dramatist 1950–1970. Bonn: Bouvier, 1978. 394 p. (Abhandlungen zur Kunst-, Musik- und Literaturwissenschaft; Bd. 273)   PT2685.A4454 Z96

English and German.

Includes index.

Bibliography: p. 362–383.

* * * * * * * * * * * * * * * * * *

1403

Weiss, Peter. Die Ästhetik des Widerstands. Frankfurt am Main: Suhrkamp, 1975. 301 p.   PT2685.E5 A65

1404

————. Aufsätze, Journale, Arbeitspunkte: Schriften zu Kunst und Literatur. Berlin: Henschelverlag, 1979. 187 p.

PT2685.E5 A93

1405

————. Bodies and shadows: two short novels. New York: Delacorte Press, 1970, c1969. 120 p.: ill.   PZ4.W435 Bo

Consists of The shadow of the coachman's body, translation of: Der Schatten des Körpers des Kutschers and Conversation of the three wayfarers, translation of: Das Gespräch der drei Gehenden.

1406

————. Dramen. Frankfurt am Main: Suhrkamp, 1968. 2 v.

PT2685.E5 A19 1968

1407

————. Exile: a novel. New York: Delacorte Press, 1968. 245 p.

PZ4.W435 Ex

In two parts: I. Leavetaking, translation of: Abschied von den Eltern; II. Vanishing point, translation of: Fluchtpunkt.

1408

———. Fluchtpunkt. Frankfurt am Main: Suhrkamp, 1962.
306 p.   PT2685.E5 F55

1409

———. Das Gespräch der drei Gehenden. Frankfurt am Main:
1968, c1963. 122 p.   PT2685.E5 G45 1968

1410

———. The investigation. New York: Atheneum, 1966. 270 p.
                                              PT2685.E5 E713

1411

———. Leavetaking and Vanishing point. London: Calder &
Boyars, 1966. 275 p.   PZ4.W435 Le3
Originally published as Abschied von den Eltern. Frankfurt:
Suhrkamp, 1961, and Fluchtpunkt. Suhrkamp, 1963.

1412

———. 'Limited bombing' in Vietnam: report on the attacks
against the Democratic Republic of Vietnam by the U.S. Air
Force and the Seventh Fleet, after the declaration of 'limited
bombing' by President Lyndon B. Johnson on March 31, 1968
by Peter Weiss and Gunilla Palmstierna-Weiss. London:
Bertrand Russell Peace Foundation, 1969. 1, 39 p.
                                              DS557.A7 W45

1413

———. Nacht mit Gästen. Frankfurt am Main: Suhrkamp, 1969.
98 p.: ill.   PT2685.E5 N3 1969

1414

———. Der neue Prozess: Stück in drei Akten. Frankfurt am
Main: Suhrkamp, 1984. 127 p.: ill.   PT2685.E5 N4 1984

1415

———. Notes on the cultural life of the Democratic Republic of
Vietnam. New York: Dell, 1970. 180 p.   DS557.A74 W43
Translation of: Notizen zum kulturellen Leben in der
Demokratischen Republik Viet Nam.

1416

————. Notizbücher: 1971–1980. Frankfurt am Main: Suhrkamp, 1981. 2 v.: ill.   PT2685.E5 N6

1417

————. The persecution and assassination of Jean-Paul Marat as performed by the inmates of the Asylum of Charenton under the direction of the Marquis de Sade. New York: Atheneum, 1966, c1965. x, 117 p.   PT2685.E5 V43 1966
     Includes music.

1418

————. Rapporte. Frankfurt am Main: Suhrkamp, 1968–71. 2 v.
         PT2685.E5 R3
     Includes bibliographical references.

1419

————. Der Schatten des Körpers des Kutschers. Frankfurt am Main: Suhrkamp, 1966. 99 p.: ill.   PT2685.E5 S3 1966

1420

————. Trotsky in exile. New York: Atheneum, 1972, c1971. 123 p.   PT2685.E5 T713 1972

1421

————. Der Turm. Stuttgart: Reclam, 1973. 61 p.
         PT2685.E5 T8

1422

Die Ästhetik des Widerstands/ herausgegeben von Alexander Stephan. Frankfurt am Main: Suhrkamp, 1983. 378 p.: ill.
         PT2685.E5 A6533 1983
     Bibliography: p. 367–377.

1423

Best, Otto F. Peter Weiss. New York: Ungar, 1976. ix, 150 p.
         PT2685.E5 Z5813 1976
     Includes index.
     Bibliography: p. 141–144.

1424
Canaris, Volker. Über Peter Weiss. Frankfurt am Main:
Suhrkamp, 1970. 184 p.   PT2685.E5 Z59

1425
Ellis, Roger. Peter Weiss in exile: a critical study of his works. Ann
Arbor, Mich.: UMI Research Press, 1987. xv, 179 p.: ill. (The-
ater and dramatic studies; no. 37)   PT2685.E5 Z66 1987
Revision of thesis (Ph.D.)—University of California-Berkeley,
1980.
Includes index.
Bibliography: p. 169–175.

1426
Meier, Reinhard. Peter Weiss: Von der Exilsituation zum politi-
schen Engagement. Zürich: Juris-Verlag, 1971. 92 p.
PT2685.E5 Z8

1427
Paul, Ulrike. Vom Geschichtsdrama zur politischen Diskussion:
über die Desintegration von Individuum und Geschichte bei
Georg Büchner und Peter Weiss. München: Fink, 1974. 228 p.
PT693.P38
Bibliography: p. 221–228.

1428
Peter Weiss/ herausgegeben von Rainer Gerlach. Frankfurt am
Main: Suhrkamp, 1984. 351 p.: ill.   PT2685.E5 Z844 1984
Bibliography: p. 331–351.

1429
Peter Weiss im Gespräch/ herausgegeben von Rainer Gerlach und
Matthias Richter. Frankfurt am Main: Suhrkamp, 1986. 355 p.
PT2685.E5 Z474 1986
Includes index.
Bibliography: p. 341–349.

1430
Vormweg, Heinrich. Peter Weiss. München: Beck, Edition Text +
Kritik, 1981. 137 p. (Autorenbücher; 21)   PT2685.E5 Z98
Bibliography: p. 133–135.

****

1431

Wellershoff, Dieter. Die Arbeit des Lebens: autobiographische Texte. Köln: Kiepenheuer & Witsch, 1985. 270 p.

PT2685.E55 Z462 1985

1432

―――. Die Auflösung des Kunstbegriffs. Frankfurt am Main: Suhrkamp, 1976. 142 p. BH39.W43
Based on lectures presented during the summer semester at the University of Salzburg, 1974.
Bibliography: p. 133-142.

1433

―――. Bau einer Laube. Neuwied, Berlin: Luchterhand, 1965. 24 p. PT2685.E55 B3

1434

―――. A beautiful day. New York: Harper & Row, 1972, c1971. 219 p. PZ4.W448 Be3·
Translation of: Ein schöner Tag.

1435

―――. Die Bittgänger. Stuttgart: Reclam, 1968. 94 p.
PT2685.E55 B5

1436

―――. Doppelt belichtetes Seestück und andere Texte. Köln: Kiepenheuer & Witsch, 1974. 303 p. PT2685.E55 D6

1437

―――. Einladung an alle. Köln: Kiepenheuer & Witsch, 1972. 272 p. PT2685.E55 E5

1438

―――. Fiktion und Praxis. Mainz: Verlag der Akademie der Wissenschaften und der Literatur; Wiesbaden: Steiner, 1969. 16 p. PN51.W35

1439

―――. Der Gleichgültige: Versuche über Hemingway, Camus, Benn und Beckett. Köln: Kiepenheuer & Witsch, 1963. 127 p.
PN774.W38

1440

————. Glücksucher: vier Drehbücher und begleitende Texte.
Köln: Kiepenheuer & Witsch, 1979. 335 p.

MLCS 86/4988 (P)

1441

————. Gottfried Benn, Phanotyp dieser Stunde. Köln: Kiepenheuer & Witsch, 1958. 253 p.   PT2603.E46 Z9

1442

————. Die Körper und die Träume. Köln: Kiepenheuer &
Witsch, 1986. 275 p.   MLCS 87/3965 (P)

1443

————. Literatur und Lustprinzip. Köln: Kiepenheuer & Witsch,
1973. 156 p.: port.   PN37.W4
„Veröffentlichungsnachweis'': p. 156.
Bibliography: p. 155.

1444

————. Literatur und Veränderung. Versuche zu einer Metakritik
der Literatur. Köln, Berlin: Kiepenheuer & Witsch, 1969.
185 p.: front.   PN58.W4

1445

————. Die Schattengrenze. Reinbek bei Hamburg: Rowohlt,
1971. 122 p.   PT2685.E55 S3 1971

1446

————. Die Schönheit des Schimpansen. Köln: Kiepenheuer &
Witsch, 1977. 310 p.   PT2685.E55 S36

1447

————. Ein schöner Tag. Reinbek bei Hamburg: Rowohlt, 1969.
150 p.   PT2685.E55 S35

1448

————. Das Schreien der Katze im Sack. Köln: Kiepenheuer &
Witsch, 1970. 182 p.: port.   PT2685.E55 S37

1449

————. Der Sieger nimmt alles. Köln: Kiepenheuer & Witsch, 1983. 514 p.   MLCS 84/2245 (P)

1450

————. Die Sirene. Köln: Kiepenheuer & Witsch, 1980. 215 p.
        PT2685.E55 S57

1451

————. Das Verschwinden im Bild. Köln: Kiepenheuer & Witsch, 1980. 285 p.   PT2685.E55 V4

1452

————. Die Wahrheit der Literatur: sieben Gespräche. München: Fink, 1980. 184 p.   PT2685.E55 Z95

1453

————. Wochenende. Sechs Autoren variieren ein Thema. Köln, Berlin: Kiepenheuer & Witsch, 1967. 223 p.   PT1334.W38

1454

Helmreich, Hans. Dieter Wellershoff. München: Beck, Edition Text + Kritik, 1982. 151 p. (Autorenbücher; 29)
        PT2685.E55 Z69 1982
    Bibliography: p. 146-151.

1455

Der Schriftsteller Dieter Wellershoff: Interpretationen und Analysen/ herausgegeben von R. Hinton Thomas. Köln: Kiepenheuer & Witsch, 1975. 191 p.: port.   PT2685.E55 Z88
    Bibliography of works by and about D. Wellershoff: p. 169-190.

1456

Vollmuth, Eike H. Dieter Wellershoff, Romanproduktion und anthropologische Literaturtheorie: zu den Romanen „Ein schöner Tag" und „Die Schattengrenze." München: Fink, 1979. 309 p.   PT2685.E55 S3538 1979
    Originally presented as the author's thesis, Münster, 1974
    Bibliography: p. 299-309.

* * * * * * * * * * * * * * *

1457
Wohmann, Gabriele. Abschied für länger. Reinbek bei Hamburg:
Rowohlt, 1969. 121 p.   PT2685.O34 A63 1969

1458
————. Ach wie gut, dass niemand weiss. Darmstadt: Luchterhand, 1980. 395 p.   PT2685.O34 A65 1980

1459
————. Alles für die Galerie. Berlin, Weimar: Aufbau-Verlag,
1972. 162 p.   PT2685.O34 A79

1460
————. Ausflug mit der Mutter. Darmstadt: Luchterhand, 1976.
138 p.   PT2685.O34 A95

1461
————. Ausgewählte Erzählungen aus zwanzig Jahren. Darmstadt,
Neuwied: Luchterhand, 1979. 2 v.   PT2685.O34 A15 1979

1462
————. Böse Streiche und andere Erzählungen. Düsseldorf:
Eremiten-Presse, 1977. 84 p. (on double leaves), 2 leaves of
plates: ill.   PT2685.O34 B6
   „Die in diesem Band erstmals versammelten Erzählungen sind
frühe Arbeiten der Autorin."

1463
————. Die Bütows. Stierstadt i. Ts.: Eremiten-Presse, 1971. 32 p.
(on double leaves): ill.   PT2685.O34 B8 1971

1464
————. Das dicke Wilhelmchen. Düsseldorf: Eremiten-Presse,
1978. 84 p.: ill.   PT2685.O34 D5

1465
————. Dorothea Wörth. Düsseldorf: Eremiten-Presse, 1975.
24 p. (on double fold): ill.   PT2685.O34 D6

1466
————. Einsamkeit. Darmstadt: Luchterhand, 1982. 170 p.
                                          MLCS 82/6599

1467
————. Endlich allein, endlich zu zwein. Düsseldorf: Eremiten-
Presse, 1976. 20 p. (on double leaves): ill.   PT2685.O34 E48

1468
————. Entziehung. Darmstadt: Luchterhand, 1974. 206 p.: ill.
PT2685.O34 E5

1469
————. Ernste Absicht. Neuwied: Luchterhand, 1970. 487 p.
PT2685.O34 E68

1470
————. Erzählungen. Ebenhausen bei München: Langewiesche-
Brandt, 1966. 143 p.   PT2685.O34 E7

1471
————. Der Fall Rufus. Stierstadt i. Ts.: Eremiten-Presse, 1971.
46 p. (on double leaves): ill.   PT2685.O34 F3

1472
————. Ein Fall von Chemie. Düsseldorf: Eremiten-Presse, 1975.
48 p. (on double leaves): ill.   PT2685.O34 F34

1473
————. Feuer bitte. Düsseldorf: Eremiten-Presse, 1978. 40 p. (on
double leaves): ill.   PT2685.O34 F45

1474
————. Frühherbst in Badenweiler. Darmstadt: Luchterhand,
1978. 265 p.   PT2685.O34 F7

1475
————. Die Gäste. Basel: Lenos-Presse, 1971. 49 p.: ill.
PT2685.O34 G3

1476
————. Gegenangriff. Neuwied: Luchterhand, 1972. 181 p.
PT2685.O34 G4

1477

————. Glücklicher Vorgang. Düsseldorf: Eremiten-Presse, 1986.
47 p.: ill.   MLCM 86/4189 (P)

1478

————. Das Glücksspiel. Darmstadt, Neuwied: Luchterhand, 1981.
234 p.   MLCS 81/1759

1479

————. Goethe hilf. Düsseldorf: Eremiten-Presse, 1983. 101 p.:
ill.   MLCS 84/7756 (P)

1480

————. Grosse Liebe. Bad Homburg: Tsamas, 1971. 90 p.: ill.
                                                      PT2685.O34 G7

1481

————. Grund zur Aufregung. Darmstadt, Neuwied: Luchterhand, 1978. 83 p.   PT2685.O34 G75

1482

————. Ein günstiger Tag. Düsseldorf: Eremiten-Presse, 1981.
83 p.   PT2685.O34 G8

1483

————. Habgier. Düsseldorf: Eremiten-Presse, 1973. 94 p. (on
double leaves): col. ill.   PT2685.034 H3

1484

————. Heiratskandidaten: ein Fernsehspiel und drei Hörspiele.
München: Piper, 1978. 188 p.   PT2685.O34 H4

1485

————. Hilfe kommt mir von den Bergen. Düsseldorf: Eremiten-
Presse, 1982. 60 p. on folded leaves: col. ill.
                                                 PT2685.O34 H54 1982

1486

————. Ich lese, ich schreibe: autobiographische Essays. Darmstadt: Luchterhand, 1984. 167 p.   MLCS 87/502 (P)

1487

————. In Darmstadt leben die Künste. Darmstadt: Schlapp, 1967. 23 l.   DD9011.D3 W6

1488

————. Ich weiss das auch nicht besser. München: Deutscher Taschenbuch-Verlag, 1980, c1974. 100 p.

MLCS 87/2775 (P)

1489

————. Der Irrgast. Darmstadt: Luchterhand, 1985. 245 p.

MLCS 86/1114 (P)

1490

————. Der Kirschbaum. Düsseldorf: Eremiten-Presse, 1984. 95 p.: col. ill.   MLCS 86/5164 (P)

1491

————. Knoblauch am Kamin. Düsseldorf: Eremiten-Presse, 1979. 48 p. (on double fold): col. ill.   PT2685.O34 K5
Limited ed. of 750 copies; this is no. 443.

1492

————. Komm lieber Mai. Darmstadt: Luchterhand, 1981. 118 p.

PT2685.O34 K6 1981

1493

————. Der kürzeste Tag des Jahres. Darmstadt: Luchterhand, 1983. 147 p.   PT2685.O34 K8 1983

1494

————. Ländliches Fest und andere Erzählungen. München: Deutscher Taschenbuch-Verlag, 1971. 126 p.

PT2685.O34 L3 1971

1495

————. Mit einem Messer: zwei Erzählungen. Düsseldorf: Eremiten-Presse, 1972. 37 p. (on double leaves): col. ill.

PT2685.O34 M5

1496

————. Die Nächste, bitte. Düsseldorf: Eremiten-Presse, 1978.
21 p. (on double leaves): ill.   PT2685.O34 N34

1497

————. Der Nachtigall fällt auch nichts Neues ein: ein Dialog.
Düsseldorf: Eremiten-Presse, 1978. 52 p.: ill.   PT2685.O34 N3

1498

————. Nachkommenschaften: ein Film. Düsseldorf: Eremiten-
Presse, 1981. 125 p.: ill.   MLCS 82/471

1499

————. Paarlauf. Darmstadt, Neuwied: Luchterhand, 1979.
291 p.   PT2685.O34 P23

1500

————. Passau, Gleis 3. Darmstadt: Luchterhand, 1984. 126 p.
MLCS 86/3037 (P)

1501

————. Paulinchen war allein zu Haus. Darmstadt: Luchterhand,
1974. 234 p.   PT2685.O34 P3

1502

————. Schönes Gehege. Darmstadt, Neuwied: Luchterhand,
1975. 324 p.   PT2685.O34 S3

1503

————. Selbstverteidigung: Prosa und anderes. Neuwied: Luchterhand, 1971. 320 p.   PT2685.O34 S4

1504

————. Sieg über die Dämmerung. München: Piper, 1974. 153 p.
PT2685.O34 S5 1974

1505

————. So ist die Lage. Düsseldorf: Eremiten-Presse, 1974. 48 p.
(on double leaves).   PT2685.O34 S57
    ,,Die ersten 200 Exemplare dieses Bandes sind numeriert und
von Gabriele Wohmann handschriftlich signiert.''

1506

————. Sonntag bei den Kreisands. Stierstadt im Taunus: Eremiten-Presse, 1970. 67 p. (on double leaves): ill.

PT2685.O34 S6

1507

————. Stolze Zeiten. Düsseldorf: Claassen, 1981. 263 p.

PT2685.O34 S68 1981

1508

————. Streit. Düsseldorf: Eremiten-Presse, 1978. 98 p. (on double leaves): ill.   PT2685.O34 S7

1509

————. Theater von innen. Olten, Freiburg: Walter, 1966. 303 p.

PQ2683.O35 T5

1510

————. Treibjagd. Stuttgart: Reclam, 1970. 87 p.

PT2685.O34 T7

1511

————. Übersinnlich. Düsseldorf: Eremiten-Presse, 1972. 28 p. (on double leaves): chiefly ill. (part col.).   PT2685.O34 U3

1512

————. Ein unwiderstehlicher Mann. Reinbek bei Hamburg: Rowohlt, 1976. 140 p.   PT2685.O34 U5

1513

————. Verliebt, oder? Darmstadt: Luchterhand, 1983. 160 p.

MLCS 84/10778 (P)

1514

————. Violas Vorbilder. Düsseldorf: Eremiten-Presse, 1980. 28 p. on folded leaves: col. ill.   PT2685.O34 V56 1980

1515

————. Vor der Hochzeit. Reinbek bei Hamburg: Rowohlt, 1980. 123 p.   PT2685.O34 V6 1980

1516
———. Wanda Lords Gespenster. Düsseldorf: Eremiten-Presse,
1979. 79 p.: ill.   PT2685.O34 W3

1517
———. Wir sind eine Familie. Düsseldorf: Eremiten-Presse, 1980.
75 p.: ill.   MLCS 87/2231 (P)

1518
———. Die Witwen. Stuttgart: Reclam, 1972. 142 p.: ill.
                                                     PT2685.O34 W5

1519
Gabriele Wohmann/ Günter Häntzschel . . . et al. München: Beck,
Edition Text + Kritik, 1982. 166 p. (Autorenbücher; 30)
                                        PT2685.O34 Z678 1982
„Auswahlbibliographie": p. 155–165.

1520
Gabriele Wohmann: Auskunft für Leser/ herausgegeben von Klaus
Siblewski. Darmstadt: Luchterhand, 1982. 185 p.
                                        PT2685.O34 Z679 1982
Includes bibliographies.

1521
Gabriele Wohmann: Materialienbuch/ Einleitung von Karl Krolow;
Bibliographie von Reiner Wohmann; hrsg. von Thomas
Scheuffelen. Darmstadt: Luchterhand, 1977. 150 p.
                                        PT2685.O34 Z68
Bibliography by and about G. Wohmann: p. 125–145.

1522
Knapp, Gerhard Peter. Gabriele Wohmann. Königstein/Ts.:
Athenäum, 1981. 212 p.   PT2685.O34 Z74
Bibliography of works by and about G. Wohmann: p. 180–201.
Includes bibliographical references and indexes.

1523

Lutz-Hilgarth, Dorothea. Literaturkritik in Zeitungen: dargestellt am Beispiel Gabriele Wohmann. Frankfurt am Main: Lang, 1984. 307 p. (Würzburger Hochschulschriften zur neueren deutschen Literaturgeschichte; Bd. 5)   PT2685.O34 Z76 1984
„Rezensionensammlung": p. 103–307.
Bibliography: p. 86–87.

1524

Wellner, Klaus. Leiden an der Familie: zur sozialpathologischen Rollenanalyse im Werk Gabriele Wohmanns. Stuttgart: Klett, 1976. 237 p. (Literaturwissenschaft, Gesellschaftswissenschaft; 17)   PT2685.O34 Z94 1976
Originally presented as the author's thesis, Hamburg, 1975, under title: Identität und Familiensystem.
Includes index.
Bibliography: p. 233–236.

****

1525

Wondratschek, Wolf. Chuck's Zimmer. Frankfurt am Main: Vertrieb Zweitausendeins, 1974. 63 p.   PT2685.O45 C5

1526

————. Früher begann der Tag mit einer Schusswunde. Ein Bauer zeugt mit einer Bäuerin einen Bauernjungen, der unbedingt Knecht werden will. München: Deutscher Taschenbuch-Verlag, 1972. 130 p.   PT2685.O45 A6 1972

1527

————. Gedichte, Lieder. Frankfurt am Main: Zweitausendeins, 1974. 95 p.: ill.   PT2685.O45 A6 1974 Bd. 1
Some poems in English.

1528

————. Das leise Lachen am Ohr eines andern. Frankfurt am Main: Zweitausendeins, 1976. 81 p.: ill.
PT2685.O45 A6 1974 Bd. 2
Some poems in English.

1529

————. Männer und Frauen. Frankfurt am Main: Zweitausendeins, 1978. 95 p.: port.   PT2685.O45 A6 1974 Bd. 3

1530

————. Maschine Nr. 9. Warwick, Eng.: University of Warwick,
1973. 84 p. (Occasional papers in German studies; no. 4)
                                              PT2685.O45 M3

German with introduction in English.
Includes bibliographical references.

1531

————. Omnibus. München: Hanser, 1972. 217 p.: ill.
                                              PT2685.O45 O4

1532

————. Paul. München: Hanser, 1971. 119 p.   PT2685.O45 P3

GERMAN DEMOCRATIC REPUBLIC

General Reference Works

1533

Bock, Stephan. Literatur Gesellschaft Nation: materielle und ideelle Rahmenbedingungen der frühen DDR-Literatur, (1949–1956). Stuttgart: Metzler, 1980. ix, 328 p.   PT3705.B6
  Includes bibliographical references and index.

1534

Cross-section: anthology of the PEN Centre German Democratic Republic. Edited on behalf of the Presidium of the PEN Centre German Democratic Republic by Wieland Herzfelde and Günther Cwojdrak. Leipzig: Edition Leipzig, 1970. 275 p.
    PT3732.C7

1535

DDR-Literatur der sechziger und siebziger Jahre: Wissenschaftliche Konferenz der Staatlichen Georgischen Universität Tbilissi und der Friedrich-Schiller-Universität Jena. Jena: Friedrich-Schiller-Universität Jena, 1985. 153 p.   PT3705.D37 1985
  German and Russian.
  Includes bibliographies.

1536

DDR-Literatur '83 im Gespräch/ herausgegeben von Siegfried Rönisch. Berlin: Aufbau-Verlag, 1984. 342 p.
    PT3706.D37 1984
  Bibliography: p. 326–342.

1537

DDR-Literatur im Tauwetter/ herausgegeben von Richard A. Zipser unter Mitarbeit von Karl-Heinz Schoeps. New York:

Lang, 1985. 3 v.: ports.   PT3732.D19 1985 v. 1-3
    Bibliography: v. 2, p. 325-329.

1538
30 Jahre DDR-Literatur/ Redaktor tomu, Norbert Honsza. Wrocław:
    Wydawnictwa Uniwersytetu Wrocławskiego, 1979. 163 p.
                                            PD9.G47 v. 41
    Includes bibliographical references.

1539
Emmerich, Wolfgang. Kleine Literaturgeschichte der DDR.
    Darmstadt, Neuwied: Luchterhand, 1981. 264 p.   PT3705.E4
    Includes index.
    Bibliography: p. 246-257.

1540
Franke, Konrad. Die Literatur der Deutschen Demokratischen
    Republik. Neubearb. Ausg. mit 3 einführenden Essays von
    Heinrich Vormweg. München: Kindler, 1974. 678 p.: ill.
                                            PT3716.F7 1974
    Includes index.
    Bibliography: p. 661-664.

1541
Geerdts, Hans Jürgen. Literatur der DDR in Einzeldarstellungen.
    Stuttgart: A. Kroner, 1972. xxiv, 571 p.   PT3716.G4

1542
Gerber, Margy. Literature of the German Democratic Republic
    in English translation: a bibliography: studies in GDR culture
    and society: a supplementary volume. Lanham, MD.: University
    Press of America, 1984. iv, 134 p.   Z2250.G45 1984

1543
Hilzinger, Sonja. „Als ganzer Mensch zu leben . . . ,"
    emanzipatorische Tendenzen in der neueren Frauen-Literatur
    der DDR. Frankfurt am Main, New York: Lang, 1985. 262 p.
    (Europäische Hochschulschriften. Reihe I, Deutsche Sprache und
    Literatur: Bd. 867)   PT3716.H55 1985
    Bibliography: p. 230-262.

1544

Huebener, Theodore. The literature of East Germany. New York:
Ungar, 1970. ix, 134 p.   PT3705.H8
Bibliography: p. 125-126.

1545

International Symposium on the German Democratic Republic
(7th: 1981: World Fellowship Center). Studies in GDR culture
and society 2: proceedings of the Seventh International
Symposium on the German Democratic Republic/ editorial
board, Margy Gerber, chief editor . . . et al. Washington, D. C.:
University Press of America, 1982. iv, 292 p.
                                    PT3701.I57 1981
English and German.
Includes bibliographical references.

1546

Köhler-Hausmann, Reinhild. Literaturbetrieb in der DDR:
Schriftsteller und Literaturinstanzen. Stuttgart: Metzler, 1984.
vi, 203 p.   PT3707.K64 1984
Bibliography: p. 192-203.

1547

Liersch, Werner. Die Liedermacher und die Niedermacher: etwas
Umgang mit Literatur. Halle: Mitteldeutscher Verlag, 1982.
138 p.   PT3706.L54 1982
Includes bibliographical references.

1548

Literarisches Leben in der DDR 1945 bis 1960: Literaturkonzepte
und Leseprogramme/ von einem Autorenkollektiv, Ingeborg
Münz-Koenen (Leitung). Berlin: Akademie-Verlag, 1979. 347 p.
                                    PT3716.L47
Includes bibliographical references and index.

1549

Die Literatur der DDR/ herausgegeben von Hans-Jürgen Schmitt.
München: Hanser, 1983. 588 p.   PT85.H33 Bd.11
Includes indexes.
Bibliography: p. 509-529.

1550

Literatur der DDR in den siebziger Jahren/ herausgegeben von
P.U. Hohendahl und P. Herminghouse. Frankfurt am Main:
Suhrkamp, 1983. 293 p.   PT3705.L58 1983
   Includes bibliographical references.

1551

Literatur im geteilten Deutschland/ herausgegeben von Paul
Gerhard Klussmann und Heinrich Mohr. Bonn: Bouvier, 1980.
viii, 166 p. (Jahrbuch zur Literatur in der DDR; Bd. 1)
                                          PT3701.L49 1980
   Includes index.
   Bibliography: p. 142–159.

1552

Mannack, Eberhard. Zwei deutsche Literaturen?: zu G. Grass,
U. Johnson, H. Kant, U. Plenzdorf und C. Wolf: mit einer
Bibliographie der schönen Literatur in der DDR (1968–1974).
Kronberg: Athenäum-Verlag, 1977. 142 p.   PT3708.M35
   Bibliography: p. 103–142.

1553

Sander, Hans-Dietrich. Geschichte der Schönen Literatur in der
DDR; ein Grundriss. Freiburg: Rombach, 1972. 354 p.
                                          PT3705.S25
   Includes bibliographical references.

1554

Taylor Institution. Library. East German literature: a catalogue
of the Library's holdings. Oxford: Taylor Institution Library,
1979. 67 p.   Z2250.T39 1979

1555

Wortmeldungen zur DDR-Literatur/ herausgegeben von Eberhard
Günther. Halle: Mitteldeutscher Verlag, 1984. 188 p.
                                          PT3716.W67 1984

1556

Writings beyond the wall: literature from the German Democratic
Republic/ edited by Edward Mackinnon, Gina Kalla, and John
Green. London: Artry Publications, Distributed by Central
Books, 1980. 112 p.: ill.   PT1113.W7

1557

Zimmermann, Peter. Industrieliteratur der DDR: vom Helden der Arbeit zum Planer und Leiter. Stuttgart: Metzler, 1984. vii, 363 p.   PT3728.Z54 1984
  Includes index.
  Bibliography: p. 336–357.

Individual Authors

1558

Becker, Jurek. Aller Welt Freund. Frankfurt am Main: Suhrkamp, 1982. 185 p.   MLCS 82/4112 (P)

1559

————. Der Boxer. Rostock: Hinstorff, 1976. 303 p.
                    PT2662.E294 B68

1560

————. Bronsteins Kinder. Frankfurt am Main: Suhrkamp, 1986. 302 p.   MLCS 86/5835 (P)

1561

————. Irreführung der Behörden. Rostock: Hinstorff, 1973. 298 p.   PT2662.E294 I7 1973b

1562

————. Jakob der Lügner. Berlin: Aufbau-Verlag, 1969. 269 p.
                    PT2662.E294 J3

1563

————. Jacob the liar. New York: Harcourt Brace Jovanovich, 1975. vii, 266 p.   PZ4.B3952 Jac3
  Translation of: Jakob der Lügner.

1564

————. Nach der ersten Zukunft. Frankfurt am Main: Suhrkamp, 1980. 271 p.   PT2662.E394 N3

1565
————. Schlaflose Tage. Frankfurt am Main: Suhrkamp, 1978.
157 p.   PT2662.E2943

1566
————. Sleepless days. New York: Harcourt Brace Jovanovich.
1979. 132 p.   PZ4.B3952 S1
Translation of: Schlaflose Tage.

****

1567
Biermann, Wolf. Affenfels und Barrikade: Gedichte, Lieder,
Balladen. Köln: Kiepenheuer & Witsch, 1986. 162 p.: ill.
MLCM 87/406 (P)

1568
————. Deutschland: ein Wintermärchen. Berlin: Wagenbach,
1972. 67 p.: front., music.   PT2662.I4 D4

1569
————. Der Dra-Dra. Berlin: Wagenbach, 1970. Score, 137 p.:
ill.   M1500.B595 D7 (Case)

1570
————. Die Drahtharfe. Berlin: Wagenbach, 1965. 77 p.
PT2662.I4 D7

1571
————. Für meine Genossen. Berlin: Wagenbach, 1972. 91 p.
M1734.B59 F8

1572
————. Das Märchen vom kleinen Herrn Moritz. München:
Parabel-Verlag, 1972. 17 l.: ill.   PZ33.B434

1573
————. Verdrehte Welt—das seh' ich gerne. Köln: Kiepenheuer
& Witsch, 1982. 195 p.: ill., music.   PT26562.I4 V4 1982

1574

————. Nachlass. Köln: Kiepenheuer & Witsch, 1977. 479 p.: ill.,
music.   PT2662. I4 N3

1575

————. The wire harp: ballads, poems, songs. New York: Harcourt,
Brace & World, 1968. 98 p.: ill.   PT2662.I4 D713 1968

1576

————. Wolf Biermann: poems and ballads. London: Pluto Press,
1977. 100 p.: music.   PT2662.I4 A6 1977
Parallel German and English texts.

1577

Biermann und die Folgen/ Günter Kertzscher . . . et al. Berlin:
Verlag Europäische Ideen, 1977. 57 p.   PT3707.B5

1578

Exil: die Ausbürgerung Wolf Biermanns aus der DDR: eine
Dokumentation/ herausgegeben von Peter Roos, unter Mitarbeit
von Armin Broeker und Carla Boulboulle; mit einem Vorwort
von Günter Wallraff. Köln: Kiepenheuer & Witsch, 1977.
319 p.: ill.   PT2662.I4 Z65
Includes bibliographical references.

1579

Laursen, Peter Busk. Om Wolf Biermanns sange og om hans
udvisning: socialistisk opposition i DDR. Arhus: Publimus, 1977.
131 p.: ill., facsims.   ML420.B53 L36
Danish and/or German.
Bibliography of works by and about W. Biermann:
p. 126–128.

1580

A Matter for our comment. Berlin: Panorama DDR, 1976 or 1977.
26 p.   JN3971.5.A92 M39 1976
Deals with Wolf Biermann's loss of DDR citizenship.

1581

Meier-Lenz, D. P. Heinrich Heine, Wolf Biermann: Deutschland,
2 Wintermärchen: ein Werkvergleich. Bonn: Bouvier, 1977.
158 p. (Abhandlungen zur Kunst-, Musik- und Literaturwissenschaft; Bd. 246)   PT2342.M4
Includes bibliographical references and index.

1582

Posadas, J. The singer Biermann, the function of criticism and the
construction of socialism. London: Revolutionary Workers Party
(Trotskyist), 1977. 1, 6, 1 p.   HX44.P6373

1583

Three contemporary German poets: Wolf Biermann, Sarah Kirsch,
Reiner Kunze. Leicester: Leicester University Press, 1985. 96 p.:
ill.   PT1174.T47 1985
English and German.
Includes indexes.
Bibliography: p. 30–32.

1584

Über Wolf Biermann. Berlin: Verlag Europäische Ideen, 1977.
166 p.   PT2662.I4 Z92
„Europäische Ideen, Sonderheft.''

1585

Wolf Biermann: Liedermacher und Sozialist/ herausgegeben von
Thomas Rothschild. Reinbek bei Hamburg: Rowohlt, 1976.
251 p.   PT2662.I4 Z97
Bibliography: p. 193–245.

****

1586

Braun, Volker. Berichte von Hinze und Kunze. Frankfurt am
Main: Suhrkamp, 1983. 89 p.   PT2662.R34 B4 1983

1587

———. Es genügt nicht die einfache Wahrheit. Frankfurt am
Main: Suhrkamp, 1976. 149 p.   PT2662.R34 E8
Includes bibliographical references.

1588

————. Gegen die symmetrische Welt. Frankfurt am Main: Suhrkamp, 1974. 90 p. PT2662.R34 G44

1589

————. Guevara, oder, Der Sonnenstaat. Wiesbaden: Drei Lilien, 1983. 67 p.: ill. (some col.). PT2662.R34 G8 1983

1590

————. Hinze-Kunze-Roman. Frankfurt am Main: Suhrkamp, 1985. 198 p. MLCS 86/1136 (P)

1591

————. Die Kipper; Hinze und Kunze; Tinka: 3 Stücke. Berlin: Henschelverlag, 1975. 208 p. PT2662.R34 A19 1975

1592

————. Kriegserklärung. Halle/Saale: Mitteldeutscher Verlag, 1967. 73 p.: ill. DS557.A61 B7

1593

————. Provokation für mich. Halle/Saale: Mitteldeutscher Verlag, 1965. 77 p. PT2662.R34 P7 1965

1594

————. Der Stoff zum Leben. Pfaffenweiler: Pfaffenweiler Presse, 1977. 32 p. (on double leaves): ill. PT2662.R34 S78
   Limited ed. of 500 copies. This is no. 226, signed by the author and artist.
   Includes bibliographical references.

1595

————. Stücke. Berlin: Henschelverlag, 1983. 375 p.
  PT2662.R34 A19 1983

1596

————. Training des aufrechten Gangs. Halle/Saale: Mitteldeutscher Verlag, 1979. 80 p. PT2662.R34 T7
   Includes bibliographical references.

1597

————. Das ungezwungne Leben Kasts. Frankfurt am Main:
Suhrkamp, 1979. 190 p.   MLCS 86/7049 (P)

1598

————. Unvollendete Geschichte. Frankfurt am Main: Suhrkamp,
1977. 97 p.   PT2662.R34 U55

1599

————. Vorläufiges. Frankfurt am Main: Suhrkamp, 1966. 85 p.
                                               PT2662.R34 V6

1600

————. Wir und nicht sie. Halle, Leipzig: Mitteldeutscher Verlag,
1979. 75 p.   MLCS 80/3421

1601

Cosentino, Christine. Zur Lyrik Volker Brauns. Königstein/Ts.:
    Forum Academicum, 1984. 169 p. (Hochschulschriften
    Literaturwissenschaft; 59)   PT2662.R34 Z62 1984
        Bibliography: p. 166–169.

1602

Im Querschnitt Volker Braun: Gedichte, Prosa, Stücke, Aufsätze/
    herausgegeben von Holger J. Schubert. Halle: Mitteldeutscher
    Verlag, 1978. 345 p., 8 leaves of plates: ill.
                                       PT2662.R34 A6 1978
        Bibliography of works by and about the author: p. 341–343.

1603

Profitlich, Ulrich. Volker Braun: Studien zu seinem dramatischen
    und erzählerischen Werk. München: Fink, 1985. 136 p.
                                       PT2662.R34 Z8 1985
        Includes index.
        Bibliography: p. 131–136.

1604

Rosellini, Jay. Volker Braun. München: Beck, Edition Text +
    Kritik, 1983. 200 p. (Autorenbücher; 31)
                                       PT2662.R34 Z85 1983
        Bibliography: p. 187–200.

1605

Volker Braun. München: Beck, Edition Text + Kritik, 1977. 65 p.
(Text + Kritik; Heft 55) PN4.T45 Heft 55
Bibliography of works by and about V. Braun: p. 58–64.

1606

Wallace, Ian. Volker Braun: Forschungsbericht. Amsterdam:
Rodopi, 1986. 132 p.: ill. (Forschungsberichte zur DDR-
Literatur; 3) PT2662.R34 Z97 1986
Bibliography: p. 81–132.

* * * * * * * * * * * * * * * * * * *

1607

Fries, Fritz Rudolf. Alexanders neue Welten: ein akademischer
Kolportageroman aus Berlin. Leipzig: Reclam, 1985, c1982.
286 p. MLCS 86/3655 (P)

1608

————. Alle meine Hotel Leben: Reisen 1957–1979. Berlin,
Weimar: Aufbau-Verlag, 1980. 197 p. MLCS 81/249

1609

————. Bemerkungen anhand eines Fundes, oder, Das Mädchen
aus der Flasche: Texte zur Literatur. Berlin: Aufbau-Verlag,
1985. 332 p. PT3716.F75 1985

1610

————. Erlebte Landschaft: Bilder aus Mecklenburg. Rostock:
Hinstorff, 1979. xxxii, 160 p.: chiefly ill. (some col.).
DD801.M34 F74 1979

1611

————. Der Fernsehkrieg. Rostock: Hinstorff, 1975. 143 p.
PT2666.R53 F4 1975

1612

————. Hörspiele. Rostock: Hinstorff, 1984. 211 p.
MLCS 84/12227 (P)

1613

————. Das Luft-Schiff: biografische Nachlässe zu den Fantasien
meines Grossvaters. Rostock: Hinstorff, 1974. 400 p.
PT2666.R53 L8

1614

————. Mein spanisches Brevier, 1976–1977. Rostock: Hinstorff,
1979. 201 p.   PT2666.R53 M44

1615

————. Das nackte Mädchen auf der Strasse. Frankfurt am Main:
Suhrkamp, 1980. 184 p.   PT2666.R53 S44 1980
   Originally published under title: Der Seeweg nach Indien.
1978.

1616

————. The road to Oobliadooh. New York: McGraw-Hill, 1968.
246 p.   PZ4.F9157 Ro
   Translation of: Der Weg nach Oobliadooh.

1617

————. Seestücke. 3. veränderte Aufl. Berlin: Betriebsschule Rudi
Arndt, 1980, c1973. 132 p.: ill.   MLCS 87/1394 (P)

1618

————. Der Seeweg nach Indien. Leipzig: Reclam, 1978. 196 p.
                                                PT2666.R53 S44 1978

1619

————. Verlegung eines mittleren Reiches. Frankfurt am Main:
Suhrkamp, 1984. 220 p.   MLCS 86/5394 (P)

1620

————. Der Weg nach Oobliadooh. Frankfurt am Main:
Suhrkamp, 1975. 231 p.   PT2666.R53 W4 1975

****

1621

Fuchs, Jürgen. Gedächtnisprotokolle. Reinbek bei Hamburg:
Rowohlt, 1977. 117 p.   PT2666.U272 G4

1622

————. Einmischung in eigene Angelegenheiten: gegen Krieg und
verlogenen Frieden. Reinbek bei Hamburg: Rowohlt, 1984.
190 p.   PT2666.U272 E5 1984
   Bibliography: p. 190.

1623
————. Fassonschnitt. Reinbek bei Hamburg: Rowohlt, 1984.
383 p.   PT2666.U272 Z465 1984

1624
————. Die Fraktionen der Jungsozialisten: Reformisten, Stamokaps,
Antirevisionisten: Darstellung und Kritik. Erlangen: Union
Aktuell, 1979. 157 p.   HX274.F8
Bibliography: p. 133–139.

1625
————. Pappkameraden. Reinbek bei Hamburg: Rowohlt, 1981.
88 p.   PT2666.U272 P3 1981

1626
————. Tagesnotizen. Reinbek bei Hamburg: Rowohlt, 1979.
79 p.   MLCS 84/10711 (P)

1627
————. Vernehmungsprotokolle: November '76–September '77.
Reinbek bei Hamburg: Rowohlt, 1978. 133 p.
                                    HV6248.F823 A35
Originally published in 1977 as a series in „Der Spiegel" under
title: Du sollst zerbrechen.

* * * * * * * * * * * * * * * * * * *

1628
Fühmann, Franz. Androklus und der Löwe. Berlin: Kinderbuchverlag, 1966. 78 p.   PZ33.F776

1629
————. Bagatelle, rundum positiv. Frankfurt am Main: Suhrkamp,
1978. 109 p.   PT2611.U436 B3

1630
————. Barlach in Güstrow. Frankfurt am Main: Röderberg-
Verlag, 1977. 98 p.: ill.   PT2611.U436 B37

1631

————. Böhmen am Meer. Rostock: Hinstorff, 1962. 52 p.: ill.
PT2611.U436 B6 (Rare Bk Coll)

1632

————. The car with the yellow star: fourteen days out of two
decades. Berlin: Seven Seas, 1968. 174 p.   PZ4.F95 Car
Translation of: Das Judenauto.

1633

————. Die Elite. Zürich: Diogenes-Verlag, 1970. 318 p.
PT2611.U436 E4

1634

————. Erfahrungen und Widersprüche: Versuche über Literatur.
Rostock: Hinstorff, 1975. 222 p.   PT403.F8

1635

————. Erzählungen, 1955–1975. Rostock: Hinstorff, 1977. 551 p.
PT2611.U436 E7

1636

————. Galina Ulanowa. Berlin: Henschelverlag, 1961. 80 p.: ill.,
ports.   GV1785.U4 F8

1637

————. Gedanken zu Georg Trakls Gedicht. Leipzig: Reclam,
1985, c1981. 98 p.   PT2642.R22 A115 1985 Bd. 2

1638

————. Gedichte und Nachdichtungen. Rostock: Hinstorff, 1978.
344 p.   PT2611.U436 G4

1639

————. Der Geliebte der Morgenröte. Rostock: Hinstorff, 1979,
c1978. 62 p.: ill.   MLCS 84/12536 (P)

1640

————. Grafik, Zeichnungen, Plastik, Dokumente. Rostock: Hinstorff, 1967. 215 p.

NB588.B35 F8 1967

1641

————. Das Hölzerne Pferd: die Sage vom Untergang Trojas und von den Irrfahrten des Odysseus, nach Homer und anderen Quellen neu erzählt. Recklinghausen: Paulus Verlag, 1968. 339 p.: col. ill. PA4029.Z5 F8

1642

————. Irrfahrt und Heimkehr des Odysseus; Prometheus; Der Geliebte der Morgenröte und andere Erzählungen. Rostock: Hinstorff, 1980. 381 p. PT2611.U436 A6 1980

1643

————. Die Irrfahrten des Odysseus; die Sage vom Untergang Trojas und von der Heimkehr des Odysseus. Recklinghausen: Bitter, 1971. 339 p.: col. ill. PZ34.1.F78

1644

————. Der Jongleur im Kino: oder. Neuwied: Luchterhand, 1971, c1970. 150 p. PT2611.U436 J6 1971

1645

————. Das Judenauto; Kabelkran und blauer Peter; Zweiundzwanzig Tage: oder, die Hälfte des Lebens. Rostock: Hinstorff, 1979. 519 p. PT2611.U436 J79

1646

————. Das Judenauto: vierzehn Tage aus zwei Jahrzehnten. Berlin: Aufbau-Verlag, 1962. 184 p. PT2611.U436 J8

1647

————. Kirke und Odysseus: ein Ballett. Rostock: Hinstorff, 1984. 52 p.: 5 ill. PT2611.U436 K5 1984

1648

————. König Ödipus. Erzählungen, 1954–1965. Frankfurt am Main: Fischer, 1972. 189 p. PT2611.U436 K6 1972

1649

————. Die Literatur der Kesselrings: ein Pamphlet. Berlin: Verlag der Nation, 1954. 55 p. DD247.K45 F8 1954

1650

―――. Lustiges Tier ABC. Berlin: Kinderbuchverlag, 1964.
68 p.: col. ill.   MLCM 87/407 (P)

1651

―――. Das Nibelungenlied. Berlin: Verlag Neues Leben, 1971.
210 p.: col. ill.   PZ14.1.F8

1652

―――. Pavlos Papierbuch und andere Erzählungen. Berlin:
Aufbau-Verlag, 1982. 190 p.   PT2611.U436 P3 1982

1653

―――. Prometheus: die Titanenschlacht. Berlin: Kinderbuchverlag, 1974. 299 p.: ill.   BL820.P68 F83

1654

―――. Reineke Fuchs. Köln: Middelhauve, 1971. 73 p.: col. ill.
PZ34.2.F8

1655

―――. Saians-fiktschen. Leipzig: Reclam, 1985. 156 p.
MLCS 86/1789 (P)

1656

―――. Die Schatten. Mit den Gedenkreden von Christa Wolf und
Uwe Kolbe. Hamburg: Hoffmann und Campe, 1986. 237 p.
PT2611.U436 A6 1986

1657

―――. Shakespeare-Märchen, für Kinder erzählt. Berlin: Kinderbuchverlag, 1968. 224 p.: col. ill., col. port.   PZ34.F77

1658

―――. Der Sturz des Engels: Erfahrungen mit Dichtung.
Hamburg: Hoffmann und Campe, 1982. 277 p.
PT2611.U436 Z88 1982
Includes bibliographical references.

1659

―――. Die Suche nach dem wunderbunten Vögelchen. Berlin:
Kinderbuchverlag, 1964. 91 p.: col. ill.   PZ33.F78 1964

1660

————. Das Tierschiff: die schönsten Tiermärchen aus aller Welt
für Kinder. Bayreuth: Loewes Verlag, 1970. 284 p.: ill.

PZ36.3.F8 1970

1661

————. Twenty-two days: or, Half a lifetime. Berlin: Seven Seas
Publishers, 1980. 258 p. PT2611.U436 Z45413 1980

1662

————. Die Verteidigung der Reichenberger Turnhalle. Stuttgart:
Reclam, 1977. 79 p. PT2611.U436 V47
Includes bibliographical references.

————

1663

Der Wahrheit nachsinnen, viel Schmerz. Leipzig: Reclam, 1985,
c1981. 2 v. PT2642.R22 A115 1985
Franz Fühmann has contributed to this work.
Includes index.

1664

Weise, Hilde. Franz Fühmann. Berlin: Berliner Stadtbibliothek,
1972. 26 p. Z8317.86.W45
This is a bibliography.

****

1665

Hacks, Peter. Adam und Eva: Komödie in einem Vorspiel und
drei Akten. Düsseldorf: Claassen, 1976. 111 p.: col. ill.

PT2668.A272 A65 1976

1666

————. Der Affe Oswald. München: Parabel, 1971. 44 p.: col. ill.

PZ36.3.H22

1667

————. Amphitryon. Komödie in drei Akten. Berlin: Eulenspiegel,
1969. 102 p. PT2615.A238 A8

1668
————. Ausgewählte Dramen 1. Berlin, Weimar: Aufbau-Verlag,
1974. 449 p.   PT2615.A238 A95 1974

1669
————. Ausgewählte Dramen 2. Berlin, Weimar: Aufbau-Verlag,
1976, 498 p.   PT2668.A272 A19 1976

1670
————. Der Bär auf dem Försterball. Köln: Middelhauve, 1972.
32 p. (chiefly col. ill.).   PZ36.3.H23

1671
————. The bear at the hunters' ball. Reading, Mass.: Addison-
Wesley, 1976. 32 p.: col. ill.   PZ7.H1146 Be
Translation of: Der Bär auf dem Försterball.

1672
————. Die Binsen; Fredegunde: zwei Dramen. Berlin: Aufbau-
Verlag, 1985. 189 p.   MLCS 86/3488 (P)

1673
————. Die Dinge in Buta. Berlin: Berliner Handpresse, 1974.
37 p.: col. ill.   PT2615.A238 D55
Limited edition of 300 copies. This is no. 198.

1674
————. Essais. Leipzig: Reclam, 1984, c1983. 479 p.
                                              MLCS 87/2 (P)

1675
————. Der Flohmarkt: Gedichte für Kinder. Zürich, Einsiedeln,
Köln: Benziger, 1973. 155 p.: ill.   PZ34.3.H23

1676
————. Historien und Romanzen: Urpoesie, oder, Das scheintote
Kind. Berlin: Aufbau-Verlag, 1985. 113 p.   MLCS 86/3154 (P)

1677
————. Ich trug eine Rose im Haar: Lieder zu Stücken. München:
Langen-Müller, 1981, c1978. 123 p.: col. ill.
                                              PT2668.A272 L5 1981

1678
———. Das Jahrmarktsfest zu Plundersweilern: Rosie träumt.
Berlin: Aufbau-Verlag, 1976. 129 p.   PT2668.A272 J3

1679
———. Die Katze wäscht den Omnibus. Hanau/M.: Dausien,
1973. 6 l.: ill.   PZ33.H107 Kat

1680
———. Lieder, Briefe, Gedichte. Wuppertal: Hammer, 1974.
135 p.   PT2668.A2172 Z47 1974

1681
———. Lieder zu Stücken. Berlin: Eulenspiegel, 1978. 123 p.: col.
ill.   MLCS 86/7086 (P)

1682
———. Margarete in Aix. Berlin: Eulenspiegel Verlag, 1974.
97 p., 4 leaves of plates: col. ill.   PT2668.A272 M3 1974

1683
———. Die Massgaben der Kunst: gesammelte Aufsätze.
Düsseldorf: Claassen, 1977. 407 p.   PT2668.A272 Z474 1977

1684
———. Meta Morfoss und Ein Märchen für Claudias Puppe.
Berlin: Kinderbuchverlag, 1975. 59 p.: col. ill.   PZ33.H1067

1685
———. Oper. Berlin: Aufbau-Verlag, 1975. 307 p.
                                   PT2668.A272 A6 1975

1686
———. Pandora: Drama nach J. W. von Goethe: mit einem Essay.
Berlin, Weimar: Aufbau-Verlag, 1981. 137 p.   MLCS 81/247

1687
———. Peter Hacks Katharinchen ging spazieren. Köln: Middelhauve, 1973. 28 p.: chiefly ill. (col.).   PZ33.H107 Pe

1688

————. Das Poetische: Ansätze zu einer postrevolutionären Dramaturgie. Frankfurt am Main: Suhrkamp, 1972. 145 p.

PN1811.H3

1689

————. Polly oder Die Bataille am Bluewater Creek. Berlin: Henschelverlag, 1966. 70 p.   PT2615.A238 P6

1690

————. Der Schuhu und die fliegende Prinzessin. Frankfurt am Main: Insel-Verlag, 1973. 67 p.   PZ34.H234

1691

————. Sechs Dramen. Düsseldorf: Claassen, 1978. 444 p.

PT2668.A272 A19 1978

1692

————. Stücke. Leipzig: Reclam, 1978. 348 p.

MLCS 84/11731 (P)

1693

————. Das Theaterstück des Biedermeier, 1815–1840. München: Printed by Author, 1951. v, 159, 7 l.   PT658.H3

1694

————. Das Windloch; Das Turmverlies: Geschichten von Henriette und Onkel Titus. Berlin: Eulenspiegel Verlag, 1978. 207 p.: ill.   PZ33.H108

1695

————. Zwei Bearbeitungen: ,,Der Frieden,'' nach Aristophanes. Frankfurt am Main: Suhrkamp, 1963. 146 p.

PT2615.A238 Z45

1696

————. Zwei Märchen. Leipzig: Reclam, 1985. 116 p.: ill.

PT2668.A272 Z456 1985

1697

Di Napoli, Thomas. The Children's literature of Peter Hacks. New
York: Lang, 1987. 321 p. (East German studies = DDR-Studien;
vol. 2)   PT2668.A272 Z64 1987
    Includes index: p. 319-321.
    Bibliography: p. 307-318.

1698

Haffner, Herbert. Heinrich Leopold Wagner, Peter Hacks, Die
Kindermörderin: Original und Bearbeitungen im Vergleich.
Paderborn: F. Schöningh, 1982. 83 p.: ill. (Modellanalysen
Literatur; Bd. 8)   PT2551.W3 A733 1982
    Bibliography: p. 81-83.

1699

Heitz, Raymond. Peter Hacks: théatre et socialisme. Berne, New
York: Lang, 1984. xi, 283 p. (Contacts. Série 1, Theatrica; 1)
    PT2668.A272 Z65 1984
    Abridged version of the author's thesis (doctoral)—Université
de Nancy.
    Summaries in German and English.
    Includes index.
    Bibliography: p. 270-278.

1700

Jäger, Andrea. Der Dramatiker Peter Hacks: vom Produktionsstück
zur Klassizität. Marburg: Hitzeroth, 1986. 14, 319 p. (Mar-
burger Studien zur Literatur; Bd. 2)
    PT2668.A272 Z67 1986
    Includes index.
    Bibliography: p. 308-319.

1701

Scheid, Judith R. „Enfant terrible" of contemporary East German
drama: Peter Hacks in his role as adaptor and innovator. Bonn:
Bouvier, 1977. vi, 184 p. (Studien zur Germanistik, Anglistik
und Komparatistik; Bd. 65)   PT2668.A272 Z83 1977
    Bibliography: p. 174-184.

1702

Schleyer, Winfried. Die Stücke von Peter Hacks: Tendenzen,
Themen, Theorien. Stuttgart: Klett, 1976. 201 p.

(Literaturwissenschaft, Gesellschaftswissenschaft; Bd. 20)
                                        PT2668.A272 Z85 1976
    Originally presented as the author's thesis, Universität
Erlangen-Nürnberg, Erlangen, 1975.
    Bibliography: p. 187–201.

1703

Schmidt, Gertrud. Peter Hacks in BRD und DDR: ein
    Rezeptionsvergleich. Köln: Pahl-Rugenstein, 1980. iv, 296 p.
                                        PT2668.A272 Z86
        Bibliography: p. 287–296.

1704

Trilse, Christoph. Peter Hacks: Leben und Werk. Westberlin:
    DEB, 1980. 288 p.: ill.   PT2615.A238 Z9 1980
    Includes bibliographical references.

1705

Zum Drama in der DDR: Heiner Müller und Peter Hacks/
    herausgegeben von Judith R. Scheid. Stuttgart: Klett, 1981.
    225 p.: ill. (Literaturwissenschaft—Gesellschaftswissenschaft; 53)
                                        PT3721.Z85 1981
        Cover title: Interpretationen zum Drama in der DDR.
    Bibliography: p. 218–224.

****

1706

Hermlin, Stephan. Abendlicht. Berlin: Wagenbach, 1979. 120 p.
                                        PT2617.E716 A63

1707

————. Ansichten über einige Bücher und Schriftsteller. Erw.
    bearb. Ausg. Magdeburg: Volk und Welt, 1947. 163 p.
                                        PN504.H4 1947

1708

————. Aufsätze, Reportagen, Reden, Interviews. München:
    Hanser, 1980. 273 p.   PT2617.E716 A6 1980
    Includes bibliographical references.

1709

————. Äusserungen: 1944–1982. Berlin: Aufbau-Verlag, 1983.
454 p.   PT2617.E716 A6 1983
Includes bibliographical references.

1710

————. Bestimmungsorte: fünf Erzählungen. Berlin: Wagenbach,
1985. 76 p.   MLCS 86/7923 (P)

1711

————. Erzählungen. 2., erw. Aufl. Berlin, Weimar: Aufbau-
Verlag, 1970. 269 p.   PT2617.E716 A15 1970

1712

————. Evening light. San Francisco: Fjord Press, 1983. 119 p.
                                 PT2617.E716 A6313 1983
Translation of: Abendlicht.

1713

————. Ferne Nähe. Berlin: Aufbau-Verlag, 1954. 132 p.: ill.
                                         DS710.H63

1714

————. Gedichte. Leipzig: Reclam, 1963. 133 p.
                                 MLCS 84/15084 (P)

1715

————. Gedichte und Prosa. Berlin: Wagenbach, 1965. 80 p.
                                 PT2617.E716 A6 1965

1716

————. Gesammelte Gedichte. München: Hanser, 1979. 110 p.
                                 MLCM 84/5377 (P)

1717

————. Der Kampf um eine deutsche Nationalliteratur. Berlin:
Deutscher Schriftsteller-Verband, 1952. 30 p. DD257.2.H42

1718

————. Lebensfrist: gesammelte Erzählungen. Berlin:
Wagenbach, 1980. 206 p.   MLCS 81/212

1719

————. Lektüre: 1960–1971. Frankfurt am Main: Suhrkamp, 1974. 223 p.   PT107.H353 1974

1720

————. Der Leutnant Yorck von Wartenburg. Frankfurt am Main: Suhrkamp, 1974. 115 p.   PT2617.A716 A6 1974

1721

————. Reise eines Malers in Paris. Wiesbaden: Limes-Verlag, 1947. 63 p.   PT2617.E716 R4

1722

————. Russische Eindrücke. Herausgegeben im Auftrag der Gesellschaft zum Studium der Kultur der Sowjetunion. Berlin: Verlag Kultur und Fortschritt, 1948. 75 p.   DK28.H4

1723

————. Scardanelli. Leipzig: Insel-Verlag, 1971. 63 p.
PT2617.E716 S3 1971

1724

————. Die Städte. München, Esslingen: Bechtle, 1966. 78 p.
PT2617.E716 S73

1725

————. Städte-Balladen. Leipzig: Reclam, 1975. 72 p.: 8 ill.
PT2617.E716 A17 1975

1726

————. Die Strassen der Furcht: Gedichte. Singen: Oberbadischer Verlag, 1947. 84 p.   PT2617.E716 S75

1727

————. Die Zeit der Gemeinsamkeit. In einer dunklen Welt. Zwei Erzählungen. Berlin: Wagenbach, 1966. 67 p.
PT2617.E716 Z4 1966

1728
Stephan Hermlin Bibliographie: zum 70. Geburtstag/ bearbeitet
von Maritta Rost und Rosemarie Geist. Leipzig: Reclam, 1985.
280 p.   Z8398.683.S73 1985
  Includes indexes.

1729
Stephan Hermlin, Texte, Materialien, Bilder/ zusammengestellt
von Hubert Witt. Leipzig: Reclam, 1985. 327 p.: 67 ill., ports.
                                                  PT2617.E716 Z89 1985

****

1730
Heym, Stefan. Ahasver. München: Bertelsmann, 1981. 319 p.
                                                  MLCS 84/2460 (P)

1731
————. Atta Troll: Versuch einer Analyse. München:
Bertelsmann, 1983. 110 p.   PT2309.A83 H49 1983
  Bibliography: p. 109–110.

1732
————. Die Augen der Vernunft. Leipzig: List, 1966. 670 p.
                                                  PS3515.E957 E95 1966

1733
————. Auskunft: neue Prosa aus der DDR. Reinbek bei Hamburg:
Rowohlt, 1977–1981, c1978. 2 v.   PT3740.H4 1977

1734
————. Der bittere Lorbeer. Roman unserer Zeit. München: List,
1966. 959 p.   PS3515.E957 C75

1735
————. The cannibals and other stories. Berlin: Seven Seas Publishers, 1958. 136 p.   PZ3.H5175 Can

1736
————. Casimir und Cymbelinchen. Berlin: Kinderbuchverlag,
1966. 59 p.   PZ34.H47

1737
————. Collin. Secaucus, N.J.: Stuart, 1980. 315 p.
                                                PT2617.E948 C613 1980

1738
————. The cosmic age, a report. New Delhi: Sinha, 1959. 116 p.
                                                Q127.R9 H4313

1739
————. Cymbelinchen: oder, Der Ernst des Lebens: vier Märchen
für kluge Kinder. München: Bertelsmann, 1975. 76 p.: ill.
                                                PZ34.H473

1740
————. Erich Huckniesel und das fortgesetze Rotkäppchen. Berlin:
Berliner Handpresse, 1977. 33 p.: col. ill.   MLCF 86/2 (P)

1741
————. The eyes of reason. Boston: Little, Brown, 1951. 433 p.
                                                PZ3.H5175 Ey

1742
————. Five days in June. Buffalo, N.Y.: Prometheus Books,
1978. 352 p.   PZ3.H5175 Fi 1978
    Translation of: 5 Tage im Juni.

1743
————. Fünf Tage im Juni. München, Gütersloh, Wien: Bertelsmann, 1974. 382 p.   PT2617.E946 F8

1744
————. Goldsborough. München: Goldmann, 1978, c1953. 542 p.
                                                PS3515.E957 G615 1978

1745
————. Hostages. New York: Putnam, 1942. 362 p.
                                                PZ3.H5175 Ho

1746
————. Im Kopf-sauber: Schriften zum Tage. Leipzig: List, 1954.
    436 p.   DD261.2.H49

1747
——. Keine Angst vor Russlands Bären. Düsseldorf: Brücken-
Verlag, 1955. 205 p.: ill.   DK28.H45

1748
——. The King David report. New York: Putnam, 1973. 254 p.
                                                             PZ3.H5175 Ki3
Translation of: Der König-David-Bericht.

1749
——. Das kosmische Zeitalter: ein Bericht. Berlin: Verlag Tribüne,
1959. 131 p.: ill.   Q171.H6

1750
——. Lassalle. München, Esslingen: Bechtle, 1969. 424 p.
                                                             PS3515.E957 U515

1751
——. The Lenz papers. Berlin: Seven Seas Publishers, 1968.
550 p.: map.   PZ3.H5175 Le4

1752
——. Märchen für kluge Kinder. München: Goldmann, 1984.
105 p.   PT2617.E948 A6 1984

1753
——. Of smiling peace. Boston: Little, Brown, 1944. 364 p.
                                                             PZ3.H5175 Of

1754
——. The queen against Defoe, and other stories. New York:
Hill, 1974. 114 p.: ill.   PZ3.H5175 Qe

1755
——. Die richtige Einstellung und andere Erzählungen. München:
Bertelsmann, 1977, c1976. 269 p.   PT2617.E948 R5 1977

1756
——. Die Schmähschrift oder Königin gegen Defoe. Zürich:
Diogenes-Verlag, 1970. 132 p.: ill.   PT2617.E948 S3

1757

————. Schwarzenberg. München: Bertelsmann, 1984. 309 p.

MLCS 84/10330 (P)

1758

————. Shadows and lights, eight short stories. London: Cassell,
1963. 186 p.   PZ3.H5175 Sh

1759

————. Uncertain friend: a biographical novel. London: Cassel,
1969. 6, 279 p.   PZ3.H5175 Un
    Based on the life of Ferdinand Lassalle.

1760

————. The wandering Jew. New York: Holt, Rinehart and
Winston, 1984, c1983. 298 p.   PT2617.E948 A7313 1984
    Translation of: Ahasver.

————————————

1761

Beiträge zu einer Biographie: eine Freundesgabe für Stefan Heym
    zum 60. Geburtstag am 10. April 1973. München: Kindler,
    1973. 56 p.: ill.   PS3515.E957 Z6

1762

Reden an den Feind: Stefan Heym/ herausgegeben von Peter
    Mallwitz. München: Bertelsmann, 1986. 351 p.

PT2617.E948 A19 1986

****

1763

Huchel, Peter. Ausgewählte Gedichte. Frankfurt am Main:
    Suhrkamp, 1973. 138 p.   PT2617.U3 A95
    Includes bibliographical references.

1764

————. The garden of Theophrastus & other poems. Manchester:
Carcanet Press; Dublin: Raven Arts Press, 1983. 183 p.

PT2617.U3 A24 1983

English and German in parallel texts.

1765

————. Gedichte. Berlin: Aufbau-Verlag, 1948. 100 p.

PT2617.U3 G4

1766

————. Gesammelte Werke in zwei Bänden. Frankfurt am Main: Suhrkamp, 1984. 2 v.: 1 map.   PT2617.U3 A127 1984
Includes bibliographical references and index.
CONTENTS: Bd. 1. Die Gedichte — Bd. 2. Vermischte Schriften.

1767

————. Gezählte Tage. Frankfurt am Main: Suhrkamp, 1973, c1972. 95 p.   PT2617.U3 G45 1973

1768

————. Die neunte Stunde. Frankfurt am Main: Suhrkamp, 1979. 70 p.   PT2617.U3 N4

1769

————. Selected poems. Cheadle, Eng.: Carcanet Press, 1974. ix, 73 p.   PT2617.U3 A24 1974

1770

————. Die Sternenreuse: Gedichte, 1925–1947. München: Piper, 1967. 93 p.   PT2617.U3 S8

————

1771

Peter Huchel/ herausgegeben von Axel Vieregg. Frankfurt am Main: Suhrkamp, 1986. 353 p.   PT2617.U3 Z83 1986
Bibliography of works by and about P. Huchel: p. 326–353.

****

1772

Kant, Hermann. Anrede der Ärztin O. an den Staatsanwalt F. gelegentlich einer Untersuchung und andere Erzählungen. Darmstadt, Neuwied: Luchterhand, 1978. 91 p.

PT2671.A5 A83 1978

1773
————. Die Aula. n. p.: Fischer Bücherei, 1968. 316 p.
PT2671.A5 A9 1969

1774
————. Der Aufenthalt. Leipzig: Reclam, 1986. 533 p.
MLCS 86/5120 (P)

1775
————. Ein bisschen Südsee. Gütersloh: Bertelsmann, 1968.
173 p.   PT2671.A5 B5 1968

1776
————. Bronzezeit: Geschichten aus dem Leben des Buchhalters
Farssmann. Darmstadt: Luchterhand, 1986. 174 p.
PT2671.A5 B7 1986

1777
————. Der dritte Nagel. Berlin: Rütten & Loening, 1981. 185 p.
MLCS 82/4163

1778
————. Das Impressum. Berlin: Rütten & Loening, 1981. 443 p.
MLCS 84/5472 (P)

1779
————. In Stockholm. Berlin: Verlag Volk und Welt, 1971.
238 p.: ill.   DL976.K3

1780
————. Schöne Elise. Leipzig: Reclam, 1983. 194 p.
MLCS 84/10473 (P)

1781
————. Eine Übertretung. Darmstadt, Neuwied: Luchterhand,
1976, c1975. 138 p.   PT2671.A5 U2 1976

1782
————. Zu den Unterlagen: Publizistik, 1957–1980. Berlin,
Weimar: Aufbau-Verlag, 1981. 414 p.   PT2671.A5 A6 1981

1783

Krenzlin, Leonore. Hermann Kant, Leben und Werk. Berlin: Verlag Das Europäische Buch, 1981, c1979. 264 p.: ill.

PT2671.A5 Z75 1981

Includes bibliographical references.

1784

Langenbruch, Theodor. Dialectical humor in Hermann Kant's novel „Die Aula": a study in contemporary East German literature. Bonn: Bouvier, 1975. 131 p. (Abhandlungen zur Kunst-, Musik- und Literaturwissenschaft; Bd. 163)

PT2671.A5 A934

Includes index.
Bibliography: p. 120-121.

****

1785

Kirsch, Rainer. Amt des Dichters: Aufsätze, Rezensionen, Notizen, 1964-1978. Rostock: Hinstorff, 1979. 184 p.: port.

PT2671.I757 A8

1786

————. Ausflug machen: Gedichte. Rostock: Hinstorff, 1980. 75 p.   MLCS 87/2388 (P)

1787

————. Auszog das Fürchten zu lernen: Prosa, Gedichte, Komödie. Reinbek bei Hamburg: Rowohlt, 1978. 261 p.

PT2671.I757 A93

1788

————. Kopien nach Originalen: Portraits aus der DDR: Der Chirurg Professor Schober, der Professor für Schweisstechnik Dr. Gilde, der Philosoph Professor Loeser, Ansicht Rossleben/Unstrut. Berlin: Wagenbach, 1974. 93 p.: ports.

DD261.2.K45

1789

————. Ordnung im Spiegel: Essays, Notizen, Gespräche. Leipzig: Reclam, 1985. 306 p.   PT505.K53 1985

1790

———. Das Wort und seine Strahlung: über Poesie und ihre Übersetzung. Berlin: Aufbau-Verlag, 1976. 119 p.

PN1059.T7 K5

****

1791

Kirsch, Sarah. Conjurations: the poems of Sarah Kirsch. Athens, Ohio: Ohio University Press, 1985. xviii, 197 p.

PT2671.I758 A24 1985

English and German.

Bibliography: p. 196–197.

1792

———. Drachensteigen. Ebenhausen: Langewiesche-Brandt, 1979. 49 p.   PT2671.I758 D7

1793

———. Erdreich. Stuttgart: Deutsche Verlags-Anstalt, 1982. 82 p.

MLCS 84/5923

1794

———. Es war dieser merkwürdige Sommer. Düsseldorf: Berliner Handpresse, 1974. 48 p. on double leaves: col. ill.

PT2671.I758 E7

Limited ed. of 300 copies. This is number 88.

1795

———. Gedichte. Ebenhausen: Langewiesche-Brandt, 1969. 79 p.

PT2671.I759 G4

1796

———. Geschlechtertausch: drei Geschichten über die Umwandlung der Verhältnisse. Darmstadt: Luchterhand, 1980. 127 p.

MLCS 87/1071 (P)

1797

———. Gespräch mit dem Saurier. Berlin: Verlag Neues Leben, 1965. 107 p., 8 leaves of plates: col. ill. MLCS 85/5004 (P)

1798

————. Irrstern. Stuttgart: Deutsche Verlags-Anstalt, 1986. 66 p.
MLCS 86/3542 (P)

1799

————. Katzenleben. Stuttgart: Deutsche Verlags-Anstalt, 1984.
92 p. MLCS 84/9237 (P)

1800

————. Landaufenthalt. Ebenhausen: Langewiesche-Brandt, 1977.
74 p. PT2671.I758 L3 1977

1801

————. La Pagerie. Stuttgart: Deutsche Verlags-Anstalt, 1980.
60 p. MLCS 87/1931 (P)

1802

————. Die Pantherfrau: fünf Erzählungen aus dem Kassetten-
Recorder. Ebenhausen: Langewiesche-Brandt, 1975, c1973.
111 p. PT2671.I758 P3 1975

1803

————. Rückenwind. Ebenhausen: Langewiesche-Brandt, 1977.
74 p. PT2671.I758 R8

1804

————. Die ungeheuren bergehohen Wellen auf See. Berlin: Eulenspiegel Verlag, 1973. 108 p.: ill. PT2671.I758 U5

1805

————. Zaubersprüche. Ebenhausen: Langewiesche-Brandt, 1976,
c1972. 73 p. PT2671.I758 Z2 1976

1806

————. Zwischen Herbst und Winter. Berlin: Kinderbuchverlag,
1975. 12 p.: all col. ill. PZ33.K459

1807
Three contemporary German poets: Wolf Biermann, Sarah Kirsch,
Reiner Kunze/ edited by Peter J. Graves. Leicester: Leicester
University Press, 1985. 96 p.: ill.   PT1174.T47 1985
English and German.
Includes indexes.
Bibliography: p. 30-32.

****

1808
Kunert, Günter. Abtötungsverfahren. München: Hanser, 1980.
92 p.   PT2621.U665 A63 1980

1809
————. Der andere Planet: Ansichten von Amerika. München,
Wien: Hanser, 1975. 207 p.   E169.02.K863 1975

1810
————. Ein anderer K. Berlin: Aufbau-Verlag, 1977. 131 p.
                                          PT2621.U665 A84

1811
————. Die Beerdigung findet in aller Stille statt. München:
Hanser, 1968. 120 p.   PT2621.U665 B4

1812
————. Betonformen. Berlin: Literarisches Colloquium, 1969.
39 p.   PT2621.U665 B45

1813
————. Bücher Nachträge. Berlin: Berliner Handpresse, 1978.
37 p.: 10 col. ill.   PT2621.U665 B8
Limited ed. of 300 copies signed by the author and artists.
This is no. 167.

1814
————. Camera obscura. München, Wien: Hanser, 1978. 136 p.
                                  PT2621.U665 C35 1978

1815

————. Diesseits des Erinnerns. München: Hanser, 1982. 247 p.

PT2621.U665 D5 1982

1816

————. Drei Berliner Geschichten. Berlin, Weimar: Aufbau-Verlag, 1979. 80 p.: 31 ill. PT2621.U665 D7

1817

————. Ein englisches Tagebuch. Berlin, Weimar: Aufbau-Verlag, 1978. 287 p. DA632.K86

1818

————. Gast aus England. München: Hanser, 1973. 157 p.

PT2621.U665 G3

1819

————. Die geheime Bibliothek. Berlin, Weimar: Aufbau-Verlag, 1973. 280 p. PT2621.U665 G4

1820

————. Günter Kunert. Berlin: Verlag Neues Leben, 1968. 31 p.: ill. PT2621.U665 G8

1821

————. Heinrich von Kleist: ein Modell. Berlin: Akademie der Künste, 1978. 36 p. (Anmerkungen zur Zeit; 18)

PT2379.K85

Speech given Nov. 13, 1977 at the Akademie der Künste, Berlin.

1822

————. Im Namen der Hüte. Berlin: Eulenspiegel-Verlag, 1976. 250 p.: ill. PT2621.U665 I4 1976

1823

————. Jeder Wunsch ein Treffer. Velber/ Hannover: Middelhauve, 1976. 76 p.: ill. PZ33.K798

1824

————. Keine Affäre. Berlin: Berliner Handpresse, 1976. 31 p. (on double leaves): 10 col. ill.   PT2621.U665 K4

   Limited ed. of 300 copies signed by the author and artists, this is no. 132.

1825

————. Kinobesuch. Leipzig: Insel-Verlag, 1976. 169 p.
                                                   PT2621.U665 K5

1826

————. Das kleine Aber. Berlin: Aufbau-Verlag, 1975. 120 p.
                                                   PT2621.U665 K6

1827

————. Kramen in Fächern: Geschichten, Parabeln, Merkmale. Berlin: Aufbau-Verlag, 1968. 193 p.   PT2621.U665 K7

1828

————. Kurze Beschreibung eines Momentes der Ewigkeit: kleine Prosa. Leipzig: Reclam, 1980. 181 p.   PT2621.U665 K8

1829

————. Leben und Schreiben. Pfaffenweiler: Pfaffenweiler Presse, 1983. 50 leaves: ill.   PT2621.U665 L4 1983

1830

————. Der Mittelpunkt der Erde. Berlin: Eulenspiegel Verlag, 1975. 118 p.: ill.   PT2621.U665 M5

1831

————. Offener Ausgang. Berlin: Aufbau-Verlag, 1972. 114 p.
                                                   PT2621.U665 O35

1832

————. Ortsangaben. Berlin: Aufbau-Verlag, 1971. 145 p.: ill.
                                                   PT2621.U665 O7

1833

————. Die Schreie der Fledermäuse. München: Hanser, 1979. 383 p.   PT2621.U665 S37

   „Quellenangaben": p. 380–383.

1834
————. Stilleben. München: Hanser, 1983. 111 p.
                                        PT2621.U665 S74 1983

1835
————. Tagträume in Berlin und andernorts. München: Hanser,
1972. 334 p.   PT2621.U665 T33

1836
————. Der ungebetene Gast. Berlin, Weimar: Aufbau-Verlag,
1965. 96 p.   PT23621.U665 U47

1837
————. Unruhiger Schlaf. München: Deutscher Taschenbuch-
Verlag, 1979. 246 p.   MLCS 87/508 (P)

1838
————. Unter diesem Himmel. Berlin: Verlag Neues Leben, 1955.
81 p.   PT2621.U665 U5

1839
————. Unterwegs nach Utopia. München: Hanser, 1977. 96 p.
                                        PT2621.U665 U54

1840
————. Verkündigung des Wetters. München: Hanser, 1966.
91 p.   PT2621.U665 V4

1841
————. Verlangen nach Bomarzo. Leipzig: Reclam, 1978. 73 p.:
12 ill.   PT2621.U665 V42 1978

1842
————. Verspätete Monologe. München, Wien: Hanser, 1981.
202 p.   PT2621.U665 V43

1843
————. Vor der Sintflut: das Gedicht als Arche Noah. München:
Hanser, 1985. 117 p.   PT2621.U665 Z76 1985

1844
————. Warum schreiben?: Notizen zur Literatur. München,
Wien: Hanser, 1976. 296 p.   PT2621.U665 W35
„Quellennachweis'': p. 295–296.

1845
————. Ziellose Umtriebe: Nachrichten vom Reisen und vom
Daheimsein. Berlin, Weimar: Aufbau-Verlag, 1979. 211 p.
                                      PT26212.U665 Z479

1846
————. Zurück ins Paradies. München: Hanser, 1984. 172 p.
                                      MLCS 86/5556 (P)

———————————————

1847
Jonsson, Dieter. Widersprüche, Hoffnungen: Literatur und Kultur-
politik der DDR: die Prosa Günter Kunerts. Stuttgart: Klett-
Cotta, 1978. 202 p. (Literaturwissenschaft, Gesellschaftswissen-
schaft; 36)   PT2621.U665 Z73 1978
Bibliography: p. 194–202.

18481
Kunert lesen/ herausgegeben von Michael Krüger. München,
Wien: Hanser, 1979. 233 p.   PT2621.U665 Z75 1979
Bibliography of G. Kunert's works: 185–222.
''Filmography'': p. 223–229.

****

1849
Kunze, Reiner. Auf eigene Hoffnung. Frankfurt am Main: Fischer,
1981. 111 p.   MLCS 82/1437

1850
————. Eines jeden einziges Leben. Frankfurt: Fischer, 1986.
125 p.   MLCS 86/5850 (P)

1851

———. Der Film Die wunderbaren Jahre: Lesefassung des Drehbuchs. Frankfurt am Main: Fischer, 1979. 143 p.: ill. (some col.). PN1997.W76 1979

1852

———. Gespräch mit der Amsel: Frühe Gedichte, Sensible Wege, Zimmerlautstärke. Frankfurt am Main: Fischer, 1984. 214 p.
MLCS 86/7855 (P)

1853

———. The lovely years. London: Sidgwick and Jackson, 1978. 8, 114 p. PT2671.U5 W813 1978
Translation of: Die wunderbaren Jahre.

1854

———. Der Löwe Leopold: fast Märchen, fast Geschichten. Frankfurt am Main: Fischer, 1970. 81 p. PZ33.K8

1855

———. Reiner Kunze. Berlin: Verlag Neues Leben, 1968. 31 p.
PT2671.U5 R4

1856

———. Sensible Wege: 48 Gedichte und ein Zyklus. Reinbek bei Hamburg: Rowohlt, 1969. 89 p. PT2671.U5 S4

1857

———. Widmungen. Bad Godesberg: Hohwacht-Verlag, 1963. 61 p. PT2671.U5 W5

1858

———. With the volume turned down, and other poems. London: London Magazine Editions, 1973. 48 p. PT2671.U5 A26

1859

———. The wonderful years. New York: Braziller, 1977. 127 p.
DD261.2.K8413
Translation of: Die wunderbaren Jahre.

1860

———. Die wunderbaren Jahre. Frankfurt am Main: Fischer,
1976. 127 p.   PT2671.U5 W8

1861

———. Zimmerlautstärke. Frankfurt am Main: Fischer, 1972.
69 p.   PT2671.U5 Z35

1862

Reiner Kunze: Werk und Wirkung/ herausgegeben von Rudolf
Wolff. Bonn: Bouvier, 1983. 160 p.: ill. (Sammlung Profile;
Bd. 2)   PT2671.U353 Z85 1983
Bibliography: p. 134–159.

1863

Three contemporary German poets: Wolf Biermann, Sarah Kirsch,
Reiner Kunze. Leicester: Leicester University Press, 1985. 96 p.:
ill.   PT1174.T47 1985
English and German.
Includes indexes.
Bibliography: p. 30–32.

****

1864

Loest, Erich. Der Abhang. Berlin: Verlag Neues Leben, 1968.
486 p.   PT2623.O425 A63

1865

———. Durch die Erde ein Riss: ein Lebenslauf. Hamburg:
Hoffmann und Campe, 1981. 413 p.   PT2672.O29 Z47

1866

———. Der elfte Mann. Halle/ Saale: Mitteldeutscher Verlag,
1969. 249 p.   PT2623.O425 E4

1867

———. Es geht seinen Gang: oder, Mühen in unserer Ebene.
Stuttgart: Deutsche Verlags-Anstalt, 1978. 294 p.
                                             PT2623.O425 E75

1868

————. Etappe Rom: 12 Geschichten. Berlin: Verlag Neues Leben, 1978. 360 p.   PT2623.O425 E8 1978

1869

————. Geordnete Rückzüge: Reisefeuilletons. Hannover: Postskriptum, 1984. 119 p.: ill.   PT2623.O425 Z465 1984

1870

————. Herzschlag. Assenheim: BrennGlas, 1984. 51 p.
                                   MLCS 86/2808 (P)

1871

————. Ich war Dr. Lev. Berlin: Eulenspiegel-Verlag, 1976. 331 p.
                                   DD256.5.L6 1976

1872

————. Das Jahr der Prüfung. Halle/ Saale: Mitteldeutscher Verlag, 1954. 393 p.   PT2623.O425 J3

1873

————. Die Mäuse des Dr. Lev. Olten: Walter-Verlag, 1984. 278 p.
                                   MLCS 84/9566 (P)

1874

————. Mit kleinstem Kaliber. Halle/ Saale: Mitteldeutscher Verlag, 1973. 210 p.   PT2672.O29 M5

1875

————. Der Mörder sass im Wembley-Stadion. Halle/ Saale: Mitteldeutscher Verlag, 1967. 237 p.   PT2672.O29 M6

1876

————. Öl für Malta. Berlin: Verlag Neues Leben, 1968. 266 p.
                                   PT2623.O425 O3

1877

————. Die Oma im Schlauchboot. Berlin: Eulenspiegel-Verlag, 1976. 144 p.: ill.   PT2623.O425 O4

1878

―――. Pistole mit sechzehn. Hamburg: Hoffmann und Campe,
1979. 259 p.   PT2672.O29 P5

1879

―――. Rotes Elfenbein. Halle/ Saale: Mitteldeutscher Verlag,
1975. 223 p.   PT2623.O425 R6

1880

―――. Saison in Key West. München: Knaus, 1986. 222 p.
                                            PT2623.O425 Z477 1986

1881

―――. Schattenboxen. Olten: Walter, 1984. 219 p.
                                                    MLCS 87/335 (P)

1882

―――. Swallow, mein wackerer Mustang: Karl-May-Roman.
Hamburg: Hoffmann und Campe, 1980. 419 p.
                                               PT2623.O425 S8 1980

1883

―――. Der vierte Zensor: vom Entstehen und Sterben eines
Romans in der DDR. Köln: Edition Deutschland Archiv im
Verlag Wissenschaft und Politik, 1984. 96 p.
                                               PT2623.O425 V5 1984
    Includes index.
    ,,Bibliographie der in der Bundesrepublik erschienenen Bücher
von Erich Loest'': p. 94.
    ,,Weiterführende Literatur zur Kulturpolitik der SED'': p. 94.

1884

―――. Völkerschlachtdenkmal. Hamburg: Hoffmann und Campe,
1984. 282 p.   MLCS 84/10334 (P)

1885

―――. Waffenkarussell. Halle: Mitteldeutscher Verlag, 1968. 240 p.
                                                        PT2672.O29 W3

1886
————. Zwiebelmuster. Hamburg: Hoffmann und Campe, 1985.
285 p. MLCS 86/1577 (P)

****

1887
Morgner, Irmtraud. Amanda: ein Hexenroman. Darmstadt: Luchterhand, 1983. 669 p. MLCS 84/2016 (P)

1888
————. Gauklerlegende. Berlin: Eulenspiegel-Verlag, 1970, 106 p.:
col. plates. PT2673.O64 G3

1889
————. Ein Haus am Rand der Stadt. Berlin: Aufbau-Verlag,
1962. 316 p. PT2673.O64 H3

1890
————. Die Hexe im Landhaus: Gespräch in Solothurn. Zürich:
Rauhreif, 1984. 124 p.: 2 ports. PT2673.O64 Z467 1984

1891
————. Hochzeit in Konstantinopel. Berlin, Weimar: Aufbau-
Verlag, 1975. 238 p. PT2673.O64 H6 1975

1892
————. Leben und Abenteuer der Trobadora Beatriz nach
Zeugnissen ihrer Spielfrau Laura: Roman in dreizehn Büchern
und sieben Intermezzos. Berlin: Aufbau-Verlag, 1974. 697 p.
PT2673.O64 L4

1893
————. Die wundersamen Reisen Gustav des Weltfahrers:
lügenhafter Roman mit Kommentaren. München: Hanser,
1972. 171 p. PT2673.O64 W8

****

1894
Müller, Heiner. Der Auftrag; der Bau; Herakles 5. Berlin: Henschelverlag Kunst und Gesellschaft, 1981. 139 p.
MLCS 84/5797

1895
————. Germania Tod in Berlin. Berlin: Rotbuch-Verlag, 1977. 94 p.: ill.   PT2673.U29 G4
Includes bibliographical references.

1896
————. Geschichten aus der Produktion. Berlin: Rotbuch-Verlag, 1974. 2 v.: ill.   PT2673.U29 A6 1974

1897
————. Herzstück. Berlin: Rotbuch-Verlag, 1983. 133 p.: ill.
PT2673.U29 H4 1983

1898
————. Die Korrektur. Leipzig: Hofmeister, 1959. 39 p.: ill.
MLCS·84/15009 (P)

1899
————. Der Lohndrucker: mit einigen Hinweisen zur Regie. Leipzig: Hofmeister, 1961. 58 p.   MLCS 85/2599 (P)

1900
————. Mauser. Berlin: Rotbuch-Verlag, 1978. 101 p.: 1 ill.
PT2673.U29 M3
Includes index.

1901
————. Philoktet. Frankfurt am Main: Suhrkamp, 1966. 72 p.
PT2673.U29 P49

1902
————. Die Schlacht; Traktor; Leben Gundlings; Friedrich von Preussen; Lessings Schlaf Traum Schrei. Berlin: Henschelverlag, 1977. 139 p.: ill.   PT2673.U29 S3

1903

———. Sophokles: Ödipus Tyrann. Nach Hölderlin. Berlin, Weimar: Aufbau-Verlag, 1969. 182 p.   PA4413.O7 M8

1904

———. Stücke. Berlin: Henschelverlag Kunst und Gesellschaft, 1975. 399 p.   PT2673.U29 S8

1905

———. Theater-Arbeit. Berlin: Rotbuch-Verlag, 1975. 127 p.: ill.
     PT2673.U29 T48

1906

———. Die Umsiedlerin: oder, Das Leben auf dem Lande. Berlin: Rotbuch-Verlag, 1975. 118 p.: ill.   PT2673.U29 U4

1907

Girshausen, Theo. Realismus und Utopie: die frühen Stücke Heiner Müllers. Köln: Prometh, 1981. 347 p.
     PT2673.U29 Z67

Bibliography: p. 337–347.

1908

Die Hamletmaschine: Heiner Müllers Endspiel/ herausgegeben von Theo Girshausen. Köln: Prometh Verlag, 1978. 178 p.: ill.
     PT2673.U29 H334

Bibliography of H. Müller's works: p. 172–176.
Bibliography: p. 177–178.

1909

Schulz, Genia. Heiner Müller. Stuttgart: Metzler, 1980. vii, 203 p.
     MLCS 87/2165 (P)

1910

Silberman, Marc. Heiner Müller. Amsterdam: Rodopi, 1980. 127 p. (Forschungsberichte zur DDR-Literatur; 2)
     PT2673.U29 Z89

Bibliography: p. 84–127.

1911

Teraoka, Arlene Akiko. The silence of entropy or universal discourse: the postmodernist poetics of Heiner Müller. New York: Lang, 1985. 240 p. (New York University Ottendorfer series; n.F., Bd. 21)   PT2673.U29 Z92 1985
    Bibliography: p. 219–240.

1912

Wieghaus, Georg. Zwischen Auftrag und Verrat: Werk und Ästhetik Heiner Müllers. Frankfurt am Main, New York: Lang, 1984. 338 p. (Europäische Hochschulschriften. Reihe I, Deutsche Sprache und Literatur; Bd. 764)   PT2673.U29 Z96 1984
    Bibliography: p. 331–338.

1913

Zum Drama in der DDR: Heiner Müller und Peter Hacks/ herausgegeben von Judith R. Scheid. Stuttgart: Klett, 1981. 225 p.: ill. (Literaturwissenschaft—Gesellschaftswissenschaft; 53)
                                                    PT3721.Z85 1981
    Cover title: Interpretationen zum Drama in der DDR.
    Bibliography: p. 218–224.

                        ****

1914

Plenzdorf, Ulrich. Buridans Esel: Legende vom Glück ohne Ende. Berlin: Henschelverlag Kunst und Gesellschaft, 1986. 156 p.
                                                    MLCS 86/5558 (P)

1915

———. Gutenachtgeschichte. Frankfurt am Main: Suhrkamp, 1983. 54 p.: col. ill.   PT2676.L39 G8 1983

1916

———. Karla; Der alte Mann, das Pferd, die Strasse: Texte zu Filmen. Berlin: Henschelverlag, 1978. 190 p.   PN1997.A1 P47

1917

———. Legende vom Glück ohne Ende. Frankfurt am Main: Suhrkamp, 1981, c1979. 318 p.   PT2676.L39 L37 1981

1918

————. Die Legende von Paul und Paula. Die neuen Leiden des jungen W.: ein Kino- und Bühnenstück. Berlin: Henschelverlag Kunst und Gesellschaft, 1974. 164 p.: ill.   PT2676.L39 L4

1919

————. Die neuen Leiden des jungen W. Frankfurt am Main: Suhrkamp, 1973. 147 p.   PT2673.L39 N4

1920

————. The new sufferings of young W. New York: Ungar, 1979. xii, 84 p.   PZ4.P7255 Ne
Translation of: Die neuen Leiden des jungen W.

———————————

1921

Flaker, Aleksandar. Modelle der Jeans Prosa: zur literarischen Opposition bei Plenzdorf im osteuropäischen Romankontext. Kronberg/Ts.: Scriptor Verlag, 1975. 256 p. (Skripten Literatur + Sprache + Didaktik; 5)   PG512.F5
Serbo-Croatian ed. published in 1976 under title: Proza u trapericama.
Includes bibliographical references.

1922

Jäger, Georg. Die Leiden des alten und neuen Werther: Kommentare, Abbildungen, Materialien zu Goethes Leiden des jungen Werthers und Plenzdorfs Neuen Leiden des jungen W. München: Hanser, 1984. 222 p.: ill. (Literatur-Kommentare; Bd. 21)   PT1980.J33 1984
Includes index.
Bibliography: p. 213–218.

* * * * * * * * * * * * * * * * * * *

1923

Reimann, Brigitte. Ankunft im Alltag. Berlin: Verlag Neues Leben, 1973. 278 p.   PT2678.E34 A8

1924
————. Franziska Linkerhand. Berlin: Verlag Neues Leben, 1974.
  582 p.   PT2678.E34 F65 1974

1925
————. Die Frau am Pranger. Berlin: Verlag Neues Leben, 1969.
  349 p.   PT2678.E34 A6 1969

1926
————. Die Geschwister. Berlin, Weimar: Aufbau-Verlag, 1966.
  178 p.   PT2678.E34 G4

1927
————. Das grüne Licht der Steppen: Tagebuch einer Sibiri-
enreise. Berlin: Verlag Neues Leben, 1965. 153 p.: ill.
                                                    DK756.R4

1928
Die geliebte, die verfluchte Hoffnung: Tagebücher und Briefe,
  1947–1972/ Brigitte Reimann, herausgegeben von Elisabeth
  Elten-Krause und Walter Lewerenz. Darmstadt: Luchterhand,
  1983. 359 p.   PT2678.E34 Z466 1983

****

1929
Schneider, Rolf. Aus zweiter Hand: literarische Parodien. Berlin:
  Aufbau-Verlag, 1958. 73 p.: ill.   PT2638.N455 A9

1930
————. Bridges and bars. London: Cape, 1967. 189 p.
                                                    PZ4.S3596 Br

1931
————. Deep waters. Berlin: Seven Seas Publishers, 1968. 194 p.
                                                    PZ4.S3596 De
Translation of: Die Tage in W.

1932

————. Dieb und König. Frankfurt: Fischer, 1969. 68 p.

PT2680.N38 D5

1933

————. Einzug ins Schloss. Berlin: Henschelverlag, 1972. 74 p.

PT2680.N38 E4

1934

————. Das Glück. Rostock: Hinstorff Verlag, 1976. 258 p.

PT2680.N38 G6

1935

————. Marienbader Intrigen: 6 Hörspiele. Frankfurt am Main: Fischer, 1985. 215 p.   MLCS 87/831 (P)

1936

————. Nekrolog: unernste Geschichten. Rostock: Hinstorff, 1973. 206 p.   PT2680.N38 N4

1937

————. November: a novel. New York: Knopf, 1981, c1979. 235 p.   PT2680.N38 N613 1981

1938

————. November: Roman. Hamburg: Knaus, 1979. 257 p.

PT2680.N38 N6

,,Pfützen voll schwarzer Unvernunft: Dokumentation zu Rolf Schneiders Roman November'' (31 p.) inserted.

1939

————. Orphee: oder, Ich reise. Rostock: Hinstorff, 1977. 132 p.

DD43.S317

1940

————. Pilzomelett und andere Nekrologe. München, Zürich: Piper, 1974. 235 p.   PT2680.N38 P5

1941

————. Die Reise nach Jarosaw. Darmstadt: Luchterhand, 1975. 266 p.   PT2680.N38 R4 1975

1942

————. Stimmen danach: Hörspiele. Rostock: Hinstorff, 1970.
321 p.   PT2680.N38 S8

1943

————. Stücke. Berlin: Henschelverlag, 1970. 346 p.
                                          PT2680.N38 A17 1970

1944

————. Die Tage in W. Rostock: Hinstorff, 1973. 362 p.
                                          PT2680.N38 T3 1973

1945

————. Unerwartete Veränderung. Rostock: Hinstorff, 1980.
159 p.   MLCS 87/2053 (P)

1946

————. Von Paris nach Frankreich: Reisenotizen. Rostock:
Hinstorff, 1975. 206 p.   DC29.S37

****

1947

Schütz, Helga. Das Erdbeben bei Sängershausen und andere
Erzählungen. Zürich: Benziger, 1974. 187 p.
                                          PT2680.U339 E7 1974

1948

————. Erziehung zum Chorgesang. Zürich: Benziger, 1981.
267 p.   PT2680.U339 J8 1981
    Previously published as: Julia, oder, Erziehung zum
Chorgesang.

1949

————. Festbeleuchtung. Berlin: Aufbau-Verlag, 1974. 163 p.
                                          PT2680.U339 F4

1950

————. In Annas Namen. Berlin: Luchterhand, 1987, c1986.
270 p.   MLCS 87/4153 (P)

1951

————. Jette in Dresden. Berlin: Aufbau-Verlag, 1977. 204 p.
PT2680.U339 J4

1952

————. Julia, oder, Erziehung zum Chorgesang. Berlin, Weimar:
Aufbau-Verlag, 1980. 313 p. MLCS 81/258

1953

————. Mädchenrätsel. Zürich: Benziger, 1978. 256 p.
PT2680.U339 J4 1978
Earlier ed. published by Aufbau-Verlag, Berlin, under title:
Jette in Dresden.

1954

————. Martin Luther: eine Erzählung für den Film. Berlin:
Aufbau-Verlag, 1983. 147 p. PT2680.U339 M3 1983

1955

————. Vorgeschichten: oder, Schöne Gegend Probstein; Das
Erdbeben bei Sängershausen und andere Erzählungen. Mün-
chen: Deutscher Taschenbuch-Verlag, 1977. 246 p.
PT2680.U339 A6 1977

****

1956

Wolf, Christa. Cassandra: a novel and four essays. New York:
Farrar, Straus, Giroux, 1984. 305 p. PT2685.O36 K313 1984
Translation of: Kassandra and Voraussetzungen einer Erzäh-
lung.

1957

————. Divided heaven. U.S.: Adler's Foreign Books, 1981.
xxxvii, 228 p. PT2685.O36 G43 1981
Translation of: Der geteilte Himmel.
Bibliography: p. 215–228.

1958

————. Fortgesetzter Versuch. Leipzig: Reclam, 1979. 345 p.
PT2685.O36 F6

1959

————. Der geteilte Himmel. Berlin, Weimar: Aufbau-Verlag,
1975. 271 p.   PT2685.O36 G4 1975

1960

————. Kassandra. Darmstadt: Luchterhand, 1983. 156 p.
MLCS 84/2091 (P)

1961

————. Kein Ort, nirgends. Berlin, Weimar: Aufbau-Verlag,
1979. 173 p.   PT2685.O36 K4 1979b

1962

————. Kindheitsmuster. Darmstadt, Neuwied: Luchterhand,
1977. 480 p.   PT2685.O36 K5 1977

1963

————. Lesen und Schreiben; neue Sammlung: Essays, Aufsätze,
Reden. Darmstadt: Luchterhand, 1980. 320 p.

PT2685.O36 L43

Includes bibliographical references.

1964

————. A model childhood. New York: Farrar, Straus, and Giroux,
1980. 407 p.   PT2685.O36 K513
Translation of: Kindheitsmuster.

1965

————. Nachdenken über Christa T. Neuwied, Berlin: Luchterhand, 1969. 235 p.   PT2685.O36 N3 1969

1966

————. No place on earth. New York: Farrar, Straus, Giroux,
1982. 129 p.   PT2685.O36 K413 1982
Translation of: Kein Ort, nirgends.

1967

————. The quest for Christa T. London: Virago, 1982. 185 p.
PT2685.O36 N313 1982
Translation of: Nachdenken über Christa T.

1968

―――. The reader and the writer: essays, sketches, memories. Berlin: Seven Seas Publishers, 1977. 222 p.

PT2685.O36 L413 1977b

Translation of: Lesen und Schreiben.

1969

―――. Till Eulenspiegel. Berlin, Weimar: Aufbau-Verlag, 1973. 222 p. PT2685.O36 T5

1970

―――. Unter den Linden: drei unwahrscheinliche Geschichten. Berlin: Aufbau-Verlag, 1974, c1973. 132 p.: 3 leaves of col. plates: col. ill. PT2685.O36 U5

1971

―――. Voraussetzungen einer Erzählung, Kassandra: Frankfurter Poetik-Vorlesungen. Darmstadt: Luchterhand, 1983. 160 p.

PT2685.O36 K338 1983

Bibliography: p. 156–160.

―――――――――

1972

Buehler, George. The death of socialist realism in the novels of Christa Wolf. Frankfurt am Main, New York: Lang, 1986. 209 p. (Europäische Hochschulschriften. Reihe I, Deutsche Sprache und Literatur, Bd. 787) PT2685.O36 Z56 1986
Bibliography: p. 188–209.

1973

Christa Wolf. München: Edition Text + Kritik, 1975. 56 p. (Text + Kritik; Heft 46) PN4.T45 Heft 46
Bibliography: p. 50–55.

1974

Christa Wolf, Materialienbuch/ herausgegeben von Klaus Sauer. Darmstadt, Neuwied: Luchterhand, 1979. 172 p.

PT2685.O36 Z6

Bibliography: p. 146–170.

1975

Erinnerte Zukunft: 11 Studien zum Werk Christa Wolfs/ herausgegeben von Wolfram Mauser. Würzburg, Königshausen: Neumann, 1985. 336 p.   PT2685.O36 Z67 1985
    Includes index.
    Bibliography: p. 316–326.

1976

Greif, Hans Jürgen. Christa Wolf: „Wie sind wir so geworden wie wir heute sind?'' Bern, Las Vegas: Lang, 1978. 152 p. (Europäische Hochschulschriften. Reihe I, Deutsche Literatur und Germanistik; Bd. 237)   PT2685.O36 Z68
    Bibliography: p. 149–152.

1977

Hilzinger, Sonja. Christa Wolf. Stuttgart: Metzler, 1986. vii, 191 p.
                                             PT2685.O36 Z68 1986
    Includes index.
    Bibliography: p. 148–187.

1978

———. Kassandra: über Christa Wolf. Frankfurt am Main: Haag + Herchen, 1984, c1982. 107 p.   PT2685.O36 Z69 1984
    Bibliography: p. 105–107.

1979

Renoldner, Klemens. Utopie und Geschichtsbewusstsein: Versuche zur Poetik Christa Wolfs. Stuttgart: Akademischer Verlag Heinz, 1981. 165 p. (Stuttgarter Arbeiten zur Germanistik; Nr. 91. Salzburger Beiträge; Nr. 3)   PT2685.O36 Z84 1981
    Abridgement of the author's thesis (doctoral)—Universität Salzburg, 1979.
    Bibliography: p. 147–163.

1980

Risse, Stefanie. Wahrnehmen und Erkennen in Christa Wolfs Erzählung „Kassandra.'' Pfaffenweiler: Centaurus-Verlagsgesellschaft, 1986. 135 p. (Reihe Sprach- und Literaturwissenschaft; Bd 10)   PT2685.O36 K336 1986
    Bibliography: p. 131–135.

1981

Weber, Heinz-Dieter. Über Christa Wolfs Schreibart. Konstanz: Universitätsverlag Konstanz, 1984. 62 p.: port. (Konstanzer Universitätsreden; 131) PT2685.O36 Z96 1984
   Bibliography: p. 50–53.

SWITZERLAND

General Reference Works

1982
Anthology of modern Swiss literature/ edited and introduced by
  H. M. Waidson. New York: St. Martin's Press, 1984. 228 p.
                                            PN849.S92 A57 1984
  Includes index.
  Bibliography: p. 222–223.

1983
Begegnungen mit vier Zürcher Autoren: Jürg Federspiel, Hugo
  Loetscher, Adolf Muschg, Hans Schumacher. Zürich: GS-
  Verlag, 1986. 64 p.   PT3878.Z8 B44 1986

1984
Die deutschsprachige Sachliteratur/ herausgegeben von Rudolf
  Radler. München, Zürich: Kindler, 1978. xix, 992 p.
                                            Z1035.3.D53
  Includes bibliographies and indexes.

1985
Fringeli, Dieter. Gut zum Druck. Literatur der deutschen Schweiz
  seit 1964. Zürich, München: Artemis, 1972. 475 p.
                                            PT3873.F68

1986
Hinter den Fassaden: Texte aus der Werkstatt Schreibender
  Arbeiter Zürich/ Kurt Badertscher . . . et al. Zürich: Rotpunkt-
  Verlag, 1979. 197 p.: ill.   PT3878.Z8 H56

1987

Honsza, Norbert. Zur literarischen Situation nach 1945 in der BRD, in Österreich und in der Schweiz. Wrocław: Państwowe Wydawn. Naukowe, 1974. 239 p.   PT401.H58
    Bibliography: p. 234–237.

1988

Literatur als Prozess. Zürich: Verlag der Arche, 1974. 175 p.: 6 plates.   PT31.L5

1989

Literatur aus der Schweiz: Texte und Materialien/ herausgegeben von Egon Ammann und Eugen Faes. Zürich: Suhrkamp, 1978. 539 p.: ill.   PT3873.L57 1978
    English, French, German, and Italian.
    „Bio-Bibliographien'': p. 533–539.

1990

Modern Swiss literature: unity and diversity/ edited by John L. Flood. New York: St. Martin's Press, 1985. ix, 146 p.
    PN849.S9 M62 1985
    Papers presented at a symposium at the University of London Institute of Germanic Studies, Mar. 22–23, 1984.
    Includes bibliographies and index.

1991

Szene 81: Beispiele Schweizer Gegenwartsliteratur/ Silvio Blatter . . . et al. Zürich: Garte Zitig, 1980. 77 p.
    MLCS 87/2253 (P)

1992

Die zeitgenössischen Literaturen der Schweiz/ herausgegeben von Manfred Gsteiger. Zürich, München: Kindler, 1974. 752 p.: ill.   PN849.S9 Z4
    Includes bibliographical references and index.

Individual Authors

1993

Bichsel, Peter. And really Frau Blum would very much like to meet the milkman: 21 short stories. New York: Delacorte Press, 1969, c1968. 88 p.   PZ4.B58 An3

Translation of: Eigentlich möchte Frau Blum den Milchmann kennenlernen.

1994
————. Der Busant: von Trinkern, Polizisten und der schönen Magelone. Darmstadt: Luchterhand, 1985. 135 p.
PT2662.I3 B87 1985

1995
————. Eigentlich möchte Frau Blum den Milchmann kennenlernen: 21 Geschichten. Olten: Walter-Verlag, 1980, c1964. 61 p.
MLCS 87/2405 (P)

1996
————. Geschichten zur falschen Zeit. Darmstadt, Neuwied: Luchterhand, 1979. 188 p.   AC35.B47

1997
————. Die Jahreszeiten. Reinbek bei Hamburg: Rowohlt, 1970. 119 p.   PT2662.I3 J3 1970

1998
————. Kindergeschichten. Neuwied: Luchterhand, 1969. 91 p.
PT2662.I3 K5

1999
————. Schulmeistereien. Darmstadt: Luchterhand, 1985. 197 p.
PT2662.I3 Z47 1985

2000
————. Des Schweizers Schweiz. Zürich: Verlag der Arche, 1969. 47 p.   DQ36.B5

2001
————. Stories for children. London, New York: Boyars, 1984. 57 p.   PZ7.B4723 St 1984
Translation of: Kindergeschichten.

2002
————. There is no such place as America. New York: Delacorte Press, 1970. 85 p.   PZ4.B58 Th
Translation of: Kindergeschichten.

2003

Banziger, Hans. Peter Bichsel: Weg und Werk. Bern: Benteli, 1984.
152 p.: ill.   PT2662.I3 Z56 1984
   Includes index.
   Bibliography: p. 117–148.

2004

Peter Bichsel: Auskunft für Leser/ herausgegeben von Herbert
Hoven. Darmstadt: Luchterhand, 1984. 160 p.
                              PT2662.I3 Z83 1984
   Bibliography of works by and about P. Bichsel: p. 151–159.

2005

Steiner-Kuhn, Susanne. Schreiben im Dazwischen-Sein: zu Robert
Walser und Peter Bichsel, mit einem Seitenblick auf J. Heinrich
Pestalozzi und Otto F. Walter. Bern: Haupt, 1982. 65 p.
                              PT3868.S7 1982
   Bibliography: p. 63–65.

****

2006

Blatter, Silvio. Flucht und Tod des Daniel Zoff: vorläufiges
Protokoll eines ländlichen Tages. Aarau: Sauerländer, 1974.
47 p.   PT2662.L36 F4

2007

———. Genormte Tage, verschüttete Zeit. Frankfurt am Main:
Suhrkamp, 1976. 109 p.   PT2662.L36 G4

2008

———. Kein schöner Land. Frankfurt am Main: Suhrkamp, 1983.
544 p.   MLCS 84/2017 (P)

2009

———. Love me tender. Frankfurt am Main: Suhrkamp, 1980.
205 p.   MLCS 87/2089 (P)

2010

———. Die Schneefälle. Zürich: Benziger, 1981. 173 p.
                              MLCS 82-44

2011

―――. Wassermann. Frankfurt am Main: Suhrkamp, 1986.
388 p.   MLCS 86/5836 (P)

2012

―――. Zunehmendes Heimweh. Frankfurt am Main: Suhrkamp,
1978. 475 p.   PT2662.L36 Z45

****

2013

Brambach, Rainer. Auch im April. Zürich: Diogenes-Verlag, 1983.
55 p.: ill.   PT2603.R183 A95 1983

2014

―――. Für sechs Tassen Kaffee und andere Geschichten. Zürich:
Diogenes-Verlag, 1978. 132 p.   PT2603.R183 F8 1978

2015

―――. Ich fand keinen Namen dafür. Zürich: Diogenes-Verlag,
1969. 52 p.   PT2603.R183 I2

2016

―――. Kneipenlieder. Zürich: Diogenes-Verlag, 1974. 67 p.: ill.
                                          PT2603.R183 K6

2017

―――. Marco Polos Koffer. Zürich: Diogenes-Verlag, 1968. 56 p.
                                          PT2603.R183 M3

2018

―――. Wirf eine Münze auf: gesammelte Gedichte. Zürich:
Diogenes-Verlag, 1977. 117 p.   PT2603.R183 W5

****

2019

Burger, Hermann. Die allmähliche Verfertigung der Idee beim
Schreiben: Frankfurter Poetik-Vorlesung. Frankfurt am Main:
Fischer, 1986. 107 p.   PT2662.U67 Z59 1986

2020

―――. Blankenburg. Frankfurt am Main: Fischer, 1986. 178 p.
MLCS 86/7476 (P)

2021

―――. Bork. Zürich, Stuttgart: Artemis, 1970. 156 p.
PT2662.U67 B6

2022

―――. Diabelli. Frankfurt am Main: Fischer, 1979. 105 p.
PT2662.U67 D5

2023

―――. Die künstliche Mutter. Frankfurt am Main: Fischer, 1982.
262 p.   MLCS 84/2458 (P)

2024

―――. Ein Mann aus Wörtern. Frankfurt am Main: Fischer,
1983. 249 p.   PT2662.U67 M36 1983

2025

―――. Paul Celan: auf der Suche nach der verlorenen Sprache.
Zürich, München: Artemis, 1974. 149 p.   PT2605.E4 Z59

2026

―――. Rauchsignale. Zürich, Stuttgart: Artemis, 1967. 64 p.
PT2662.U67 R3

2027

―――. Schilten: Schulbericht zuhanden der Inspekto-
renkonferenz. Zürich: Artemis, 1976. 300 p.   PT2662.U67 S34

―――――――――――

2028

Schauplatz als Motiv: Materialien zu Hermann Burgers Roman
Schilten/ Beiträge Uli Daster. . . et al. Zürich, München:
Artemis, 1977. 186 p.: ill.   PT2662.U67 S3437
Bibliography: p. 185–186.

****

2029
Burkart, Erika. Augenzeuge. Zürich: Artemis, 1978. 244 p.
PT2662.U68 A97

2030
————. Fernkristall. Tobel: Verlag an der Hartnau, 1972. 23 p.
PT2603.U738 F4

2031
————. Die Freiheit der Nacht. Zürich: Artemis, 1981. 83 p.
MLCM 84/2073

2032
————. Ich lebe. Zürich: Artemis, 1964. 68 p.
PT2603.U738 I2

2033
————. Jemand entfernt sich. Zürich: Benziger Verlag, 1972.
24 p.   PT2662.U68 J4

2034
————. Das Licht im Kahlschlag. Zürich, München: Artemis,
1977. 79 p.   PT2662.U68 L5

2035
————. Mit den Augen der Kore. St. Gallen: Tschudy-Verlag,
1962. 176 p.   PT2662.U68 M5

2036
————. Moräne. Olten, Freiburg i. Br.: Walter-Verlag, 1970.
392 p.   PT2662.U68 M6

2037
————. Rufweite. Zürich, München: Artemis, 1975. 235 p.
PT2603.U738 R8

2038
————. Die Spiele der Erkenntnis. Zürich: Artemis, 1985. 300 p.
MLCS 86/1104 (P)

2039

―――. Sternbild des Kindes. Zürich: Artemis, 1984. 76 p.

MLCM 86/4586 (P)

2040

―――. Die Transparenz der Scherben. Zürich, Einsiedeln, Köln: Benziger, 1973. 96 p. PT2662.U68 T7

2041

―――. Der Weg zu den Schafen. Zürich: Artemis, 1979. 356 p.

MLCS 84/14638 (P)

2042

―――. Die weichenden Ufer. Zürich, Stuttgart: Artemis, 1967. 76 p. PT2662.U68 W4

―――――――

2043

Vogt-Baumann, Frieda. Von der Landschaft zur Sprache: die Lyrik von Erika Burkart. Zürich, München: Artemis, 1977. 104 p. (Züricher Beiträge zur deutschen Literatur- und Geistesgeschichte; 47) PT2603.U738 Z9

Bibliography: p. 104.

****

2044

Diggelmann, Walter Matthias. Aber den Kirschbaum, den gibt es. Zürich, Einsiedeln, Köln: Benziger, 1975. 225 p.

PT2664.I46 A63

2045

―――. Balladen von süchtigen Kindern. Pfaffenweiler: Pfaffenweiler Presse, 1976. 42 p. (on double leaves): col. ill.

PT2664.I46 B3

Edition of 200 numbered copies signed by the author and the artist. This is no. 55.

2046

―――. Feststellungen: ein Lesebuch: Texte 1963 bis 1978. Zürich: RPV, 1978. 146 p. MLCS 84/12636 (P)

2047

————. Filippinis Garten. Zürich: Benziger, 1978. 175 p.

PT2664.I46 F54

2048

————. Freispruch für Isidor Ruge. Frankfurt am Main: Fischer, 1971, c1967. 207 p.   PT2664.I46 F7 1971

2049

————. DDR: Tagebuch einer Erkundungsfahrt. Zürich: Benziger, 1977. 120 p.   MLCS 86/3706 (D)

2050

————. Hexenprozess. Die Teufelsaustreiber von Ringwil. Bern: Benteli, 1969. 156 p.   HV6535.S93 R53

2051

————. Die Hinterlassenschaft. München: Piper, 1965. 301 p.

PT2664.I46 H5

2052

————. Ich heisse Thomy. Frankfurt am Main: Fischer, 1973. 131 p.   PT2664.I46 I24

2053

————. Ich und das Dorf: ein Tagebuch in Geschichten. Frankfurt am Main: Fischer, 1972. 251 p.   PT2664. I46 I25

2054

————. Der Reiche stirbt. Zürich, Köln: Benziger, 1977. 182 p.

PT2664.I46 R425

2055

————. Reise durch Transdanubien. Zürich, Einsiedeln, Köln: Benziger, 1974. 259 p.   PT2664.I46 R43

2056

————. Schatten: Tagebuch einer Krankheit. Zürich: Benziger, 1979. 121 p.   PT2664.I46 Z515

2057

————. Spaziergänge auf der Margareteninsel. Zürich: Benziger, 1980. 164 p.   MLCS 87/2584 (P)

2058

————. Tage von süsslicher Wärme. Zürich: Benziger, 1982. 250 p.   MLCS 84/2222 (P)

2059

————. Die Vergnügungsfahrt. München: Goldmann, 1978. 218 p.   PT2664.I46 V4 1978

2060

————. Das Verhör des Harry Wind. München: Goldmann, 1979, c1962. 252 p.   PT2664.I46 V5 1979

2061

————. Zwanzig Geschichten. Leipzig: Reclam, 1986. 273 p.   MLCS 87/3116 (P)

2062

————. Zwölf Erzählungen und ein Roman: Die Rechnung und andere Erzählungen: Aber den Kirschbaum, den gibt es. Leipzig: Reclam, 1976. 298 p.   PT2664.I46 Z46

****

2063

Dürrenmatt, Friedrich. Achterloo: Komödie in zwei Akten. Basel: Reiss, 1983. 122 leaves.   MLCL 84/134 (P)

2064

————. Albert Einstein: ein Vortrag. Zürich: Diogenes-Verlag, 1979. 66 p.   QC16.E5 D78

"... ergänzte Fassung des Vortrags zur Feier anlässlich des 100. Geburtstags Albert Einsteins, gehalten in der Eidgenössischen Technischen Hochschule, Zürich, am 24. Februar 1979."

Bibliography: p. 65–66.

2065
———. An angel comes to Babylon & Romulus the Great. Ann
Arbor, Mich.: Reprinted for Grove Press by University
Microfilms International, 1978, 174 p.
                                              PT2607.U493 E53 1978
     Translation of: Ein Engel kommt nach Babylon and Romulus
der Grosse, respectively.

2066
———. Der Auftrag, oder, Vom Beobachten des Beobachters der
Beobachter: Novelle in vierundzwanzig Sätzen. Zürich: Diogenes-
Verlag, 1986. 132 p.   MLCS 86/7462 (P)

2067
———. Das Bild des Sisyphos. Zürich: Verlag der Arche, 1968.
48 p.   PT2607.U493 B5

2068
———. Die Ehe des Herrn Mississippi: eine Komödie. New York:
Holt, Rinehart and Winston, 1973. x, 159, xxxviii p.
                                              PT2607.U493 E48 1973

2069
———. Ein Engel kommt nach Babylon: eine fragmentarische
Komödie in drei Akten: Neufassung 1980. Zürich: Diogenes-
Verlag, 1980. 141 p.   MLCS 84/8918 (P)

2070
———. Four plays: Romulus the Great. The marriage of Mr.
Mississippi. An angel comes to Babylon. The physicist. New
York: Grove Press, 1965. 349 p.   PT2607.U493 A24 1965

2071
———. Die Frist: eine Komödie. Zürich: Verlag der Arche, 1977.
119 p.   MLCS 82/2629

2072
———. Gesammelte Hörspiele. Zürich: Verlag der Arche, 1964,
c1954. 317 p.   PT2607.U493 A19 1964

2073

————. Gespräch mit Heinz Ludwig Arnold. Zürich: Verlag der Arche, 1976. 86 p.   PT2607.U493 Z52

,,Das Gespräch zwischen Friedrich Dürrenmatt und Heinz Ludwig Arnold wurde am 7. und 8. März 1975 in Neuchâtel geführt.''

2074

————. Grieche sucht Griechin: eine Prosakomödie. Frankfurt am Main: Ullstein, 1968. 149 p.   PT2607.U493 G7

2075

————. Die Heimat im Plakat: ein Buch für Schweizer Kinder. Zürich: Diogenes-Verlag, 1963. 1 v.: chiefly ill.

NC1659.D8 A48

2076

————. Herkules und der Stall des Augias. Zürich: Verlag der Arche, 1963. 88 p.: ill.   PT2607.U493 H4

2077

————. The judge and his hangman; The quarry: two Hans Barlach mysteries. Boston, Mass.: Godine, 1983. 162, xv p.

PT2607.U493 R513 1983

Translations of: Der Richter und sein Henker and Der Verdacht.

2078

————. Komödien. Zürich: Verlag der Arche, 1957–1970, c1963. 3 v.   PT2607.U493 A19 1957

2079

————. Justiz. Zürich: Diogenes-Verlag, 1985. 369 p.

MLCS 86/1108 (P)

2080

————. König Johann. Nach Shakespeare. Zürich: Verlag der Arche, 1968. 101 p.   PT2607.U493 K6

2081

————. Lesebuch. Zürich: Verlag der Arche, 1978. 323 p.

PT2607.U493 A6 1978

2082

————. Der Meteor. Zürich: Verlag der Arche, 1966. 71 p.
PT2607.U493 M4

2083

————. The meteor: a comedy in two acts. Ann Arbor, Mich.:
Reprinted for Grove Press by University Microfilms
International, 1978, c1974. 63 p.   PT2607.U493 M413 1978
Translation of: Der Meteor.

2084

————. Der Mitmacher: ein Komplex: Text der Komödie,
Dramaturgie, Erfahrungen, Berichte, Erzählungen. Zürich:
Verlag der Arche, 1976. 288 p.   PT2607.U493 M5

2085

————. Monstervortrag über Gerechtigkeit und Recht nebst einem
helvetischen Zwischenspiel. Zürich: Verlag der Arche, 1969.
120 p.   PT2607.U493 M6

2086

————. Once a Greek. New York: Knopf, 1965. 179 p.
PZ4.D84 On

2087

————. Die Panne. London: Oxford University Press, 1967. 7,
123 p.: front., port.   PT2607.U493 P3 1967

2088

————. The physicists. London: Cape, 1973. 67 p.
PT2607.U493 P53 1973
Translation of: Die Physiker.

2089

————. Die Physiker: eine Komödie in zwei Akten. London,
Melbourne: Macmillan, 1966. lxxvi, 140 p.
PT2607.U493 P5 1966

2090

————. Play Strindberg: the Dance of death choreographed. Ann
Arbor, Mich.: University Microfilms International, 1978, c1973.
76 p.   PT2607.U493 P5513 1978

Translation of: Play Strindberg: Totentanz nach August Strindberg.

2091

————. Play Strindberg: Totentanz nach August Strindberg.
Zürich: Verlag der Arche, 1969. 67 p.   PT2607.U493 P55

2092

————. Plays and essays. New York: Continuum, 1982. xxii,
312 p.   PT2607.U493 A6 1982

2093

————. Porträt eines Planeten. Zürich: Verlag der Arche, 1971.
85 p.   PT2607.U493 P6

2094

————. The quarry. Greenwich, Conn.: New York Graphic Society,
1962, c1961. 162 p.   PZ4.D84 Qar2

2095

————. Der Richter und sein Henker. Reinbek bei Hamburg:
Rowohlt, 1970. 116 p.: ill.   PT2607.U493 R5 1970

2096

————. Sätze aus Amerika. Zürich: Verlag der Arche, 1970. 72 p.
                                           E169.O2.D82

2097

————. Die Stadt, Prosa I–IV. Zürich: Verlag der Arche, 1952.
183 p.   PT2607.U493 S7

2098

————. Stoffe I–III. Zürich: Diogenes-Verlag, 1981. 356 p.
                                           PT2607.U493 A6 1981

2099

————. Stranitzky und der Nationalheld. Zürich: Verlag der Arche,
1959. 48 p.: ill.   PT2607.U493 S75

2100

————. Der Sturz. Zürich: Verlag der Arche. 1971. 119 p.
                                           PT2607.U493 S78

2101

―――. Theater-Schriften und Reden. Zürich: Verlag der Arche,
1966. 2 v.   PN1623.D8
„Quellen und Daten'': v. 1, p. 354–357.

2102

―――. Theaterprobleme. Zürich: Verlag der Arche, 1973, c1955.
46 p.   PN1631.D8 1973

2103

―――. Titus Andronicus. Zürich: Verlag der Arche, 1970. 79 p.
                                          PT2607.U493 T5

2104

―――. Traps. New York: Knopf, 1960. 114 p.   PZ4.D84 Tr

2105

―――. Der Verdacht. Boston: Houghton Mifflin, 1964. ix, 204 p.
                                          PT2607.U493 V38 1964

2106

―――. Das Versprechen. Zürich: Verlag der Arche, 1958. 244 p.
                                          PT2607.U493 V4

2107

―――. Das Versprechen: Requiem auf den Kriminalroman.
London: Harrap, 1967. 185 p.: ill. (incl. port., music), 4 plates.
                                          PT2607.U493 V4 1967
Map on end-papers. Text in English. Originally published,
Zürich: Schifferli, 1958.
Bibliography: p. 15–17.

2108

―――. The visit: a tragi-comedy. London: Cape, 1973. 109 p.
                                          PT2607.U493 B43 1973
Translation of: Der Besuch der alten Dame.

2109

―――. Writings on theatre and drama. London: Cape, 1976.
183 p.   PN1623.D82

These essays are taken from F. Dürrenmatt's two-volume work Theater-Schriften und Reden and Dramaturgisches und Kritisches.
Bibliography: p. 18–19.

2110
————. Zusammenhänge: Essay über Israel: eine Konzeption. Zürich: Verlag der Arche, 1976. 240 p.   DS115.5.D83

2111
Angermeyer, Hans Christoph. Zuschauer im Drama: Brecht, Dürrenmatt, Handke. Frankfurt am Main: Athenäum, 1971. 144 p.   PT668.A55

2112
Arnold, Armin. Friedrich Dürrenmatt. Berlin: Colloquium-Verlag, 1979. 98 p. (Köpfe des zwanzigsten Jahrhunderts; Bd. 57)
       PT2607.U493 Z56 1979
    Bibliography: p. 95–96.

2113
Badertscher, Hans. Dramaturgie als Funktion der Ontologie: eine Untersuchung zu Wesen und Entwicklung der Dramaturgie Friedrich Dürrenmatts. Bern: Haupt, 1979. 131 p. (Sprache und Dichtung; n.F. Bd. 27)   PT2607.U493 Z564
    Bibliography: p. 127–129.

2114
Banziger, Hans. Frisch und Dürrenmatt. Bern, München: Francke, 1976, c1960. 312 p.   PT2611.R814 Z58 1976
    Includes bibliographical references and index.

2115
Both, Wolfgang. Vom religiösen Drama zur politischen Komödie: Friedrich Dürrenmatt „Die Wiedertäufer" und „Es steht geschrieben": ein Vergleich. Frankfurt am Main, Bern, Las Vegas: Lang, 1978. 479 p. (Europäische Hochschulschriften. Reihe I, Deutsche Literatur und Germanistik; Bd. 276)
       PT2607.U493 W533
    Bibliography: p. 468–479.

2116
Fickert, Kurt J. To heaven and back: the new morality in the plays of Friedrich Dürrenmatt. Lexington: University Press of Kentucky, 1972. 70 p. (Studies in the Germanic languages and literatures, no. 5)   PT2607.U493 Z7
    Bibliography: p. 67.

2117
Friedrich Dürrenmatt. München: Edition Text und Kritik, 1976–1977. 2 v. (Text + Kritik; 50/51, 56)
                                              PN4.T45 v. 50–51, 56
    Includes ,,Bibliographie zu Friedrich Dürrenmatt, von Winfried Hönes'': v. 1, p. 93–108.

2118
Gertner, Hannes. Das Komische im Werk Friedrich Dürrenmatts: Versuch einer Erklärung des Komischen, seiner verschiedenen Formen und Funktionen im Werk Friedrich Dürrenmatts. Frankfurt am Main, New York: Lang, 1984. iii, 143 p. (Europäische Hochschulschriften. Reihe I, Deutsche Sprache und Literatur; Bd. 782)   PT2607.U493 Z726 1984
    Originally presented as the author's thesis (doctoral)— Universität Marburg, 1984.
    Bibliography: p. 137–143.

2119
Gottwald, Sigrun R. Der mutige Narr im dramatischen Werk Friedrich Dürrenmatts. New York: Lang, 1983. xii, 331 p. (New Yorker Studien zur neueren deutschen Literaturgeschichte; Bd. 3)   PT2607.U493 Z728 1983
    Bibliography: p. 319–331.

2120
Hansel, Johannes. Friedrich Dürrenmatt Bibliographie. Bad Homburg v. d. H., Berlin, Zürich: Gehlen, 1968. 87 p.
                                                    Z8246.2.H32

2121
Jenny, Urs. Dürrenmatt: a study of his plays. London: Eyre Methuen, 1978. 206 p.   PT2607.U493 Z7613
    Translation with revisions of Friedrich Dürrenmatt.
    Includes index.

2122

Knopf, Jan. Friedrich Dürrenmatt. München: Beck, Edition Text und Kritik, 1980. 193 p. (Autorenbücher; 3)

PT2607.U493 Z77 1980

Bibliography: p. 185–190.

2123

Loeffler, Michael Peter. Friedrich Dürrenmatts Der Besuch der alten Dame in New York: ein Kapitel aus der Rezeptionsgeschichte der neueren Schweizer Dramatik. Basel, Stuttgart: Birkhäuser, 1976. 122 p., 1 leaf of plates: ill.

PT2607.U493 B4245

Bibliography: p. 117–122.

2124

Rümler-Gross, Hanna. Thema und Variation: eine Analyse der Shakespeare- und Strindberg-Bearbeitungen Dürrenmatts unter Berücksichtigung seiner Komödienkonzeption. Köln: Böhlau, 1985. ix, 285 p. (Kölner germanistische Studien; Bd. 20)

PT2607.U493 Z85 1985

Originally presented as the author's thesis (doctoral)—Universität zu Köln, 1981.

Bibliography: p. 247–285.

2125

Schüler, Volker. Dürrenmatt, Der Richter und sein Henker, Die Physiker: Dichterbiographie und Interpretation. Hollfeld/Ofr.: Beyer, 1976. 112 p. (Analysen und Reflexionen; Bd. 13)

PT2607.U493 R536 1976

Includes bibliographical references.

2126

————. Dürrenmatt, Der Verdacht, Der Besuch der alten Dame: Untersuchungen und Anmerkungen. Hollfeld/Ofr.: Beyer, 1975. 103 p. (Analysen und Reflexionen; Bd. 16)

PT2607.U493 B428

Bibliography: p. 102.

2127

Seifert, Walter. Friedrich Dürrenmatt: Der Richter und sein Henker: zur Analyse und Didaktik des Kriminalromans. München: Oldenburg, 1975. 120 p.: maps.   PT2607.U493 R537

Bibliography: p. 118–120.

2128
Tiusanen, Timo. Dürrenmatt: a study in plays, prose, theory.
Princeton, N.J.: Princeton University Press, 1977. xiii, 486 p.,
4 leaves of plates: ill.   PT2607.U493 Z89
   Includes index.
   Bibliography: p. 443–467.

2129
Treib, Manfred. August Strindberg und Edward Albee: eine
vergleichende Analyse moderner Ehedramen: mit einem Exkurs
über Friedrich Dürrenmatts Play Strindberg. Frankfurt am
Main: Lang, 1980. 186 p. (Europäische Hochschulschriften.
Reihe XVIII, Vergleichende Literaturwissenschaften; Bd. 23)
                                                    PS3551.L25 Z894 1980
   Bibliography: p. 175–186.

2130
Weber, Emil. Friedrich Dürrenmatt und die Frage nach Gott: zur
theologischen Relevanz der frühen Prosa eines merkwürdigen
Protestanten. Zürich: Theologischer Verlag, 1980. 293 p.
                                                    PT2607.U493 Z945
   Bibliography: p. 283–293.

2131
Whitton, Kenneth S. The theatre of Friedrich Dürrenmatt: a study
in the possibility of freedom. London: Wolff; Atlantic Highlands,
N.J.: Humanities Press, 1980. 242 p.
                                                    PT2607.U493 Z95 1980
   Includes indexes.
   Bibliography: 228–236.

2132
Wales, University College, Aberystwyth. Library. Friedrich
Dürrenmatt: catalogue of an exhibition illustrating his work,
prepared in conjunction with his visit to this College as holder
of the Welsh Arts Council international writers' prize.
Aberystwyth: The Library, 1976. 1, 14 p.
                                                    PT2607.U493 Z94 1976
   Bibliography: p. 12–14.

****

2133
Eggimann, Ernst. Arbeiter-Bibel-Kreis. München: Kaiser, 1973.
18 p.   PT2665.G47 A9

2134
———. Emmental. Zürich: Rentsch, 1983. 111 p.: ill.
DQ841.E49 E34 1983

2135
———. Heikermant. Zürich: Verlag der Arche, 1971. 56 p.
PT2665.G47 H37

2136
———. Henusode. Zürich: Verlag der Arche, 1968. 48 p.
PT2665.G47 H4

2137
———. Jesus-Texte. Zürich: Verlag der Arche, 1972. 80 p.
PT2665.G47 J4

2138
———. Die Landschaft des Schülers. Zürich: Verlag der Arche,
1973. 77 p.   PT2665.G47 L3

2139
———. Meditation mit offenen Augen. München: Kaiser, 1974.
79 p.   BL627.E19
Bibliography: p. 6.

2140
———. Psalmen. Wiesbaden: Limes, 1967. 80 p.
PT2665.G47 P8

2141
———. Vor dem jüngsten Jahr. Zürich: Verlag der Arche, 1969.
171 p.   PT2665.G47 V6

****

2142
Ehrismann, Albert. Eine Art Bilanz. 65 Gedichte aus 45 Jahren.
Mit einem Geburtstagsbrief von Hans Schumacher. Zürich: Gute
Schriften, 1973. 86 p.   PT2609.H767 A9
    Includes bibliographical references.

2143
————. Die Gedichte des Pessimisten und Moralisten Albert
Ehrismann. Rörschach: Nebelspalter-Verlag, 1972. 62 p.
                                                PT2609.H767 G4

2144
————. Heimkehr der Tiere in der Heiligen Nacht. Zürich: Verlag
der Arche, 1965. 64 p.   PT2609.H767 H4

2145
————. In dieser Nacht. Herrliberg-Zürich: Bühl-Verlag, 1946.
15 p.   PT2609.H767 I6

2146
————. Inseln sind keine Luftgespinste. Zürich: Werner Classen,
1977. 88 p.   PT2609.H767 I65
    Bibliography of A. Ehrisman's works: p. 88.

2147
————. Kolumbus kehrt zurück, eine dramatische Legende.
Zürich: Büchergilde Gutenberg, 1947. 77 p.: ill.
                                                PT2609.H767 K6

2148
————. Mich wundert, dass ich fröhlich bin. 65 Gedichte. Zürich:
Werner Classen, 1973. 128 p.   PT2609.H767 M5

2149
————. Nachricht von den Wollenwebern. Zürich: Artemis, 1964.
64 p.   MLCS 87/3271 (P)

2150
————. Schmelzwasser. Rörschach: Nebelspalter-Verlag, 1978.
71 p.   PT2609.H767 S35
    Bibliography of the author's works: p. 71.

2151

————. Später, Aonen später. Rörschach: Nebelspalter-Verlag, 1975. 87 p.   PT2609.H767 S6

Bibliography of the author's works: p. 87.

2152

————. Wetterhahn, altmodisch. Zürich, Stuttgart: Artemis, 1968. 63 p.   PT2609.H767 W4

2153

————. Wir haben Flügel heut. Zürich: Artemis, 1962. 64 p.   PT2609.H767 W5

* * * * * * * * * * * * * * * * * *

2154

Federspiel, Jürg. The ballad of Typhoid Mary. New York: Dutton, 1983. 171 p.   PT2666.E37 B313 1983

Translation of: Die Ballade von der Typhoid Mary.

2155

————. Die Ballade von der Typhoid Mary. Frankfurt am Main: Suhrkamp, 1982. 153 p.   MLCS 82/6438

2156

————. Belfridge, oder Das Eigentor. Frankfurt am Main: Suhrkamp, 1971. 133 p.   PT2666.E37 B4

2157

————. Die beste Stadt für Blinde und andere Berichte. Zürich: Suhrkamp, 1980. 224 p.   AC35.F36

2158

————. An earthquake in my family. New York: Dutton, 1986. 249 p.   PT2666.E37 A254 1986

Stories selected from Orangen und Tode, Der Mann, der Glück brachte, and Paratuga kehrt zurück.

2159

————. Die Märchentante. München: Piper, 1971. 96 p.   PT2666.E37 M33

2160

————. Museum des Hasses; Tage in Manhattan. München:
Piper, 1969. 267 p.   PT2666.E37 M8

2161

————. Orangen und Tode. München: Deutscher Taschenbuch-
Verlag, 1966. 120 p.   PT2666.E37 O7

2162

————. Orangen vor ihrem Fenster. Berlin: Verlag Volk und Welt,
1977. 190 p.   PT2666.E37 O74

2163

————. Paratuga kehrt zurück. Darmstadt: Luchterhand, 1973.
148 p.   PT2666.E37 P3

2164

————. Träume aus Plastic. Einsiedeln, Zürich, Köln: Benziger,
1972. 184 p.   NX65.F43

2165

————. Wahn und Müll: Berichte und Gedichte. Zürich: Limmat,
1983. 130 p.   PT2666.E37 W33 1983

****

2166

Fringeli, Dieter. Dichter im Abseits: Schweizer Autoren von
Glauser bis Höhl. Zürich, München: Artemis 1974. 183 p.
                                                   PT3868.F68
    Includes index.
    Bibliography: p. 179–180.

2167

————. Durchaus: neue Gedichte. Düsseldorf: Eremiten-Presse,
1975. 60 p.: col. ill.   PT2666.R55 D8

2168

————. Gut zum Druck. Literatur der deutschen Schweiz seit
1964. Zürich, München: Artemis 1972. 475 p.   PT3873.F68

2169

————. Ich bin nicht mehr zahlbar. Zürich: Verlag der Arche, 1978. 77 p.   PT2666.R55 I2

2170

————. Mein Feuilleton: Gespräche, Aufsätze, Glossen zur Literatur. Breitenbach: Jeger-Moll, 1982. 480 p.

PT2666.R55 A6 1982

2171

————. Nachdenken mit und über Friedrich Dürrenmatt: ein Gespräch. Breitenbach: Jeger-Moll, 1977. 30 p.: ill.

PT2607.U493 Z723 1977

2172

————. Ohnmachtwechsel und andere Gedichte aus 20 Jahren. Zürich: Verlag der Arche, 1981. 137 p.   PT2666.R55 O3

2173

————. Die Optik der Trauer. Alexander Xaver Gwerder: Wesen und Wirken. Bern: Kandelaber-Verlag, 1970. 176 p.: facsim., port.   PT2613.W4 Z7
   Bibliography: p. 174–176.

2174

————. Reden und andere Reden: Politik und Sprache. Basel: Nachtmaschine, 1979. 95 p.   MLCS 86/5128 (J)

2175

————. Von Spitteler zu Muschg: Literatur der deutschen Schweiz seit 1900. Basel: Reinhardt, 1975. 143 p.   PT3868.F7
   Bibliography: p. 141–143.

2176

————. Was auf der Hand lag. Liestal: Heinzelmann & Kunz, 1974. 48 p.: col. ill.   PT2666.R55 W3 1974
   Limited ed. of 500 numbered copies. This is no. 127.

2177

————. Das Wort reden. Olten, Freiburg i. Br.: Walter, 1971. 63 p.   PT2666.R55 W6

2178
————. Zwischen den Orten. Breitenbach: Jeger-Moll, 1965.
45 p.: ill.   PT2666.R55 Z9

****

2179
Frisch, Max. Als der Krieg zu Ende war. New York: Dodd, Mead,
1967. 154 p.   PT2611.R814 A66

2180
————. Andorra: a play in twelve scenes. New York: Hill and
Wang, 1964, c1962. 88 p.   PT2611.R814 A713

2181
————. Andorra: Stück in 12 Bildern. Frankfurt am Main:
Suhrkamp, 1976, c1961. 126 p.   PT2611.R814 A7 1976

2182
————. Antwort aus der Stille. Stuttgart, Berlin: Deutsche Verlags-
Anstalt, 1937. 130 p.   PT2611.R814 A75 1937

2183
————. Ausgewählte Prosa. New York: Harcourt, Brace & World,
1968. xxv, 123 p.   PT2611.R814 A16 1968

2184
————. Biedermann und die Brandstifter: ein Lehrstück ohne
Lehre. Berlin: Suhrkamp, 1959, c1958. 173 p.
                                                    PT2611.R814 B5

2185
————. Biografie: ein Spiel. Frankfurt am Main: Suhrkamp, 1969.
117 p.   PT2611.R814 B54 1969

2186
————. Biography: a game. New York: Hill and Wang, 1969.
90 p.   PT2611. R814 B543
      Translation of: Biografie: ein Spiel.

2187

————. Blätter aus dem Brotsack. Zürich: Atlantis, 1969. 92 p.
PT2611.R814 B55 1969

2188

————. Blaubart: eine Erzählung. Frankfurt am Main: Suhrkamp,
1982. 171 p. MLCS 82/6802

2189

————. Bluebeard: a tale. San Diego: Harcourt Brace Jovanovich,
1983. 134 p. PT2611.R814 B5613 1983
Translation of: Blaubart.

2190

————. The Chinese wall. New York: Hill and Wang, 1961.
121 p. PT2611.R814 C53
Translation of: Die chinesische Mauer.

2191

————. Die chinesische Mauer. Frankfurt am Main: Suhrkamp,
1967. 102 p. PT2611.R814 C5 1967

2192

————. Dienstbüchlein. Frankfurt am Main: Suhrkamp, 1974.
157 p. PT2611.R814 D5

2193

————. Don Juan, oder, Die Liebe zur Geometrie. Frankfurt am
Main: Suhrkamp, 1966. 101 p. PT2611.R814 D6 1966

2194

————. Dramaturgisches. Ein Briefwechsel mit Walter Höllerer.
Berlin: Literarisches Colloquium, 1969. 42 p.
PT2611.R814 D7

2195

————. Erinnerungen an Brecht. Berlin: Friedenauer Presse, 1968.
21 p. PT2603.R397 Z6192

2196

————. The firebugs: a learning-play without a lesson. New York: Hill and Wang, 1963, c1959. 85 p.   PT2611.R814 F53 1963
Translation of: Biedermann und die Brandstifter.

2197

————. Four plays: The great wall of China; Don Juan, or, The love of geometry; Philipp Hotz's fury; Biography: a game. London: Methuen, 1969. 298 p.   PT2611.R814 A22

2198

————. Frühe Stücke: Santa Cruz; Nun singen sie wieder. Frankfurt am Main: Suhrkamp, 1966. 138 p.   PT2611.R814 F7

2199

————. Gantenbein. San Diego: Harcourt Brace Jovanovich, 1982, c1965. 304 p.   PT2611.R814 M413 1982
Translation of: Mein Name sei Gantenbein.
Reprint. Originally published: A wilderness of mirrors. London: Methuen, 1965.

2200

————. Gesammelte Werke in zeitlicher Folge. Frankfurt am Main: Suhrkamp, 1976. 12 v.   PT2611.R814 1976
Includes bibliographical references.

2201

————. Graf Oderland: Eine Moritat in zwölf Bildern. New York: Harcourt, Brace & World, 1966. xi, 119 p.
                                        PT2611.R814 G7 1966

2202

————. Homo faber: ein Bericht. Boston: Houghton Mifflin, 1973. ix, 358 p.   PT2611.R814 H6 1973
Bibliography: p. viii–ix.

2203

————. Homo Faber: a report. Harmondsworth: Penguin, 1974. 218 p.   PZ3.F9186 Ho10
Translation of: Homo faber.

2204

―――. Man in the Holocene: a story. New York: Harcourt Brace
Jovanovich, 1980. 113 p.: ill.   PZ3.F9186 Man
Includes bibliographical references.

2205

―――. Der Mensch erscheint im Holozän: eine Erzählung.
Frankfurt am Main: Suhrkamp, 1979. 142 p.: ill.
PT2611.R814 M44

2206

―――. Montauk. New York: Harcourt Brace Jovanovich, 1983,
c1976. 143 p.   PT2611.R814 Z513 1983

2207

―――. Nun singen sie wieder: Versuch eines Requiems. London,
Toronto: Harrap, 1967. 16 p.: front., port.
PT2611.R814 N8 1967

2208

―――. Öffentlichkeit als Partner. Frankfurt am Main: Suhrkamp,
1967. 152 p.   PT2611.R814 O34

2209

―――. Rip van Winkle. Stuttgart: Reclam, 1969. 62 p.
PT2611.R814 R5

2210

―――. Die Schwierigen. Zürich: Atlantis, 1970. 207 p.
PT2611.R814 S3 1970

2211

―――. Sketchbook, 1946–1949. New York: Harcourt Brace
Jovanovich, 1977. xii, 301 p.   PT2611.R814 Z5213
Translation of: Tagebuch 1946–1949.

2212

―――. Stich-Worte. Frankfurt am Main: Suhrkamp, 1975. 251 p.
PT2611.R814 S68
Includes indexes.

2213
————. Stiller. Leipzig: Reclam, 1986, c1954. 406 p.
                                        MLCS 87/621 (P)

2214
————. Tagebuch mit Marion. Zürich: Atlantis, 1947–50. 2 v.
                                        PT2611.R814 T3

2215
————. Tagebuch 1946–1949. Frankfurt am Main: Suhrkamp,
  1965. 463 p.   PT2611.R814 Z52 1965

2216
————. Tagebuch 1966–1971. Frankfurt am Main: Suhrkamp,
  1972. 431 p.   PT2611.R814 Z524 1972

2217
————. Triptych: three scenic panels. New York: Harcourt Brace
  Jovanovich, 1981. 73 p.   PT2611.R814 A19 1981
  Translation of: Triptychon.

2218
————. Triptychon: drei szenische Bilder. Frankfurt am Main:
  Suhrkamp, 1981. 139 p.   PT2611.R184 T7 1981

2219
————. A wilderness of mirrors. New York: Random House,
  1966, c1965. 304 p.   PZ3.F9186 Wi2
  Translation of: Mein Name sei Gantenbein.

2220
————. Wilhelm Tell für die Schule. Frankfurt am Main: Suhrkamp, 1971. 124 p.: ill.   DQ92.F75

2221
————. Zürich-Transit. Skizze eines Films. Frankfurt am Main:
  Suhrkamp, 1966. 76 p.   PT2611.R814 Z8

2222

Adamson, Carl L. The contemporaneity of Max Frisch's novels: counter-existentialism and human commitment. Wichita, Kan.: Wichita State University, 1973. 13 p.   AS36.W62 no. 97
"Slightly revised version of a lecture delivered in Topeka, Kan., at the March 23, 1973 meeting of the Kansas Foreign Language Association."
Includes bibliographical references.

2223

Banziger, Hans. Frisch und Dürrenmatt. 7., neu bearb. Aufl. Bern, München: Francke, 1976, c1960. 312 p.
PT2611.R814 Z58 1976
Includes bibliographical references and index.

2224

————. Zwischen Protest und Traditionsbewusstsein: Arbeiten zum Werk und zur gesellschaftlichen Stellung Max Frischs. Bern, München: Francke, 1975. 121 p.   PT2611.R814 Z59
Includes bibliographical references and index.

2225

Begegnungen: eine Festschrift für Max Frisch zum siebzigsten Geburtstag. Frankfurt am Main: Suhrkamp, 1981. 225 p.
PT2611.R814 Z62

2226

Bücher, Bilder, Dokumente: Begleitheft zur Ausstellung in der Zentralbibliothek Zürich, 15. Februar–26. März 1977: Die Ausstellung wurde zusammengestellt von der Deutschen Bibliothek in Frankfurt anlässlich der Verleihung des Friedenspreises des Deutschen Buchhandels 1976 an Max Frisch. Zürich: Zentralbibliothek, 1977. 53 p.   PT2611.R814 Z65
Includes bibliographical references.

2227

Dahms, Erna M. Zeit und Zeiterlebnis in den Werken Max Frischs: Bedeutung und Technische Darstellung. Berlin, New York: de Gruyter, 1976. ix, 210 p. (Quellen und Forschungen zur Sprach- und Kulturgeschichte der germanischen Völker; n.F., 67 (191))
PT2611.R814 Z64
Includes indexes.
Bibliography: p. 193–202.

2228

Egger, Richard. Der Leser im Dilemma: die Leserrolle in Max Frischs Romanen „Stiller,'' „Homo faber'' und „Mein Name sei Gantenbein.'' Bern, New York: Lang, 1986. 237 p. (Zürcher germanistische Studien; Bd. 6)   PT2611.R814 Z643 1986
   Originally presented as the author's thesis (doctoral)— Universität Zürich, Wintersemester 1985-86.
   Bibliography: p. 233-237.

2229

Ellerbrock, Jochen. Identität und Rechtfertigung: Max Frischs Romane unter besonderer Berücksichtigung des theologischen Aspektes. Frankfurt am Main, New York: Lang, 1985. 309 p. (Europäische Hochschulschriften. Reihe XXIII, Theologie; Bd. 249)   PT2611.R814 Z644 1985
   Bibliography: p. 299-309.

2230

Frischs „Andorra''/ herausgegeben von Walter Schmitz und Ernst Wendt. Frankfurt am Main: Suhrkamp, 1984. 321 p.
                         PT2611.R814 A726 1984
   Bibliography: p. 288-321.

2231

Frischs „Don Juan, oder, Die Liebe zur Geometrie''/ herausgegeben von Walter Schmitz. Frankfurt am Main: Suhrkamp, 1985. 335 p.: ill.   PT2611.R814 D634 1985
   Bibliography: p. 330-335.

2232

Frischs „Homo faber''/ herausgegeben von Walter Schmitz. Frankfurt am Main: Suhrkamp, 1983. 360 p.: ill.
                         PT2611.R814 H633 1983
   Bibliography: p. 334-337.

2233

Frühwald, Wolfgang. Max Frisch: Andorra; Wilhelm Tell: Materialien, Kommentare. München: Hanser, 1977. 197 p.: ill.
                         PT2611.R814 A7235
   Includes index.
   Bibliography: p. 170-191.
   Bibliography of M. Frisch's works: p. 196-197.

2234

Groot, Cegienas de. Zeitgestaltung im Drama Max Frischs: die Vergegenwärtigungstechnik in Santa Cruz, die Chinesische Mauer und Biografie. Amsterdam: Rodopi, 1977. 346 p. (Amsterdamer Publikationen zur Sprache und Literatur; Bd. 33)

PT2611.R814 Z675 1977

Originally presented as the author's thesis, Vrije Universiteit Amsterdam.

Summary in Dutch.

Bibliography: p. 329–339.

2235

Hage, Volker. Max Frisch: mit Selbstzeugnissen und Bilddokumenten. Reinbek bei Hamburg: Rowohlt, 1983. 147 p.: ill.

PT2611.R814 Z678 1983

Includes index.

Bibliography: p. 141–146.

2236

Hanhart, Tildy. Max Frisch, Zufall, Rolle und literarische Form: Interpretationen zu seinem neueren Werk. Kronberg/Ts.: Scriptor Verlag, 1976. vii, 135 p. PT2611.R814 Z68 1976

Originally presented as the author's thesis, Zürich, 1975.

Bibliography of works by M. Frisch: p. 129–130.

Bibliography: p. 130–135.

2237

Jaques-Bosch, Bettina. Kritik und Melancholie im Werk Max Frischs: zur Entwicklung einer für die schweizer Literatur typischen Dichotomie. Bern, New York: Lang, 1984. 170 p. (Europäische Hochschulschriften. Reihe I, Deutsche Sprache und Literatur; Bd. 790) PT2611.R814 Z698 1984

Originally presented as the author's thesis (doctoral)— Universität Zürich, Switzerland.

Bibliography: p. 165–170.

2238

Kiernan, Doris. Existenziale Themen bei Max Frisch: die Existenzialphilosophie Martin Heideggers in den Romanen Stiller, Homo faber und Mein Name sei Gantenbein. Berlin, New York: de Gruyter, 1978. 224 p. (Quellen und Forschungen

zur Sprach- und Kulturgeschichte der germanischen Völker;
n.F., 73 (197))   PT2611.R814 Z743 1978
  Originally presented as the author's thesis, University of
California, Berkeley, 1976.
  Includes index.
  Bibliography: p. 211–217.

2239

Max Frisch: Ansprachen anlässlich der Verleihung des
Friedenspreises des Deutschen Buchhandels. Frankfurt am Main:
Verlag der Buchhändler-Vereinigung, 1976. 64 p. (Friedenspreis
des Deutschen Buchhandels; 1976)   PT2611.R814 Z7477

2240

Max Frisch: Aspekte des Prosawerks. Bern, Las Vegas: Lang, 1978.
367 p. (Studien zum Werk Max Frischs; Bd. 1)
                                                   PT2611.R814 Z748
  Includes index.
  Bibliography: p. 309–351.

2241

Naumann, Helmut. Der Fall Stiller: Antwort auf eine Herausforderung: zu Max Frischs „Stiller.'' Rheinfelden: Schäuble,
1978. v, 240 p. (Deutsche und vergleichende Literaturwissenschaft; Nr. 2)   PT2611.R814 S735
  Bibliography: p. 229–240.

2242

Pender, Malcolm. Max Frisch, his work and its Swiss background.
Stuttgart: Akademischer Verlag Heinz, 1979. iii, 277 p. (Stutt-
garter Arbeiten zur Germanistik; Nr. 67)
                                                   PT2611.R814 Z767
  Bibliography: p. 267–277.

2243

Perspectives on Max Frisch/ Gerhard F. Probst and Jay F. Bodine,
editors. Lexington, Ky.: University Press of Kentucky, 1982.
225 p.   PT2611.R814 Z768 1982
  Bibliography: p. 177–223.

2244

Rausser, Fernand. Fünf Orte im Leben von Max Frisch. Frankfurt
am Main: Suhrkamp, 1981. 74 p.: chiefly ill.
                                    PT2611.R814 Z785

2245

Schenker, Walter. Die Sprache Max Frischs in der Spannung
zwischen Mundart und Schriftsprache. Berlin: de Gruyter, 1969.
142 p.   PT2611.R814 Z82 1969

2246

Scholz-Petri, Gisela. Max Frisch: zur Funktion von Natur und
Politik in seinen Tagebüchern. Darmstadt, Berlin: Agora, 1980.
263 p. (Canon: literaturwissenschaftliche Schriften; Bd. 6)
                                    PT2611.R814 Z8243 1980
Originally presented as the author's thesis (doctoral)—Ruhr-
Universität Bochum.
Bibliography: p. 259-263.

2247

Schuchmann, Manfred E. Der Autor als Zeitgenosse: gesellschaft-
liche Aspekte in Max Frischs Werk. Frankfurt am Main, Bern,
Las Vegas: Lang, 1979. 273 p. (Europäische Hochschulschriften.
Reihe I, Deutsche Literatur und Germanistik; Bd. 296)
                                    PT2611.R814 Z825 1979
Originally presented as the author's thesis, Frankfurt am
Main, 1978.
Bibliography: p. 254-273.

2248

Schuhmacher, Klaus. Weil es geschehen ist: Untersuchungen zu
Max Frischs Poetik der Geschichte. Königstein/Ts.: Hain, 1979.
167 p.   PT2611.R814 Z826 1979
Originally presented as the author's thesis, Freiburg im
Breisgau, 1978.
Bibliography: p. 155-167.

2249

Stephan, Alexander. Max Frisch. München: Beck, Edition Text +
Kritik, 1983. 178 p. (Autorenbücher; 37)
                                    PT2611.R814 Z86 1983
Bibliography of works by and about Max Frisch: p. 165-176.

2250

Werner, Markus. Bilder des Endgültigen, Entwürfe des Möglichen: zum Werk Max Frischs. Bern, Frankfurt am Main: Lang, 1975. 90 p. (Europäische Hochschulschriften. Reihe I, Deutsche Literatur und Germanistik; Bd. 111)   PT2611.R814 Z92
Bibliography: p. 87–90.

2251

Zeitz, Bernhard. Die Rechtsauffassung in der Dichtung von Max Frisch. Würzburg: 1972. xi, 135 p.   PT2611.R814 Z97

****

2252

Ganz, Raffael. Im Zementgarten. Zürich: Orell Füssli, 1971. 154 p.
PT2613.A65 I4

2253

———. Orangentraum: Erzählungen aus Marokko. Zürich: Artemis, 1961. 248 p.   PT2613.A65 O7

2254

———. Sandkorn im Wind. Zürich: Füssli, 1980. 239 p.
PT2613.A65 S2 1980

2255

———. Schabir. Zürich, Stuttgart: Artemis, 1966. 221 p.
PT2613.A65 S3

****

2256

Gomringer, Eugen. The book of hours, and Constellations. New York: Something Else Press, 1968. 1 v. (unpaged).
PT2667.O48 S713
Translation of: Das Stundenbuch and Die Konstellationen.

2257

———. Eugen Gomringer: 1970–1972. München: Edition UND, 1973. 42 leaves.   PT2667.O48 A17 1973

2258

————. Josef Albers: sein Werk als Beitrag zur visuellen Gestaltung im 20. Jahrhundert. Starnberg: Keller, 1971. 205 p.: plates (part col.). N6888.A5 G6 1971

2259

————. Konstellationen, Ideogramme, Stundenbuch. Stuttgart: Reclam, 1977. 157 p. PT2667.O48 K6
Bibliography: p. 153–156.

2260

————. Poesie als Mittel der Umweltgestaltung. Itzehoe: Hansen & Hansen, 1969. 48 p. PN1274.G6

2261

————. Das Stundenbuch. München: Huber, 1965. 79 p.
PT2667.O48 S7

2262

————. Worte sind Schatten: die Konstellationen 1951–1968. Reinbek bei Hamburg: Rowohlt, 1969. 305 p.
PT2667.O48 W6

****

2263

Guggenheim, Kurt. Alles in allem. Zürich: Artemis, 1952. 3 v.
PT2613.U43 A8

2264

————. Alles ist der Rede wert: Worte zum neuen Tag. Frauenfeld: Huber, 1977. 104 p. BJ1583.G83

2265

————. Das Ende von Seldwyla. Zürich: Artemis, 1965. 381 p.
PT2374.Z4 G8

2266

————. Entfesselung. Zürich, Leipzig: Guggenbuhl & Huber, Schweizer Spiegel Verlag, 1935. 263 p.
PT2613.U43 E6 1935

2267

————. Einmal nur: Tagebuchblätter. Frauenfeld: Huber, 1981–
1983. 3 v.   PT2613.U43 Z465 1981

2268

————. Die frühen Jahre. Zürich: Artemis, 1962. 214 p.
                                                      PT2613.U43 Z53

2269

————. Das Fussvolk der Literatur. Zürich: Schweizerische Wer-
bestelle für das Buch des Schweizerischen Buchhändler- und
Verlegervereins, 1972. 18 p. (on double leaves).
                                                       PT2613.U43 F8

2270

————. Gerufen und nicht gerufen. Zürich: Benziger, 1973. 324 p.
                                                       PT2613.U43 G4

2271

————. Der goldene Würfel. Zürich, Stuttgart: Artemis, 1967.
231 p.   PT2613.U43 G6

2272

————. Der heilige Komödiant. Einsiedeln, Zürich, Köln: Benziger,
1972. 117 p.   PQ1915.S33 G8

2273

————. Heimat oder Domizil? Die Stellung des deutschschweize-
rischen Schriftstellers in der Gegenwart. Zürich: Artemis, 1961.
38 p. (Schriften zur Zeit, Heft 25)   DQ36.G85

2274

————. Die heimliche Reise. Zürich: Artemis, 1945. 211 p.
                                                       PT2613.U43 H4

2275

————. Der labyrinthische Spazierweg: Goethes Reise nach Zürich,
nach Stafa und auf den Gotthard im Jahre 1797. Frauenfeld:
Huber, 1975. 143 p., 10 leaves of plates (3 fold.): ill.
                                                         PT2067.G8

2276

————. Mignon und Peregrina: Begegnungen. Bremen: Jacobi, 1970. 184 p.   PT2613.U43 M47

2277

————. Minute des Lebens: Roman um die Freundschaft zwischen Zola und Cézanne. Zürich: Artemis, 1969. 270 p.
PT2613.U43 M5

2278

————. Nachher: vier Erzählungen. Zürich: Benziger, 1974. 139 p.   PT2613.U43 N3

2279

————. Riedland. Zürich: Gute Schriften, 1971. 154 p.
PT2613.U43 R5 1971

2280

————. Salz des Meeres, Salz der Tränen. Zürich: Artemis, 1964. 252 p.   PT2613.U43 S2

2281

————. Sandkorn für Sandkorn. Zürich: Artemis, 1959. 235 p.
QL31.F3 G8

2282

————. Sieben Tage. Zürich: Schweizer Spiegel Verlag, 1936. 260 p.   PT2613.U43 S5 1936

2283

————. Tagebuch am Schanzengraben. Zürich: Artemis, 1963. 125 p.: ill.   PT2613.U43 T3

2284

————. Warum gerade ich? Worte für die Kranken. Zürich, Stuttgart: Artemis, 1968. 68 p.   R727.4.G75

2285

————. Wilder Urlaub. New York: Holt, 1949. iv, 104 p.
PT2613.U43 W5 1949

2286

―――. Das Zusammensetzspiel. Frauenfeld, Stuttgart: Huber.
    1977. 219 p.   PT2613.U43 Z454

****

2287

Jaeggi, Urs. Brandeis. Darmstadt, Neuwied: Luchterhand, 1978.
    269 p.   PT2670.A32 B7

2288

―――. Grundrisse. Darmstadt: Luchterhand, 1981. 275 p.
                                                   MLCS 82/1436

2289

―――. Die Komplicen. Berlin: Freitag, 1982. 199 p.: ill.
                                             PT2670.A32 K6 1982

2290

―――. Versuch über den Verrat. Darmstadt: Luchterhand, 1984.
    337 p.   PT2670.A32 V4 1984

2291

―――. Was auf den Tisch kommt, wird gegessen: Aufsätze.
Darmstadt: Luchterhand, 1981. 201 p.   MLCS 87/4727 (H)

****

2292

Leutenegger, Gertrud. Gouverneur. Frankfurt am Main: Suhr-
    kamp, 1981. 228 p.   MLCS 82/41

2293

―――. Kontinent. Frankfurt am Main: Suhrkamp, 1985. 161 p.
                                             PT2672.E86 K6 1985

2294

―――. Lebewohl, gute Reise: ein dramatisches Poem. Frankfurt
am Main: Suhrkamp, 1980. 140 p.: port.   PT2672.E86 L4

2295

————. Komm ins Schiff. Frankfurt am Main: Suhrkamp, 1983.
87 p.   MLCS 84/2025 (P)

2296

————. Ninive. Frankfurt am Main: Suhrkamp, 1977. 171 p.
                                             PT2672.E86 N5

2297

————. Das verlorene Monument. Frankfurt am Main: Suhrkamp, 1985. 107 p.   MLCS 87/663 (P)

2298

————. Vorabend. Frankfurt am Main, Zürich: Suhrkamp, 1975.
207 p.   PT2672.E86 V6

2299

————. Wie in Salomons Garten. Düsseldorf: Eremiten-Presse,
1981. 51 p.: col. ill.   MLCS 87/3812 (P)

****

2300

Loetscher, Hugo. Abwässer: ein Gutachten. Zürich: Verlag der
Arche, 1963. 224 p.   PT2672.O3 A65

2301

————. Die Entdeckung der Schweiz und anderes: Romanaus-
schnitte und Erzählungen. Zürich: Gute Schriften, 1976. 59 p.
                                             PT2672.O3 E5

2302

————. Herbst in der grossen Orange. Zürich: Diogenes, 1982.
164 p.   MLCS 84/7684 (P)

2303

————. How many languages does man need? New York, N.Y.:
Graduate School and University Center, City University of New
York, 1982. 101 p. (Pro Helvetia Swiss lectureship; 1)
                                             P106.L58 1982
„Hugo Loetscher biography and bibliography": p. 99–100.

2304

————. Der Immune. Darmstadt, Neuwied: Luchterhand, 1975.
420 p.   PT2672.O3 I4

2305

————. Die Kranzflechterin. Zürich: Verlag der Arche, 1964.
263 p.   PT2672.O3 K7

2306

————. Noah: a novel. London: Owen, 1970. 4, 140 p.
PZ4.L828 No

2307

————. Noah: Roman einer Konjunktur. Berlin: Union Verlag,
1976. 129 p.   PT2672.O3 N6 1976

2308

————. Die Papiere des Immunen. Zürich: Diogenes, 1986. 504 p.
MLCS 86/7673 (P)

2309

————. Wunderwelt: eine brasilianische Begegnung. Darmstadt,
Neuwied: Luchterhand, 1979. 162 p.   PT2672.O3 W86

2310

————. Zehn Jahre Fidel Castro: Reportage und Analyse. Zürich:
Verlag der Arche, 1969. 127 p.   F1788.22.C3 L6

****

2311

Marti, Kurt. Abendland. Darmstadt: Luchterhand, 1981, c1980.
99 p.   MLCS 87/2204 (P)

2312

————. Abratzky. Neuwied: Luchterhand, 1971. 112 p.
PT2673.A473 A63

2313

————. Das Aufgebot zum Frieden. Basel: Reinhardt, 1969.
111 p.

BT736.4.M3

2314

————. Bundesgenosse Gott. Basel: Reinhardt, 1972. 107 p.

BS1245.4.M3

2315

————. Bürgerliche Geschichten. Darmstadt: Luchterhand, 1981.
156 p.   PT2673.A473 B8 1981

2316

————. Gedichte am Rand. Köln: Kiepenheuer & Witsch, 1968.
84 p.   PT2673.A473 G4 1968

2317

————. Geduld und Revolte: die Gedichte am Rand. Stuttgart:
Radius-Verlag, 1984. 94 p. (Reihe, Dichtung im ausgehenden
zwanzigsten Jahrhundert; Bd. 5)   MLCS 84/11529 (P)

2318

————. Grenzverkehr: ein Christ im Umgang mit Kultur, Literatur
und Kunst. Neukirchen-Vluyn: Neukirchener Verlag des Erzie-
hungsvereins, 1976. 194 p.   BR115.C8 M24

2319

————. Heil Vetia: poetischer Diskurs. 2., erw. Aufl. Basel: Lenos,
1981. 55 p.: ill.   MLCS 82/1408

2320

————. Leichenreden. Neuwied, Berlin: Luchterhand, 1969. 65 p.

PT2673.A473 L4

2321

————. Das Markus-Evangelium. Ausgelegt für die Gemeinde.
Basel: Reinhardt, 1967. 368 p.   BS2585.4.M3

2322

————. Meergedichte, Alpengedichte. Berlin: Fietkau, 1975. 33 p.

PT2673.A473 M4

2323

————. Mein barfüssig Lob. Darmstadt: Luchterhand, 1987. 74 p.

MLCS 87/4152 (P)

2324

————. Der Mensch ist nicht für das Christentum da: ein Streitgespräch über Gott und die Welt zwischen einem Christen und einem Agnostiker. Hamburg: Lutherisches Verlagshaus, 1977. 119 p.   BL2778.M34
Includes bibliographical references.

2325

————. Moderne Literatur, Malerei und Musik. Zürich: Flamberg, 1963. 409 p.: music.   PN774.M3

2326

————. Nancy Neujahr & Co. Leverkusen: Literarischer Verlag Braun, 1976. 64 p.   PT2673.A473 N3

2327

————. Paraburi. Eine Sprachtraube. Bern: Zytglogge, 1972. 43 p.   PT2673.A473 P3

2328

————. Politische Gottesdienste in der Schweiz: fünf Beispiele. Basel: Reinhardt, 1971. 127 p.   BV198.M365

2329

————. Politisches Tagebuch. Gütersloh: Gütersloher Verlagshaus Mohn, 1977. 148 p.   BX9439.M33 A34

2330

————. Republikanische Gedichte. Neuwied: Luchterhand, 1971, c1959. 48 p.   PT2673.A473 R4 1971

2331

————. Die Riesin: ein Bericht. Darmstadt: Luchterhand, 1975. 140 p.   PT2673.A473 R5

2332

————. Rosa loui: vierzig gedicht ir bärner umgangsschprach. Neuwied: Luchterhand, 1967. 58 p.   PT2673.A473 R6

2333
——. Ruhe und Ordnung: Aufzeichnungen, Abschweifungen, 1980–1983. Darmstadt: Luchterhand, 1984. 245 p.: ill.
PT2673.A473 A16 1984

2334
——. Schon wieder heute: gesammelte Gedichte, 1959–1980. Darmstadt: Luchterhand, 1982. 144 p.   MLCS 84/5497

2335
——. Die Schweiz und ihre Schriftsteller—die Schriftsteller und ihre Schweiz. Zürich: EVZ-Verlag, 1966. 88 p.   PT3868.M3

2336
——. Tagebuch mit Bäumen. Darmstadt: Luchterhand, 1985. 105 p.   MLCS 86/1426 (P)

2337
——. Theologie im Angriff. Zürich: Verlag der Arche, 1969. 47 p.   BR125.M39

2338
——. Trainingstexte. Zürich: Regenbogen-Verlag, 1967. 26 l.: (in portfolio).   PT2673.A473 T7

2339
——. Undereinisch: gedicht ir bärner umgangsschprach. Darmstadt, Neuwied: Luchterhand, 1973. 92 p.   PT2673.A473 U5

2340
——. Wo chiemte mer hi?: gedicht und schtückli (minidramen) ir bärner umgangsschprach. Münsingen: Fischer, 1984. 128 p.
MLCS 86/7927 (P)

2341
——. Zärtlichkeit und Schmerz: Notizen. Darmstadt, Neuwied: Luchterhand, 1979. 136 p.   PT2673.A473 Z2

2342
——. Zum Beispiel: Bern 1972. Darmstadt: Luchterhand, 1973. 185 p.   PT2673.A473 Z528

****

2343
Meier, Gerhard. Der andere Tag: ein Prosastück. Bern: Zytglogge,
1974. 106 p.   PT2673.E47 A8

2344
————. Die Ballade vom Schneien. Gümligen: Zytglogge, 1985.
130 p.   MLCS 86/3575 (P)

2345
————. Der Besuch. Bern: Zytglogge, 1976. 152 p.
                                                 PT2673.E47 B4

2346
————. Borodino. Gümligen: Zytglogge, 1982. 134 p.
                                                 MLCS 84/5943

2347
————. Einige Häuser nebenan. Wien: Bartsch, 1973. 76 p.
                                                 PT2673.E47 E5

2348
————. Es regnet in meinem Dorf. Olten, Freiburg i. Br.: Walter,
1971. 62 p.   PT2673.E47 E8

2349
————. Das Gras grünt. Bern: Benteli, 1964. 51 p.
                                                 PT2673.E47 G7

2350
————. Im Schatten der Sonnenblumen. Bern: Kandelaber Verlag,
1967. 64 p.   PT2673.E47 I4

2351
————. Kübelpalmen träumen von Oasen: 60 Skizzen. Bern:
Kandelaber Verlag, 1969. 84 p.   PT2673.E47 K8

2352
————. Papierrosen: gesammelte Prosaskizzen. Gümligen: Zytglogge,
1976. 116 p.   PT2673.E47 P3
   Selections from the author's Kübelpalmen träumen von Oasen
and Es regnet in meinem Dorf.

2353

———. Der schnurgerade Kanal. Bern: Zytglogge, 1977. 162 p.

MLCS 84/11368 (P)

2354

———. Toteninsel. Gümligen: Zytglogge, 1979. 141 p.

PT2673.E47 T67

2355

Hoffmann, Fernand. Heimkehr ins Reich der Wörter: Versuch über den Schweizer Schriftsteller Gerhard Meier. Luxemburg: Verlag der Abteilung für Kunst und Literatur des Grossherzöglichen Institutes von Luxemburg, 1982. 109 p.

PT2673.E47 Z69 1982

Includes bibliographical references.

****

2356

Meier, Herbert. Anatomische Geschichten. Zürich, Einsiedeln, Köln: Benziger, 1973. 109 p.   PT2673.E48 A8

Bibliography of the author's works: p. 111–112.

2357

———. Bräker: eine Komödie. Zürich: Neue Schauspiel AG, 1978. 55 p.   PT2673.E48 B7

2358

———. Manifest und Reden. 2. erg. Aufl. Zürich: Flamberg-Verlag, 1969. 82 p.   PT2673.E48 M3 1969

2359

———. Sequenzen: ein Gedichtbuch. Zürich, Einsiedeln, Köln: Benziger, 1969. 80 p.   PT2673.E48 S4

2360

———. Skorpione: ein Fernsehstück. Zürich: Benziger, 1964. 50 p.   MLCS 87/602 (P)

2361
———. Stauffer-Bern. Frauenfeld: Huber, 1975. 142 p.: ill.
PT2673.E48 S78

2362
———. Stiefelchen: ein Fall. Zürich, Einsiedeln, Köln: Benziger,
1970. 182 p.   PT2673.E48 S8

2363
———. Der verborgene Gott: Studien zu den Dramen Ernst
Barlachs. Nürnberg: Glock und Lutz, 1963. 168 p.
PT2603.A53 Z7

2364
———. Verwandtschaften. Einsiedeln: Benziger, 1963. 238 p.
PT2673.E48 V4

2365
———. Von der Kultur. Zürich: Verlag der Arche, 1973. 40 p.
NX65.M44

2366
———. Wohin geht es denn jetzt: Reden an Etablierte und ihre
Verachter. Zürich: Flamberg, 1971. 108 p.
MLCS 87/530 (P)

****

2367
Meyer, E. Y. Eine entfernte Ähnlichkeit. Frankfurt am Main:
Suhrkamp, 1975. 152 p.   PT2673.E92 E5
Includes index.

2368
———. Die Hälfte der Erfahrung: Essays und Reden. Frankfurt
am Main: Suhrkamp, 1980. 197 p.   PT2673.E92 H34 1980

2369
———. In Trubschachen. Frankfurt am Main: Suhrkamp, 1979.
217 p.   PT2673.E92 I5 1979

2370

————. Plädoyer: für die Erhaltung der Vielfalt der Natur beziehungsweise für deren Verteidigung gegen die ihr drohende Vernichtung durch die Einfalt des Menschen. Frankfurt am Main: Suhrkamp, 1982. 175 p. PT2673.E92 P4 1982

2371

————. Ein Reisender in Sachen Umsturz. Frankfurt am Main: Suhrkamp, 1972. 124 p. PT2673.E92 R4

2372

————. Die Rückfahrt. Frankfurt am Main: Suhrkamp, 1977. 426 p. PT2673.E92 R8

2373

————. Sundaymorning: Theaterstück, Berndeutsch. Bern: Erpf, 1984. 109 p. MLCS 86/7866 (P)

———————

2374

E. Y. Meyer/ herausgegeben von Beatrice von Matt. Frankfurt am Main: Suhrkamp, 1983. 314 p.: ill. PT2673.E92 Z63 1983
E. Y. Meyer was the recipient of the Gerhart-Hauptmann-Preis in 1983.
Includes bibliographies.

****

2375

Muschg, Adolf. Albissers Grund. Berlin: Verlag Volk und Welt, 1976. 411 p. PT2673.U78 A8 1976
Some text in English with German translation.

2376

————. Die Aufgeregten von Goethe. Politisches Drama in 40 Auftritten. Zürich: Verlag der Arche, 1971. 79 p.
PT2673.U78 A9

2377

————. Besprechungen, 1961–1979. Basel, Boston, Stuttgart: Birkhäuser, 1980. 148 p. PT2673.U78 B4

2378

―――. The blue man and other stories. New York: Braziller,
1985. 141 p.   PT2673.U78 A23 1985

2379

―――. Empörung durch Landschaften: vernünftige Drohreden.
Zürich: Rauhreif, 1985. 129 p.   PT2673.U78 E49 1985

2380

―――. Entfernte Bekannte. Frankfurt am Main: Suhrkamp, 1976.
169 p.   PT2673.U78 E5

2381

―――. Fremdkörper. Zürich: Verlag der Arche, 1968. 219 p.
PT2673.U78 F7

2382

―――. Gegenzauber. Zürich: Verlag der Arche, 1967. 487 p.
PT2673.U78 G4

2383

―――. Gottfried Keller. München: Kindler, 1977. 412 p.: ill.
PT2374.Z4 M8 1977
Includes indexes.
Bibliography: p. 403–408.

2384

―――. High fidelity. Basel: Lenos-Presse, 1973. 86 p.
PT2673.U78 H5

2385

―――. Im Sommer des Hasen. Frankfurt am Main: Suhrkamp,
1975. 316 p.   PT2673.U78 I4 1975

2386

―――. Das Kerbelgericht. Zürich: Verlag der Arche, 1969. 54 p.
PT2673.U78 K4

2387

―――. Leib und Leben. Frankfurt am Main: Suhrkamp, 1982.
213 p.   MLCS 82/6600

2388

―――. Das Licht und der Schlüssel: Erziehungsroman eines Vampirs. Frankfurt am Main: Suhrkamp, 1984. 518 p.

MLCS 87/350 (P)

2389

―――. Liebesgeschichten. Frankfurt am Main: Suhrkamp, 1972. 170 p.

PT2673.U78 L5

2390

―――. Literatur als Therapie?: ein Exkurs über das Heilsame und das Unheilbare: Frankfurter Vorlesungen. Frankfurt am Main: Suhrkamp, 1981. 204 p.: 1 port.

PN56.P93 M87 1981

2391

―――. Mitgespielt. Zürich: Verlag der Arche, 1969. 380 p.

PT2673.U78 M5

2392

―――. Noch ein Wunsch. Frankfurt am Main: Suhrkamp, 1979. 140 p.

PT2673.U78 N6

2393

―――. Papierwände. Bern: Kandelaber Verlag, 1970. 103 p.

DS822.5.M87

2394

―――. Rumpelstilz: ein kleinbürgerliches Trauerspiel. Zürich: Verlag der Arche, 1968. 82 p.

PT2673.U87 R8

2395

―――. Der Turmhahn und andere Liebesgeschichten. Frankfurt am Main: Suhrkamp, 1987. 215 p.

MLCS 87/3969 (P)

2396

―――. Übersee: drei Hörspiele. Stuttgart: Reclam, 1982. 95 p.

PT2673.U78 U2 1982

2397

―――. Unterlassene Anwesenheit. Leipzig: Reclam, 1984. 222 p.

MLCS 84/13085 (P)

2398

———. Von Herwegh bis Kaiseraugst: wie halten wir es als Demokraten mit unserer Freiheit?: Rede. Zürich: Limmat-Verlag, 1975. 61 p.   PT2355.H5 Z8

2399

Ammann, Georges. Gespräch mit Adolf Muschg. Basel: Reinhardt, 1969. 28 p.   PT2673.U78 Z57

2400

Über Adolf Muschg/ herausgegeben von Judith Ricker-Abderhalden. Frankfurt am Main: Suhrkamp, 1979. 357 p.
                                    PT2673.U78 Z9
  Bibliography of A. Muschg's works: p. 333–341.
  Bibliography: p. 342–357.

2401

Voris, Renate. Adolf Muschg. München: Beck, Edition Text + Kritik, 1984. 143 p.   PT2673.U78 Z93 1984
  Bibliography: p. 139–142.

****

2402

Nizon, Paul. Aber wo ist das Leben: ein Lesebuch. Frankfurt am Main: Suhrkamp, 1983. 175 p.   PT2674.I9 A63 1983

2403

———. Am Schreiben gehen: Frankfurter Vorlesungen. Frankfurt am Main: Suhrkamp, 1985. 136 p.: ill.   PT2674.I9 Z54 1985
  Includes bibliographical references.

2404

———. Diskurs in der Enge. Aufsätze zur Schweizer Kunst. Bern: Kandelaber Verlag, 1970. 124 p.   N7141.N58

2405

———. Friedrich Kuhn. Zürich: Verlag Um die Ecke, 1970. 72 p.: ill., 15 plates, fold. plate (in pocket).   N7153.K8 N58 1970

2406

————. Im Hause enden die Geschichten; Untertauchen: Protokolle einer Reise. Frankfurt am Main: Suhrkamp, 1978. 187 p.   PT2674.I9 A15 1978

2407

————. Das Jahr der Liebe. Frankfurt am Main: Suhrkamp, 1981. 230 p.   MLCS 81/1869

2408

————. Stolz. Frankfurt am Main, Zürich: Suhrkamp, 1975. 191 p.   PT2674.I9 S8

2409

————. Swiss made. Portraits, Hommages, Curricula. Einsiedeln, Zürich, Köln: Benziger, 1971. 132 p.: ill.   N7141.N59

2410

————. Untertauchen: Protokoll einer Reise. Frankfurt am Main: Suhrkamp, 1972. 77 p.   PT2674.I9 U5 1972

2411

Paul Nizon/ herausgegeben von Martin Kilchmann. Frankfurt am Main: Suhrkamp, 1985. 304 p.: ill.   PT2674.I9 Z79 1985
Bibliography: p. 291–304.

****

2412

Schmidli, Werner. Der alte Mann. Basel: Gute Schriften, 1972. 56 p.   PT2680.M47 A7 1972

2413

————. Fundplätze. Zürich, Köln, Einsiedeln: Benziger, 1974. 378 p.   PT2680.M17 F8

2414

————. Ganz gewöhnliche Tage. Zürich: Benziger, 1981. 180 p.
PT2680.M47 G3 1981

2415

————. Gebet eines Kindes vor dem Spielen. Bern: Lukianos
Verlag, 1970. 70 p.   PT2680.M47 G4

2416

————. Gustavs Untaten. Einsiedeln: Benziger, 1976. 195 p.
                                                 PT2680.M47 G8

2417

————. Der Junge und die toten Fische. Einsiedeln: Benziger,
1966. 251 p.   PT2680.M47 J8

2418

————. Der Mann am See. Zürich: Nagel & Kimche, 1985. 268 p.
                                              MLCS 86/1105 (P)

2419

————. Meinetwegen soll es doch schneien. Zürich, Einsiedeln,
Köln: Benziger, 1967. 240 p.   PT2680.M47 M4

2420

————. Mir hört keiner zu. Basel: Lenos-Presse, 1971. 47 p.:
front.   PT2680.M47 M5

2421

————. Sagen Sie nicht: beim Geld hört der Spass auf. Einsiedeln,
Zürich, Köln: Benziger, 1971. 104 p.   PT2680.M47 S25

2422

————. Das Schattenhaus. Zürich, Einsiedeln, Köln: Benziger,
1969. 326 p.   PT2680.M47 S3

2423

————. Warum werden Bäume im Alter schön. Zürich: Benziger,
1984. 199 p.   MLCS 87/383 (P)

2424

————. Zellers Geflecht. Köln: Benziger, 1979. 299 p.
                                         PT2680.M47 Z16 1979

****

2425
Vogt, Walter. Alle Irrenhäuser sind gelb. Liebefeld: Lukianos-
Verlag, 1967. 10 l.   PT2684.O38 A8

2426
———. Altern. Zürich: Benziger, 1981. 275 p.
                                    PT2684.O38 A82 1981

2427
———. Booms Ende. Zürich: Benziger, 1979. 207 p.
                                    PT2684.O38 B6

2428
———. Briefe aus Marokko. Zürich: Verlag der Arche, 1974.
   111 p.   PT2684.O38 Z53 1974

2429
———. Husten: Wahrscheinliche und unwahrscheinliche Geschichten. Zürich: Diogenes Verlag, 1968. 157 p.
                                    PT2684.O38 H8

2430
———. Der Irre und sein Arzt. Zürich: Verlag der Arche, 1974.
   151 p.   PT2684.O38 I7

2431
———. Klartext. Zürich: Verlag der Arche, 1973. 47 p.
                                    PT2684.O38 K5

2432
———. Maskenzwang. Zürich: Benziger, 1985. 255 p.
                                    MLCS 86/1100 (P)

2433
———. Mein Sinai-Trip. Eine Laienpredigt. Zürich: Verlag der
Arche, 1973. 47 p.   BV4254.G3 V63

2434
———. Melancholie. Die Erlebnisse des Amateur-Kriminalisten
Beno von Stürler. Zürich: Diogenes Verlag, 1967. 239 p.
                                    PT2684.O38 M4

2435

————. Metamorphosen. Zürich: Benziger, 1984. 162 p.

MLCS 86/5393 (P)

2436

————. Pilatus und Faust. Bern: Zytglogge, 1972. 47 p.

PT2684.O38 P5 1972

2437

————. Die roten Tiere von Tsavo. Zürich: Verlag der Arche, 1976. 202 p.   MLCS 84/8604 (P)

2438

————. Schizogorsk. Zürich: Verlag der Arche, 1977. 212 p.

PT2684.O38 S3

2439

————. Spiele der Macht. Basel: Lenos-Presse, 1972. 57 p.: ill.

PT2684.O38 S6

2440

————. Die Talpi kommen. Aarau, Frankfurt am Main: Sauerländer, 1973. 96 p.   PZ33.V567

2441

————. Vergessen und erinnern. Zürich: Benziger, 1980. 206 p.

PT2684.O38 V47

2442

————. Der Vogel auf dem Tisch. Zürich: Verlag der Arche, 1978. 159 p.: ill.   PT2684.O38 V6 1978

2443

————. Der Wiesbadener Kongress. Zürich: Verlag der Arche, 1972. 220 p.   PT2684.O38 W5

2444

————. Wüthrich. Selbstgespräch eines sterbenden Arztes. Zürich: Diogenes Verlag, 1966. 194 p.   PT2684.O38 W8

****

2445

Walter, Silja. Der achte Tag: Schauspiel in vier Akten. Zürich: Jordan-Verlag, 1984. 69 p.   MLCS 86/5431 (P)

2446

————. Beim Fest des Christus: Messe-Meditationen. Zürich: Verlag der Arche, 1975. 127 p.: ill.   PT2685.A52 B4

2447

————. Der brennende Zeitvertreib: Pfingstspiel. Zürich: Verlag der Arche, 1976. 60 p.   PT2685.A52 B7

2448

————. Der Fisch und Bar Abbas. Zürich: Verlag der Arche, 1967. 160 p.   PT2685.A52 F5

2449

————. Frau mit Rose: oder, Basler Lebenstanz. Zürich: Verlag der Arche, 1978. 82 p.   PT2685.A52 F7

2450

————. Gesammelte Gedichte. Zürich: Verlag der Arche, 1972. 99 p.   PT2685.A52 A17 1972

2451

————. Gesammelte Spiele. Zürich: Verlag der Arche, 1963. 282 p.   PT2685.A53 G4

2452

————. Das Hymnenjahr. Zürich: Verlag der Arche, 1975. 80 p.   PT2685.A52 H9

2453

————. Ich bin nicht mehr tot. Zürich: Verlag der Arche. 1974. 79 p.   PT2685.A52 I3

2454

————. Die Jahrhundert-Treppe: Solothurner Chronikspiel (1481–1981). Zürich: Verlag der Arche, 1981. 111 p.: ill.   MLCS 82/238

2455

————. Jan, der Verrückte: ein Spiel. Zürich: Verlag der Arche, 1978. 82 p.   PT2685.A523 J3 1978
   Originally performed on the Swiss and German stage under the title: ‚‚ Jan, der Idiot.''

2456

————. Das Kloster am Rande der Stadt. Der Tag der benediktinischen Nonne. Zürich: Verlag der Arche, 1971. 87 p.: ill.
                                                      BX4210.W35

2457

————. Die Schleuse. Zürich: Verlag der Arche, 1972. 200 p.
                                                      PT2685.A52 S3

2458

————. Sie warten auf die Stadt. Zürich: Verlag der Arche, 1973, c1963. 70 p.: ill.   PT2685.A52 S5 1973

2459

————. Der Tanz des Gehorsams, oder, Die Strohmatte. Zürich: Verlag der Arche, 1970. 159 p.: ill., 4 plates.   PT2685.A52 T3

2460

————. Tanz vor dem Herrn: neue Wortgottesdienste. Zürich: Verlag der Arche, 1974. 166 p.   PT2685.A52 T34
   Includes bibliographies.

2461

————. Der Turm der Salome. Zürich: Verlag der Arche, 1976. 56 p.: ill.   PT2685.A52 T8
   Bibliography of the author's works: p. 56.

2462

————. Würenloser Chronikspiel. Zürich: Verlag der Arche, 1970. 96 p.   PT2685.A52 W8

2463

Kramer, Toni. Der Mensch zwischen Individuum und Kollektiv: das Menschenbild im Werk Silja Walters. Bonn: Bouvier, 1977. 183. p. (Studien zur Germanistik, Anglistik und Komparatistik; Bd. 62)   PT2685.A52 Z74
  Bibliography: p. 176–183.

2464

Rothlisberger, Max. Silja Walters Zeugnis. Bonn: Bouvier, 1977. 233 p. (Studien zur Germanistik, Anglistik und Komparatistik; Bd. 34)   PT2685.A52 Z87
  Includes index.
  Bibliography of works by and about S. Walter: p. 226–233.

* * * * * * * * * * * * * * * * * * *

2465

Wiesner, Heinrich. Das Dankschreiben. Basel: Lenos-Presse, 1975. 219 p.   PT2685.I363 D3

2466

————. Heinrich Wiesners Kürzestgeschichten. Basel: Lenos-Presse, 1980. 199 p.   MLCS 87/2616 (P)

2467

————. Die Kehrseite der Medaille: neue lakonische Zeilen. München: Piper, 1972. 81 p.: ill.   PT2685.I363 K4

2468

————. Lakonische Zeilen. München: Piper, 1965. 63 p.
                PT2685.I363 L3

2469

————. Lapidare Geschichten. München: Piper, 1967. 142 p.: ill.
                PT2685.I363 L34

2470

————. Neue Kürzestgeschichten. Rorschach: Nebelspalter, 1985. 116 p.: ill.   MLCS 86/3587 (P)

2471

———. Notennot: Schulgeschichten. Basel: Lenos-Presse, 1973.
67 p.: ill.   LB1033.W53

2472

———. Der Riese am Tisch. Basel: Lenos-Presse, 1979. 169 p.
                                    PT2685.I363 R5
Bibliography of the author's works: p. 2.

2473

———. Schauplätze: Chronik. 2., überarb. Aufl. Basel: Lenos-
Presse, 1976. 168 p.   PT2685.I363 S3 1976

2474

———. Das verwandelte Land: ein Lesebuch. Liestal: Ludin,
1977. 128 p.: ill. (Literarische Schriftenreihe Baselland; Bd. 11)
                                    PT2685.I363 V4
Bibliography of the author's works: p. 128.

☆ U.S. GOVERNMENT PRINTING OFFICE : 1989 - 237-001 : QL 3